Copyright

Al

The characters and events portrayed in this book are fictitious. Any similarity to real persons, living or dead, is coincidental and not intended by the author.

No part of this book may be reproduced, or stored in a retrieval system, or transmitted in any form or by any means, electrical, mechanical, photocopying, recording, or otherwise, without express written permission of the copyright holder.

ISBN- 13: 9798873536603

Cover designed by Joshua G P Gwynne
Cover copyright David F Buxton

Printed in the United Kingdom

Dedicated to:

Kirstin
Without your inspiration, support and encouragement
these books would never have happened.

I would like to say a special thank you to:
Margaret & Dougie
For your help, advice and belief in me.

I would also like to thank:
Jenny Buxton
For being Mum

Craig & Paul among others,
For listening to my droning

Chapter One

"Ohhh... I wish you would get yourself up and get out of the house!" the voice whined from a distant room, closely followed by the slamming of various kitchen cupboard doors. The voice continued, the volume rising as the owner headed towards the living room only to be halted by a loud bang that shook the whole house. The living room door had slammed shut with such force that it not only jolted Oliver out of his daydream but physically dislodged him from the settee.

The door was thrown open by an enraged mother, "How dare you slam the door on me when I am talking!"

The young lad pleaded his innocence as the dog clambered from her bed beside the settee and shot out of the room, desperate to find some safe shelter.

The figure stood over Oliver, hands on hips, shaking her head, her foot impatiently tapped on the floor for what felt like ages. The reddened angry face finally growled, "go and get some air in your lungs," his mother raised her hand and pointed to the door, "let your skin see some of the glorious sunshine, get some vitamin D surging through you."

Oliver heavily plonked himself back onto the corner of the settee, drew his knees up under his chin and wrapped his arms around them, and sulkily pulled himself into a tight ball.

His mum could see any further conversation would be a waste, "I hate the summer break and the endless weeks of you lot under my feet." She moaned. The figure huffily turned and marched out of the door, the occasional garbled word could be identified as his mum muttered and burbled into the background. A shout rang out from the distance as Kiera sauntered back in, "Why don't you go and see your friends?" the voice continued, shouting into the ether, hoping the words would reach the intended target. The next verbal grenade landed as the footsteps disappeared into the depths of the kitchen, "You never take the dog out, why don't you take Kiera for a walk?".

Oliver was outraged by the implication, 'I never walk her!' he grumbled to himself, 'I am the ONLY one who walks the blasted dog!'. His frustration boiled up, Oliver's face turned red with rage as he screamed out, "I told you my rubbish trainers are falling apart.". He angrily clenched his fists, "I asked for some new blue and white 'Treadmaster GKs' ages ago, but you just blasted ignored me." punching the arm of the settee as he growled.

Oliver's words seemingly fell on deaf ears, his response obviously ignored as various loud crashes and bangs continued unhindered as the kitchen implements were being stashed away. Waiting until the next time they were grabbed, as the owner fought to create an edible meal. A fight his mum never won!

Oliver's temper raged as he spied the fruit bowl, on the highly polished mahogany sideboard. A half smile flicked across his face, 'REVENGE' he thought to himself, he dashed over and picked out the largest orange he could find. 'I am sick of people picking on me.', he thought to himself. 'The carefully arranged fruit,' he thought as he grasped an orange, 'you know the old girl will do her nut!'. Oliver did not even like oranges, but he knew his mum hated things out of place. The whole family would snigger as they would watch her move an item by millimetres, stand back, tut and move it again and again until it was perfectly in position. Oliver knew his mum would immediately notice a gap and would have to rearrange the fruit.

Oliver planted himself firmly on the leather settee and waited, the whingeing voice worked itself up to an almost deafening crescendo as his mum stormed back into the room. "Look, your bike is out in the garden, why don't you go for a…?" Mum took a deep breath as she double glanced at the fruit bowl. The sight stopped her in her tracks and made her shake her head and tut in disgust. "Why are you and Michael soooo different?" She griped as she subconsciously rearranged the bowl.

Oliver had no chance to even consider the question before the voice erupted again. "I can't ever get him to stay in!". Oliver heard the exaggerated tut as she removed all the fruit and started to place them one by one back in the bowl, "and I can't get you to go out!" she moaned as she patiently toyed with the various items.

Oliver shot a scowl at his mother, 'Because I hate the fact 'darling Michael' and blasted Spinks relentlessly bully me, that's why I don't like going out, you stupid woman!' His inner voice screamed. Oliver knew exactly what his mum would reply if he said anything. The answer was always the same, "Well stand up and hit them back!" was her usual unhelpful reply.

Oliver tutted angrily as the droning continued outside, 'retaliate?' he thought to himself, 'when I do try to retaliate, what happens?' He subconsciously slowly shook his head from side to side, 'the little git goes running off and tells his mother, then she comes charging around here like some enraged hippopotamus!'. Oliver smiled as he imagined an enraged hippopotamus, with bright red lipstick smeared around its mouth. 'Her bum wobbling like a big jelly as she marches up the path, accompanied by an extraordinarily overpowering stench of rotting food and stale sweat. She waddles up to *my* mum and explodes in a rage of exaggeration, often with her face turning purple with anger as she wiggles and waggles her finger all over the place, accompanied by wild body gestures.' Oliver closed his eyes as he imagined the scene, 'Then what happens?'. Oliver took a deep breath, 'I get into trouble... *again*!", he released the huge lungful of air as the internal monologue continued, "I just can't win," he thought, "I just can't blasted well win!"

Mum stood back and subconsciously nodded her approval at the now perfectly arranged bowl. "Grandad is at home by now, why don't you jump on your bike and go to see him?" she griped with exasperation over her shoulder. "You know how much he loves to see you and enjoys your company." were her parting words as she disappeared into the kitchen.

Oliver was caught up in his own little world. "I've got an idea –

Why don't you just shut up?!" He muttered to himself, 'it's *my* holiday and if I don't want to do anything...' Oliver fidgeted, ' I won't flipping well do ANYTHING!' he screamed in his head as he extended his legs across the cushion. His thumbs joined together at the top of the fruit and pushed down, tearing through the scented skin and the pith before ripping them apart. A pressurised squirt of stinging orange juice hit him square in the eye, just as the perfumed mist assaulted his nostrils causing his nose and eyes to sting and run. Oliver began to devour some of the sweet fruit segments as the second part of his trap was set. He casually dropped the skin into the cereal bowl he had purposely left on the floor, pulled his knees up under his chin, wrapped his arms around them and pulled them close and waited.

His attention was once again grabbed by a familiar voice shouting outside, the voice of his nemesis and archenemy, Alfie Spinks, his brother Michael's best friend. The pair of bullies were a huge agitation in what would otherwise be viewed as a perfect life. To add insult to injury, Spinks only lived three doors away! Oliver felt his forehead crease into deep furrows, 'I wish he did not live around here,' his inner voice screamed in frustration as he pondered, "or on Earth for that matter?" as pictures of Mars flashed across the screen.

Oliver had no idea what made Alfie behave the way he did; and had no real interest in discovering the root cause either, what he did know was the bullying felt relentless. Spinks never passed a chance to pick on Oliver, making sure everybody in listening distance could hear him belittle the lad. Spinks would go out of his way to creep up and land a sneaky flick, a pinch or a crafty punch on Oliver, and always when people were not looking. Spinks would casually slap the back of Oliver's head as he walked past, nudge Oliver's arm as he was writing essays in class, late tackle him when playing football, even when they were on the same team! He would often delight in grabbing Oliver by the wrist with both hands and twisting in opposite directions, quickly and expertly administering a painful 'burn' in the blink of an eye.

"Alfie Spinks." Just the thought of his name sent a shiver down Oliver's spine and made him squirm. "Alfie Robert Spinks… Hang on a minute." Oliver thought to himself, "His initials!", a smile stretched across Oliver's face as a thought flashed across his mind. "A.R.S... his initials spell arse!". The realisation made him chortle, his shoulders involuntarily jerked up and down. "Arse!" he shouted as he started to laugh uncontrollably, Oliver jumped to his feet and started jiggling as he started a tuneless chant.

The dog was jolted out of her doze, greeted with a blurred vision of a strange, demented alien form, jiggling and jumping about, shouting out strange words in front of her. It made no sense to the poor dog, but Kiera was fixated and never being one to pass up a chance to join in, she scrabbled off her comfy spot and, with her tail helicoptering, stretched her paws out in front of her, before she bounded over to Oliver and joined in by jumping up and down, barking loudly along with Oliver's chant.

"What's all this blasted noise?" Oliver's Mum demanded as she steamed through from the kitchen and scowled at the sight before her. "Kiera STOP!" she snapped crossly as she clicked her fingers and gestured at the dog to lie down. A command that the dog ignored completely, she was having too much fun dancing with Oliver and did not want to stop. His mums' gaze fell upon an erroneous item on the floor. "Ohhhh Oliver, for God's sake boy, I have just washed up, why is there a cereal bowl and spoon beside the settee?". Her face turned red with anger at the sight, "How many times do I..."
Oliver did an imaginary fist pump, his trap worked, as he loudly interrupted, "Err, yes mum... I know mum... ehh... sorry mum... bye mum!" as he jumped around the settee and shot out of the living room before his ear could be bent anymore, with Kiera in hot pursuit. Oliver charged through the bright hallway, an image caught his eye and made him stop dead in his tracks. It was his own reflection, captured on the huge, stylised mirror that reached from floor to ceiling. The lad flexed the muscles in his torso and turned from one side to another, "I wish I was a

bit taller," he tutted as he rose up on the balls of his feet. "Like Dad. I wish I was as tall as Dad." Oliver drew a deep breath, "then Spinks would think twice before he picked on me." he exhaled slowly as he looked at his head, "Ginger Nuts?" he mumbled to himself as he pulled strands of his hair taut and examined it closely. "How can Spinks call me 'Ginger Nuts'?" he grumbled to himself, "I'm not GINGER!" he exclaimed loudly, even Michael is more ginger than I am!" He tugged another clump. "I am not even strawberry blonde!" he continued as the dog sat beside him. "I know that because Mum has that special shampoo dye that clearly states, 'Strawberry Blonde', and my hair is much yellower than hers!".

Oliver was the youngest and the smallest in his year, everybody seemed to be taller than he was. Even his twin seemed to be bigger, although Michael was only a full twenty minutes older! For twins they could not be more unlike each other, Michael was physically very different, a wild mop of mousey coloured curly hair framed his chiselled features and a more prominent nose than Oliver's; and was always getting up to no good. Oliver secretly wished for the new term to start. The new school year would mean an influx of first year pupils. They would be younger, it must follow that they would be shorter, he would be able to look down on people for a change! He arched his back as he continued to stare at his reflection, he idly turned his shoulders one way and then the other as he stared at his reflection, "I just hate being skinny!". He turned away and, as he took a step forward, his foot met with a rogue training shoe, causing him to trip and stumble. "Grrr... was that you, you blasted dog?" he growled as he kicked his foot out and angrily punted the shoe out of the way before glancing crossly at the dog beside him.

The young lad bounded up the stairs, his feet thumping down heavily on each of the wooden steps, making such a loud clomp it made his mum shout at him. Oliver shot into the bathroom, washed his hands and face before slipping out of his pyjamas, idly letting them drop to the floor. He would often wonder if there was such a thing as a 'tidying fairy' in the house, because his pyjamas were *never* where he left them!

Oliver bounded to the corner of the bathroom, opened the airing cupboard door only to have his favourite T-shirt fall out, 'another good omen!' Oliver thought to himself as he continued to push his toothbrush around his mouth with his other hand. He hated cleaning his teeth, but his mum always checked by insisting she smelled his breath to make sure he had dragged the mint mush around his gob. Besides, it was easier to clean his teeth than incur the wrath of mum! Although he did often wonder how Michael seemed to get away without being checked, his toothbrush was always drier than the Atacama Desert, and his breath always stank. 'Maybe that is why mum never checks his breath!' He thought, making him smile as he shrugged his shoulders.

Outside Kiera was waiting obediently for him. She had circled tightly three times before planting her prone body right in front of the bathroom door, resting her chin on the floor and closing her eyes - creating a perfect trip hazard! A creak on the stairs made the dog lazily open one eye and slowly turn her head in the direction of the noise; only to witness Michael sneaking up. She sighed, placed her chin back down and closed her eyes once more. Michael slipped into the bedroom that he shared with Oliver, tiptoed across the carpeted floor and climbed into the wardrobe… The trap was set!

Oliver gingerly stepped over Kiera and as he did so she opened her eyes once again, stood up lazily and dutifully followed him into his bedroom. Oliver threw the t-shirt on to his bed, drifted over to the set of drawers, rescued a pair of pants and grabbed some socks and drew them on. He never seemed to own a matching pair, perhaps the reason being his mum! She would dump a pile of underwear on each of the boy's beds and they were supposed to match the socks and put them in the drawer, but Oliver being Oliver, there was always something more important or fun to do!

Oliver opened the bottom drawer and grabbed a pair of jeans, balanced precariously on one leg as he held the trousers open and tried to guide the raised foot in. He was so off balance that he ended up jumping and leaping uncontrollably around, but gravity got the better of him, causing him to lose his balance and fall flat on his face. Oliver managed to pull the jeans up and fasten the blasted things, sat up and reached for the side of his bed. He eagerly grabbed the edge and pulled himself up and rested his chin on his duvet. He glanced over to where he had chucked his t-shirt and noticed a box underneath it. The lad jumped up, grabbed the shirt and stared in amazement at the now exposed cardboard, his face dropped as he immediately recognised the logo and corporate colours of the very trainers he had been pestering his mum for. Oliver threw on his t-shirt as he rushed to open the box and reveal its prized contents. He eagerly pulled out the paper and cardboard inserts, his face beamed as he loosened the laces and placed them on his feet. He pulled the laces tight and tied them into a double bow before standing up and slowly wandered about the floor, staring down with amazement as he did so. Oliver could not wait to get outside and get to grandad's house to show them off. He dashed to the wardrobe for a jumper, threw open the door and nearly jumped out of his skin with fright as a body dived at him from the darkness.

"Victory will be mine!" Michael screamed from behind a hideous face mask that he had grabbed on the way to his hiding place. The yellow-fanged mouth part looked as if it was dripping with a thick mix of mucus and saliva and, as he lunged at Oliver, he thrust his filthy claws towards him.

"No, you don't; not this time!" growled Oliver, as he swiftly stepped to one side and lifted his arm to block the dirty-fingered thug. His brother made a mad grab for Oliver's throat, and contact was made. The pair wrestled as Kiera, who would never miss a good tumble, rose on her hind legs, barking as she tried desperately to get between the pair and into the heart of the action as the boys battled and grappled with each other. Oliver lost his footing and started to tumble backwards towards the ground. Gravity did its worst; he could not help himself as his head was forced towards the carpet.

"This is going to hurt!" he thought, as his head got nearer the ground, the closer he got, the slower time went. He closed his eyes tightly as he braced himself for the inevitable impact.

Chapter Two

Emperor Nero shouted for a clerk immediately on hearing the news of a suspected Druid uprising, he was all too aware that the situation in Britain was fast becoming untenable if he did not act decisively. He called for his scribe and instructed him to issue instructions for one of his favourite and most trusted governors, a fearless general, a man who was almost as psychotic as himself. The instruction; to attend him immediately. Nero knew he had to assert all the power and might of Rome directly on the island of Britannia to the northwest that had proved problematic for generations, full of dangerous barbarians. A land that had given Rome such costly trouble over the years. Former emperors had forced her boundaries to ebb and flow. Rome had applied brute force but the Briton's never fully capitulated, the Empire's campaigns seemed to have been compromised for one reason or another, so the Emperor had implemented various ways to finish these troublesome beings - attempting a cunning plan to take the lands. Rome would seduce each of its ignorant tribal leaders in turn and lead them into a union with Rome, making them believe these peasant leaders were equal to the Emperor himself and would come under the protection of the Empire. Part of the trap would involve seducing them into signing binding contracts that favoured Rome in the long run. In effect the tribal puppet kings not only embraced Rome, the technology, the fashions and the Roman way of life, they really did belong to Rome. The kings paid taxes, obeyed Rome's instructions, her laws and most of all, offered no resistance. If the tribal king broke the Empire's laws, failed to pay taxes or died with no legitimate male heirs, the lands and wealth automatically become the Emperor's.

On receiving Nero's directive, the clerk immediately ran from the Emperor's chambers, sprinted through the labyrinth of rooms and corridors as he searched desperately for the

Sergeant of the Guard, who in turn dispatched his men to find Gaius Suetonius Paulinus with the greatest haste.

Suetonius was not difficult to find. He was resting at home in his villa on a southern hill overlooking Rome itself. Its position was deemed to be one of the best in the known world, as it was always bathed in glorious sunshine all year round.

The approach to the villa was a long, cobbled track, lined with poplar trees, giving much needed shade from the summer sun that could be ferocious and relentless, and hiding the countless rows of grape vines that graced the front of the property. Ancient olive trees grew to the rear thus Suetonius was surrounded by the two favourite staples of a privileged Roman existence.

The villa itself was an impressive two storey building set in exquisitely manicured, landscaped gardens, a large wing on either side created an impressive U shape. The main entrance was set in the centre and a large water feature and fountain meant that you had to approach from a certain angle, and circle around the water feature as you came around the front. This made the house look even more impressive as you circled around. Its roof was made of terracotta tiles that absorbed the sun's rays and reflected the character of its owner – the sharp lines were immaculate and pristine. Every detail was designed to take your breath away and reflect the enormous wealth of the occupier. Although not all the wealth had been earned legitimately!

Every room was lavished with the most expensive furniture, gold fittings and exquisite, reclined seats adorned with fine silks. The walls were expertly decorated, hand painted with scenes from Rome's glorious history or representations of his favourite pastimes, depending on the room's use. The centre of each floor had a mosaic that had been laid by the best designers in the Empire. Each mosaic was of a different god, their motto enclosing them in a stylish circle. The army of slaves that Suetonius owned to wait on his every need, whim and desire moved around the villa almost silently, as they went about their work. Each one did not want to disturb their master and suffer his displeasure. All were careful not to look at him directly, always making sure they averted their eyes in his presence. Conversations never happened in the main rooms because if he heard your voice, he would issue savage beatings, being careful not to kill (slaves cost money!) or sell you on to another master or to Gladiator School without warning.

Suetonius was busying himself in the inner chambers of the sprawling villa. The view from the open doors and flanking windows of the room was of the central gardens, embellished with exotic plants and a bubbling water feature with an image of Bacchus, the god of wine, surrounded by cherubs. The General was attending to domestic matters and dealing with some laborious correspondence when he became aware of a commotion towards the front of the house. He closed his eyes and listened to footsteps getting louder as the owner of the feet ran along a corridor, heading towards Suetonius's inner sanctum. Andronimus, the house head-slave, finally found his master, and puffing heavily, he knocked on the door frame, cleared his throat and gasped, "Excuse me sir, I am deeply sorry to bother you, but there is a messenger at the door. Are you receiving anybody today?"

Suetonius threw his head back, while keeping his eyes firmly closed, "What does he want?" he enquired bluntly.

The unfit house head-slave fought for breath. "He won't say sir, but he is dressed in the uniform of the Emperor's private guard," Andronimus declared as he wheezed heavily. "I asked if there was a message, but he refused to say. All he would tell me was that he has a scroll for you and you alone."

His master tutted heavily. "Show him through!" an agitated Suetonius mumbled.

Andronimus scrambled back to the front door, caught the eye of the tense looking man, "This way," he abruptly urged the messenger, as he lowered his head, turned around to face the direction he had just come from and started running through the entrance hall and back up the corridor. The messenger obediently started to walk behind, Andronimus glanced over his shoulder and gesticulated wildly with his left hand. "Keep up!" the eager slave commanded and as he looked forward again, he realised the messenger was dawdling behind. "Master won't wait..." he continued as he temporarily forgot he was just a slave, as he hurried back to his master. The pair eventually reached the room that Suetonius occupied, Andronimus stepped to one side and waved the man through.

The messenger halted for a moment as he reached the doorway and waited for an introduction, which was not forthcoming. He paused, cleared his throat before smartly taking four paces into the room as Suetonius's gestured for him to approach his desk. He halted and pulled himself up sharply to attention, "Hail Caesar!" he shouted as he looked ahead and raised his right arm in a traditional Roman military salute.

Suetonius fleetingly looked up at the man in front of him, "Hail!" he replied, slightly raising his right hand in response and looked back down at the papers that were laid out on the desk in front of him.

"The Emperor demands your presence at your earliest convenience, Sir!" The messenger ventured as he passed the scroll to the General.

Suetonius looked up at the hand that grasped the sealed parchment, "Is this a request, a demand or an order?" he enquired sarcastically as he reached out and took the letter from the messenger. He broke the Emperor's seal, unrolled the scroll and scanned the sketchy handwriting.

"I believe the Emperor *demands* your presence at your earliest convenience, Sir," repeated the soldier as he continued to stand to attention, his chin up and gazing into the middle distance.

"Very well!" sighed the General before shouting, "Andronimus, have my horse saddled for me!" The General rose out of the chair as he addressed the messenger. "Thank you, you may go, you have executed your orders."

The messenger remained at attention, "My orders are that I am..." the man swallowed hard, the General's reputation for temper was well documented, as he continued, "I am to escort you to the palace, Sir!"

Suetonius patience snapped; he hated the thought of an escort. In his experience escorts were usually sent to escort prisoners. "BY WHOM, MAN?" he screamed in the soldiers' face, but did not wait for a reply as he continued to bellow, "I AM A GENERAL AND YOU DARE TO TRY TO ORDER ME?"

The soldier started to shake at the wrath that spewed from Suetonius as the General reached for his gladius sword and started to pull the blade from the elaborate scabbard. The Guard had seen action and had been involved in many fierce battles before being hand-picked as one of Nero's own personal guards, but the General's action made him wince, much to the General's inner amusement. Suetonius looked the soldier up and down with a look of distaste, "Nero's Guard!" he exclaimed, "Snivelling wretch," he snorted in disgust as he looked at the man with repulsion. "GET OUT!" he screamed. The order caused the soldier to impulsively salute, turn sharply, and depart the room smartly, grateful he was leaving with his life!

Andronimus waited for a minute or two. He knew his master well, and he would calm down quickly. Experience told him it was never wise to bother him too swiftly as the Master could turn on you faster than a whip could crack. The slave gingerly knocked on the door frame before informing the General, "I have taken the liberty of having Apollo saddled and he is waiting for you at the front entrance, Master." His words had fallen on deaf ears. The General had left the room and was now looking out of the large window on the front aspect of the villa, observing the soldier and the other members of the escort that had been sent for him, as they exited the front gates of the Villa and galloped off towards the great city. The slave knocked again and repeated his news.

Suetonius nodded slowly as the words penetrated. "Good," he muttered as he turned to the faithful slave. "I will not be eating here tonight. The Emperor demands my company." As his master passed, Andronimus bowed his head subserviently and acknowledged the news. Suetonius dismissed the slave as he disappeared into his dressing room to prepare for the meeting.

Apollo was a fine black beast. His body was a mass of rippling muscle with a fine black mane and tail that had been plaited. The splendid, majestic animal had poise in its demeanour. To some it appeared quite skittish, volatile and unpredictable. The horse always carried himself as if he were about to burst into full flight. Suetonius had to use all his skill and strength to keep the highly strung animal under control, and he loved it. He felt as if they were kindred spirits, both of them independent and strong willed.

Suetonius finally reached the city gates. The guards waved the General through as he slowly approached. He held his cloak open to reveal he was unarmed at every guard post. He rode through the streets and as he did so, he appreciated just how honoured and fortuitous he was to have his house in the hills. The stench of raw sewage in the streets almost made him retch. Having been raised in the city he would have imagined he would be used to the gagging smell. The Roman love of strange dishes and sauces like garum (a sauce made from rotting fish guts and heads that was fermented in the hot summer sun) certainly did not help. It was only a momentary reaction though and quickly passed, it always happened when he rode through the city gates after a period of time. He had become acclimatised to the fresh air in the hills, although sometimes he would catch a whiff of the city if the winds blew towards his house, but for the most part he lived where the air was delightfully fresh, often the only assault on the nostrils was from sweet perfume from the jasmine that had been positioned and was growing around the villa's windows.

Apollo moved with grace and purpose through the cluttered streets His head was up as he observed and listened to all the bustle of the crowds as they busily went about their lives, his muscled legs exaggerating every step. His front legs lifted high, looking as if he were about to paw the ground with every step. He deftly avoided carts delivering goods, people stepping out of the wooden high-rise buildings and staggering off the pavements and into his path. Barking, snapping dogs rushed out of the open-fronted shops towards him, but he never missed a step. His sure-footed hooves planted each shoe delicately down, avoiding the stepping-stones that had been strategically placed so that the hordes of Roman citizens could cross safely without having to step into the stinking, rotting mud. As the roads narrowed towards the splendid Senate buildings, he walked past the training area of Octavius Severus Cronos whose name hung in bold letters above the front gate. The most famous gladiator of the time, he was a slave who had won his freedom. He trained with his gladiators in full view of the adoring fans, women would often stop and gaze longingly at the rippling muscles of their favourite fighters. The pugilists would exercise using machines designed to sharpen mental reflexes and increase physical strength, train with various weapons and wrestle almost naked in the scorching heat. The sight of the fierce men with well-honed physiques struck fear into the hearts of opponents. Several arenas around the city advertised the upcoming events on posters glued to the sides of buildings. Wondrous hunting scenes where wild starving animals were the hunters and slaves were the prey. The slaves really were ripped to pieces! The infamous gladiators were usually slaves who were trained in different disciplines such as the Retiarius who was armed with a trident and a net, the Hopomachus who was armed with spears, the Secutor who fought with a shield and a gladius – the short sword used by the military, and the Thraex who carried a small shield, and a curved blade called a sica. All were at their utmost physical fitness and faced each other to fight for glory and the admiration of the crowds or die in the attempt. The more blood and gore the crowds saw, the better the games, and the more excited they became.

Suetonius eventually arrived at his destination, rode through the front gates of the palace and up to the front of the building. He threw his right leg over the neck of his mount, slid out of the basic saddle, and landed sure-footed on the marbled floor, as a slave cautiously approached Apollo and reached for his bridle. The slaves were well aware that Suetonius had been summoned by Nero and all bowed submissively as he strode through the corridors behind Nero's chief of staff, who had been waiting for his arrival. Numerous doors were opened and closed behind them as they ventured further and deeper into the Palace itself, before finally being ushered towards Nero's private rooms. The seasoned General parted a thick, heavy, purple curtain with his left arm, entered a large room and spied the Emperor half reclining on a pile of cushions. "Hail Nero!" he barked as he drew his clenched right fist into his chest and bent down on his left knee in front of the toga-clad Emperor.

"Hail, Gaius Suetonius Paulinus!" the Emperor muttered, sounding very bored and disinterested, as he raised his right hand in a half-hearted salute, before rising to his feet and starting to stride across the mosaiced floor. "Come Suetonius... Join me," Nero requested as he gestured his arm towards his opulent apartments. The pair exchanged pleasantries as they took a goblet of wine each from a tray held by a slave who remained silent and statuesque, as they moved around from room to room before finally settling in the dining room. The eating area consisted of low tables and reclining couches strategically placed around the space. As the pair positioned themselves, legs and feet up on the couches, they faced each other as Nero casually informed Suetonius, "I am sure you have heard about the 'slight issue' we have with Britannia? Or rather, with the Celts, who firmly believe they still own the land and have rights to be there," he said as he grabbed a stuffed dormouse from a platter and filled his mouth before continuing, "The present District Governor has betrayed me, and is, well... How can I put this?" Nero paused as a psychopathic grin stretched his face at the thought of the man's imminent sudden demise, "His post is vacant, or at least will be. I have sent some of my personal guard to help him with his ... 'resignation' shall we say!" Nero declared as he outstretched his arm and inspected his well-manicured fingernails.

Suetonius watched the Emperor as he chose his words carefully. "Help him?" he ventured, with a knowing, sly smile.

"Mmmm," nodded the Emperor. "He, and his immediate

family of course, will be joining their ancestors a lot sooner than they ever imagined!' Nero commented in an emotionless, cold manner. "What else did you think would happen to someone who betrays me?"

Suetonius's ears pricked up. Politics at that time was one of self-preservation as well as self-promotion. "May I be so forward as to ask how he betrayed his emperor?" he probed.

The simple question sparked a rage in Nero. "*How?*" he screamed. "*How?*" The despot could almost feel the veins burst in his temples. "*He failed me, that's how!*" he continued as his face turned purple and he punched his fists on a table. Almost immediately his rage was gone. He turned to the slave who stood by the door, clicked his fingers, and instructed that more food and wine be served. One slave approached the pair and poured fine red wine into the elaborately engraved silver goblets they had been drinking from. The casual small talk continued as slaves moved efficiently around the pair in virtual silence, removing finished dishes, and presenting new delicacies to them, as they reclined on silk-covered couches, propped up on their sides by cushions, swapping stories and anecdotes like a pair of very good, long-standing friends. A myriad of sumptuous dishes was laid out on the table before them. The differences between these two was almost negligible, but they did have some striking things in common, a very disturbing similarity. The pair of them were proven to be extremely dangerous murderers. Each had demonstrated psychopathic traits. They had no remorse, no empathy, and showed no emotion when they extinguished a life. In fact, they both positively relished the pleasure as they committed the act. Nero had even murdered his own mother in order to succeed to the throne.

As the pair continued to discuss Nero's ideas and plans, a small serving girl had reached for an empty platter, as she did so she accidentally stepped on a sharp fragment of mosaic tile which cut her bare foot. The slicing pain caused her to jump suddenly. As she did so she sent Suetonius's wine goblet flying. The contents spilled on Suetonius's toga, sandals and on to a dish of baked sparrows, sending Suetonius into a blind rage. "*Come here!*" Suetonius screeched at the girl as he jumped to his feet.

The girl slowly walked towards the General, her hands clasped in front of her, her head bowed as she stared at the ground mumbling, "Sorry, sorry, I am so sorry, please don't hurt me."

Suetonius refused to listen as he drew his pugio dagger and pointed it at her, "Here, grasp the blade," he growled through gritted teeth. "At the hilt," he demanded.

The young girl's trembling hand reached out and she wrapped her fingers around the sharp blade.

Suetonius stared hard at the girl's innocent face. "Grasp it hard in the palm of your hand!" he screeched as she trembled with fear. "*Harder!*" he yelled.

He could see her knuckles turn white as she held the blade with all her strength. Her whole body started to shake, as a sadistic smile broke across his face. With one decisive stroke he pulled the dagger towards him, slicing deeply into her flesh, blood spilling from the opening wound as he did so. The girl screamed as the pain registered on her face.

"Shut up!" Suetonius yelled at her as he grabbed her hair with his left hand and plunged the bloody blade in his right hand into her throat. "Who gave you permission to scream?" he growled, as he sliced the blade towards the back of her neck. Her face turned white; her eyes rolled back into her head as she dropped to the floor. Suetonius withdrew the blade as she slumped down, calmly wiping it clean on the dress of the dying girl before he nonchalantly returned it to its sheath.

The silence was broken by Nero as he slowly clapped his hands, applauding the General as he calmly returned to his couch and panicked slaves removed the dead girl.

Nero clumsily clambered off the couch and staggered to his feet, the combination of wine, food and not moving for a while had taken its toll. "There was something I wanted to discuss with you., Nero smirked. "I had a list of prospective candidates for the post of Governor in Britain." The despot signalled for a slave to approach with a vase, fished around with his clothing before starting to pee into the receptacle as he continued to talk, "But I now know the answer to the question." He paused as he stared hard at the General, "You are needed by Rome. Are you ready to serve me and make me great?" he requested as he finished peeing and stretched out once again on the reclined chair.

Suetonius was not stupid. The demand was posed as a question, but there was only one answer. Well, only one possible answer if you wanted to stay alive! After all you would be a long time dead, and Roman Emperors had some very interesting, as well as very painful, long, slow ways of killing you. Considering that, as far as Nero was concerned, life was cheap, very cheap!

Suetonius walked towards the despot, stopped and bent down on one knee, bowing his head, "Of course, my Emperor!" he barked as he stared at the Emperor's sandalled feet. He was experienced enough to know that Nero was quite mad and was becoming more unsteady and unpredictable by the day, as rumours of his depravity escalated. He would have you murdered if you so much as looked at his body without his permission. "What would my Emperor have me do?"

Nero turned, "Britannia!" he mumbled as he turned and wandered towards the balcony which overlooked Rome below. His golden crown of laurel leaves caught the sun's bright rays. "Britannia!" he repeated, "Go and show the true force of our mighty Empire. Remind the barbaric hordes who their leader is!" Nero's grasp on his goblet tightened, his knuckles whitened as his rage flared again. "Those tin pot groups are fighting amongst themselves." The madman stared out to the horizon as he demanded, "Divide and rule Suetonius, divide and rule!" He screamed as the vessel started to lose its shape under his ever-tightening grasp. "Kill every man, woman, and child. Raze their straw buildings to the ground and WIPE THEM FROM HISTORY!" he screamed as he threw the goblet against a wall, narrowly missing one of the waiting slaves.

Nero breathed heavily and he paused as his rage subsided, "The elite Ninth Legion is ready to move. I have issued orders for them to receive you. The Sixth have already been posted towards the north, use them too. They are awaiting your command." With that Nero took a step forward and held out his hand, "Do my bidding!"

Suetonius leaned forward to bring his face in line with the hand, and without looking up, kissed the ring of Rome which adorned Nero's index finger.

Nero turned and marched out of the room, leaving Suetonius alone in the space, still on one knee and still looking down at the ground with just the sickly smell of burning incense filling his nostrils. Eventually he stood up, but only when he was sure Nero had gone. Nero was a very unstable and violent man. The rumours of his violent temper had foundation. Suetonius did not want to fall foul of the Emperor and end up losing any part of his body, or his life come to that. Nero was capable of anything by his own hand. Earlier that day, just a couple of hours before their meeting, he had cut the fingers off a musician who played a wrong note as the Emperor was singing. Nero saw himself as a god, and theatre was his kingdom. He believed that he was blessed as an actor, poet, musician, and singer. You had to adore and praise him, or your life could end very prematurely!

As Suetonius rose, his mind wrestling with the enormity of the request, he turned and marched out of the chamber. As he strode to the end of the corridor, he was intercepted by a scribe who held out the Emperor's orders inscribed on a roll of parchment and sealed with a large lump of wax that bore the Emperor's stamp. Not a word was exchanged as he relieved the scribe of the scroll. The scribe simply bowed his head before scuttling off into a side room.

Suetonius paced through the palace with purpose, demanded Apollo be brought around to the front entrance for him to make his leave. The slickly run palace household was way ahead of him. As he reached the palace door, Apollo was prepared, bridled and waiting. A slave stood in front of the beast, holding the horse's bridle and was very careful not to look directly at the new Governor of the troubled island to the north. The sealed orders were placed into a loculus bag, a satchel which fastened to the side of a saddle. He stood on the left of the horse, facing its rump. With one swift movement, he vaulted and landed in the saddle, with the reins in his hands, he pulled Apollo's head round to the left and kicked his heels in. The sprightly stallion sprang into life; his head lifted and dropped a couple of times as if he was nodding, as he viewed the route ahead. His powerful legs quickly took Suetonius to a canter as they headed to the gates.

"Governor of that forsaken land, what, by all the gods, have I done to deserve this tribulation!" he thought to himself as the anger raged inside him. "I will make this task pay. I will have rewards greater than those before me!" His inner voice continued a torrent of abuse as he slowed to a trot and navigated the crowded streets. Around him were the usual sights of the night, thieves, drunks, numerous fights, brothels and prostitutes advertising their trade where, by day, honest traders went about their business. The sounds of traders shouting their wares had been replaced by screams of the night, but still the same stench of the overcrowded city was ever present. He scarcely recognised the dangers as his mind raced, the stomach-turning stench of rotting fish no longer turned his very full stomach as he hurried to reach home.

Suetonius did not venture into Rome very often. The politics of the Senate were the only things in Rome that excited him and made him feel alive. The plotting, planning and backstabbing was almost a farce, if the results had not been so serious. Nero refused to listen to the Senators, which, in itself, was a very dangerous thing to do. After all, the Senate could remove him, even dispose of him. It was well known that many an Emperor had become a victim of a rather nasty accident. Some had even ended their lives resembling pincushions with the number of stabs that they had endured! What Nero relied on was fear. He knew every single man was afraid of him. Fear, Nero thought, would protect him and keep the Senate under his direct control, they would never rebel as a group because he constantly played one off against the other, dividing them and causing distrust between them prevented them rising against him. They were all weak in his eyes.

The result was that the times the Senate met were becoming more and more infrequent. Now they only really met when Nero had demands to make of them. The ones who held the real power were those who had the ear of the Emperor, and Suetonius definitely had Nero's ear. He was adept at judging the future and he skilfully applied the lessons from his military career. Although to the casual observer it seemed more luck rather than planning, playing the political game had made him spectacularly rich and powerful. The officer in him had taught him to always be prepared, to trust nobody. He learned very quickly to keep people on his side and could read people extremely well. He was very aware that people seemed to be attracted to him, coupled with the use of simple psychological techniques. People fell under his spell and his influence. Suetonius always made a point of asking open questions about people, and encouraged them to talk about their favourite topic, *themselves.*

He made a point of remembering little details about those he needed to keep on his side or dominate. He would often record details in a book, referring to his notes before meetings if he needed to. Small things like the name of the person's wife, children and home made him look as if he cared, as if he gave a damn. Which, of course he did not. The one thing he never let slip, was the fact that he did not care about anybody except himself, and by using a barrage of open questions he would deflect any questions about him or his personal life. He did not care if they were alive or dead, if they were sick, deformed or ill, but he always looked interested, with a nod every now and then and a well-timed, wry smile, making sure he kept his secrets very, very secret. He smiled to himself as his thoughts started to form into a plan. As he could see it the advantages of this command far outweighed the negatives. He finally returned through his villa's entrance doors. "As this journey ends another fantastic, opportunist journey is just about to begin!" he mumbled to himself as he dismounted Apollo and strode through the front door of his fine villa.

Chapter Three

The meandering streams were the source of life to Jannon, his wife and his numerous relatives that made up the village, his village. The homestead they resided in was long established and well chosen; water was key to everything. The commodity was scarce in some summers, but the local beavers upstream had created an impressive dam, with a large lodge in the centre to protect their young. This resulted in a steady flow of water in the driest of summers, and almost guaranteed enough to irrigate the crops if required. All they had to do was block the flowing streams and the water was diverted through various channels across the small fields. Once the ground had been watered, the obstruction was removed; allowing the water to continue on its original path.

The Trinovantes had become a very proficient tribe of farmers, their abilities to cultivate land that was considered almost barren, was famous among the majority of the Celtic tribes, both near and far. Jannon often pondered on this well-founded reputation and concluded that it must be due to the appreciation of nature itself, working in harmony and having a deep working knowledge of the surrounding fauna and flora, seasonal weather patterns and the soil itself.

His wife's brother, Kearney, would often scoff at Jannon's reasoning and simply proclaim that every success was due to the gods, and that blindly obeying the sacred rituals of the druids was key. Jannon, however, was not convinced by Kearney's simple reasoning and preferred to keep an open mind, something Kearney was obviously not capable of doing! Jannon would occasionally raise issues and question his wife's relative in attempts to test his mental aptitude, much to the annoyance of Mardina, Jannons' wife. The results were always the same when the two clashed, the heavily built brother would habitually shout louder and louder as his face turned almost crimson with rage and out of frustration he would gesticulate wildly, often banging his fists on the simple furniture. He would make wild accusations and claim that Jannon did not have the same level of belief, this was obviously the only reason why any 'bad luck' they endured was solely down to Jannon. Kearney would then leave the conversation with a big defining 'humph' and walk off into the distance throwing anything he could lay his hands on, or kick any loose object within striking distance. He would then sulk for a few days, not that his silence had any detrimental effect on Jannon, or the rest of the clan for that matter, in fact it was nice to have a bit of peace and quiet!

The homestead was not huge, by any stretch of the imagination, with seven roundhouses, numerous pens or stalls of varying sizes for livestock, a sunken grain pit and a small, square latrine hut that covered a very large hole for human waste! Apart from the fields that were planted with oats and grains, the compound had a small garden, usually tended by the girls and younger women of the group. This was just as important as the main crops in the fields as it was where herbs for flavouring food and drinks as well as the plants that provided medicines, were cultivated. The variety of plants was both necessary and a little bit of a luxury. Wild fruits, such as wild strawberries, blackberries and hazelnut had been encouraged to grow around the perimeter so that the children could harvest the fruits towards the end of the summer rather than foraging for miles.

Jannon had inherited the role of head of the family when his father passed away, an appointment that nearly always went to the eldest son. This law meant that he would reside in the largest of the seven roundhouses and had overall responsibility for the extended family living around him. It was his father's domain and his mother still lived in the building after his father's demise, so she could be cared for as she became less able to fend for herself with the advancement of time.

Jannon opened his eyes and threw his arms up over his head as a he stretched out his body on the raised platform that was covered with various animal skins and acted as his bed. He gave a big yawn as he stared into the dark room before rolling over onto his side and laid his eyes on the most beautiful woman he had ever seen. He gently reached out and touched her cheek before tickling the tip of her nose, causing her to slowly open her eyes. A big smile filled her face as she looked upon Jannon as he watched her. He reached his hand down and touched her stomach. 'Well?" he grinned, "How's my son?" he lovingly demanded.

His wife tutted at the remark, "I have borne you enough sons," she retorted as she playfully hit his shoulder. "This one is going to be a little girl!"

Jannon rubbed his eyes as he sat up on the bed. "Strapping sons are more use to me; girl!" he teased as he stood and started to dress, looking around in the dim light as he did so. "Mother?" he shouted as he climbed into the plaid trousers Mardina had skilfully created. She had used wool from their sheep, using a variety of vegetables to dye threads different colours before weaving them into cloth. She had then taken that cloth and fashioned it into items of clothing, including his trousers. "Fire's out woman!" Jannon boldly stated into the darkness. His words were met with a moan from a figure who slowly rose and started to shuffle around, collecting kindling as she did so before making her way towards the fire pit in the middle of the room. Mardina wrapped a woven shawl around her shoulders. The baby growing inside her was resting on her bladder and if she did not move quickly there was a very real chance she would not make it to the toilet hut. "Don't leave before I am back!" she called to her husband as she deftly darted across the floor and out into the chilled air, "You are in big trouble!"

Jannon looked over to his mother, who had glanced up from the from the smoking tinder with a smile on her face.

Jannon puzzled over his wife's last statement as he observed the fire coming to life. "What?" he asked his mother incredulously, but the question was met with a shrug from the old woman as she wandered over to a pile of dried wood, that was stored in a small area near the door and fetched some to fuel the fire. He looked around as the flames started to rise and illuminate the room, the flickering revealed a few cherub-like faces of their children poking out from the heap of cloth blankets and furs, where they remained sound asleep. The sight made him smile as he picked up a pitcher of weak mead and took a few large gulps. Although the water in the streams were free flowing, the homestead knew water could make them sick, and without natural springs nearby they did not take any risks. They did not know about particular diseases or water-borne parasites, but the women of the household would boil water to brew weak ales and mead. The heady stronger drink was reserved mainly for the evenings, the weaker ones were for daily consumption. The brewing process not only flavoured the water, but the yeast used to turn the sugars into alcohol had the advantage of preserving the fluid and was drunk by all, even the children.

Jannon slipped his jerkin on just as a desperate call came from outside, "Jannon, Jannon!" The shout made Jannon glance at his mother, who in turn had a look that was a mixture of worry, surprise, and glee, perhaps the baby was coming!

The leader dashed for the weathered hides that covered the entrance to the roundhouse, brushing them aside as he ran into the bright sunlight, his eyes quickly adjusted to see his wife pointing at the horizon. Mardina's cries had drawn the attention of the rest of the homestead, and men and women appeared in various degrees of dress. Some of them had little faces peering from behind their parents to see what the fuss was. Jannon peered at the horizon to see a couple of mounted figures slowly heading towards them, both cloaked in white, the first rider was much the larger of the two, the second carried a long staff with a banner attached.

"Mardina, get inside and get the kids dressed," he ordered. "We have guests, and I think I know who they are!" he divulged as he spun around, only to be greeted by a big beaming smile. "Aiden!" he exclaimed as he eagerly threw his arms wide to catch the lad who was now charging towards him. Jannon caught his first born, hugged him tightly as he kissed his head, "You are coming into your eleventh summer, big enough now to come and spend some time working with us men, for sure."

His wife heard his words and fired a cross look at her man, "No you don't!" She growled, "And, I still want that word with you."

Jannon looked up at his spouse, unfurled his arms from around Aiden and playfully rubbed the lad's hair with his right hand. Aiden looked up at his father's face. As their eyes met, Jannon winked and sent the boy on his way. The man looked over and purposely strode toward his heavily pregnant wife. As he reached her, he leaned in towards her and smiled "I love it when you're angry!" he murmured, "Your eyes have a real sparkle!"

Mardina was cross, but Jannon had a real knack of disarming her temper.

He turned towards the smaller houses, each external wattle and daub wall was painted with a different hue, which gave the homestead a certain charm. Jannon decreed that everyone was to prepare for the unexpected guests as he recognised one of the riders. "Tarc the Druid Master is approaching!" he acknowledged with a bright smile as the men drew closer.

Jannon always enjoyed the company of the Druid Master, his tales and stories contained legends of mythical beings and strange doings, delivered in a manner that enthralled all within earshot. As Druid Master, Tarc was highly skilled in medicine, he had a deep knowledge of the human body and how to repair it using potions and poultices. Druids were also well versed in the laws that helped to keep a peace between the tribes, uneasy as it was at times. Tarc's most prestigious role was as a 'shaman', a living link between man and the gods. He would consume a mysterious potion that would cause him to start chanting and dancing. This became more and more vigorous as he danced faster and more manically. It climaxed with his body being taken over by a spirit that allowed him to directly communicate the will of the gods, remonstrating with those who had displeased them and acknowledging those who had shown dedication.

Jannon could not believe that the Druids' arrival coincided with the expected date of his next offspring. He chatted excitedly to the spiritual master and exclaimed that it was indeed good fortune for Mardina that Tarc had arrived.

Tarc dismounted his steed and handed the reins to a villager, who dutifully led the animal away to a small pen, as the Druid moved with a regal elegance among the gathered extended family. "Thank you for your invite to stay Jannon," he graciously acknowledged, "but we are making our way to Donnchad's palace for the celebration of Beltane," he explained, "but I will gladly accept an offer of shelter for a short time!"

Jannon nodded at the request and rapidly made arrangements for the Druid and his apprentice to stay.

Chapter Four

The rain fell in deafening torrents and the earth trembled as the mighty Roman military continued to load the machinery designed to carry out the will of the Emperor and smash the resident tribes, onto a flotilla of shallow-bottomed boats. Each ship master supervised the loading of his vessel, ensuring all the weight was evenly distributed. The last thing any of them wanted was an unbalanced ship out in the English Channel, where storms could blow up in moments and tides could suddenly swell and sweep you away, or even capsize the unprepared. The distance might well be short, but the channel was recognised as one of the most treacherous crossings in the known world. The constant driving rain had temporarily stopped the military plan in its tracks. The weather was starting to test the patience of every man, but no one quite as much as much as Suetonius. His lack of tolerance and fiery bad temper preceded him and was never doubted by all who had the dubious pleasure of knowing the General. He and his officers had all taken refuge in harbourside offices while the organised bedlam of the boats being laden went on around them. Suetonius took advantage of the delay by running through orders and his detailed plans once more with his officers as they waited for the off. The scores of ship masters barked commands as the harbourmaster screamed his directions, desperate to make himself heard over the sailors, the driving rain and howling winds. Suetonius suddenly fell silent, stood bolt upright and froze as the sound of a neighing horse reached his ears. "Apollo!" he exclaimed loudly as he dropped the papers, sprinted out of the tent and into the storm with no further explanation.

The General dodged, elbowed and barged past people, ordering them out of the way, his leather-booted feet smashed through deep puddles as he desperately made his way towards the origin of the distressed sounds. Suetonius jumped on to the wooden deck of the ship and ran to a gaping chasm in the deck, through which goods, equipment and animals were being lowered to the storage deck below. "STOP!" he screamed as he leaned over the edge and witnessed the sight of a very distraught Apollo, bucking and pawing the wooden deck, throwing his head, desperate to try and free himself. A combination of slaves, port workers and soldiers, were busy acting on the ship masters' orders, all trying to cajole and manhandle the beast into a stall. In a single moment they stopped, turned and looked upwards as they strained to identify the person responsible for the shouting.

Whilst they peered at the figure above, the horse reared up, tearing the ropes clear from their fastenings and bucked violently. As it lashed out, its hoofs caught a young slave heavily in the back, causing the boy to shoot through the air and smash into the ship's hull. His ribs crashed with a sickening crunch into a row of metal studs, that held the keel to the ship's ribs, before his lifeless body fell to the deck. The men instinctively ran over to the lad as Suetonius sprinted to the stairwell, jumped down the stairs and dashed towards the horse. His speed slowed as he reached Apollo. He reached out gently and clasped one of the ropes, talking quietly to his pride and joy as he did so. The horse quickly calmed at the sound of the familiar voice. The General gently touched the only entity he had ever felt any real affection for, stroking the beast's neck as he hushed him softly. Lost in the moment he completely ignored the men trying hopelessly to revive the heaped body. Eventually he led the beast forward into the stall and tied Apollo's reins and halter lead to a rail, stroking and gently patting the animal's black-haired body as did so until he was satisfied the animal was secured, safe and settled. The General made his leave and patted Apollo's rump as he exited the stall, inhaling a deep breath through his nose in order to draw in the faint aroma of horse as he did so.

He marched directly over to the men who were crouching where the boy lay, one of them gently scooped the limp body up in his arms as tears rolled down his face. The General was incensed with rage and anger. "What the hell were you bloody idiots doing with MY HORSE?" he growled, desperate not to spook Apollo. He pointed at three soldiers who had run over to try and control the situation, "Get up the stairs and get to my tent NOW!" he snapped.

The heavy, driving rain showed no sign of easing as the drenched figures dragged their weary bodies to the offices that the General had commandeered while he waited for the weather to break. The guard ushered them into Suetonius' office and the three marched in smartly and came to attention in front of his desk where he was reviewing a pile of papers. The only sound to be heard was the water falling from their drenched clothes as it smacked onto the wooden floor, as the three men stood shoulder to shoulder in front of Suetonius, patiently waiting for him to finish reading. The General glanced up briefly and glared at the soldiers before looking back at the huge pile of parchments splayed out on his desk. "Well?" he demanded as he glanced through the sheets that he was shuffling. The question was met with silence, the men had no idea as to what the General was alluding. A silence that was deafening as the three started to look at each other uneasily. The General dropped the papers from his hand as he slowly stood up, staring hard at each of the faces in turn before clearing his throat. "I asked you a question," he snapped as he stepped away from the desk and wandered around the desk to where the three were standing. "I want to know who was responsible for upsetting my horse in the ship's hold?" he demanded as he turned and started to pace in front of the men. "Who was it?"

The question was again met with silence as the three did not grasp exactly what the General was asking. Eventually one of the soldiers blurted out, "I am not sure sir, the horse was spooked, we were trying to get it safely into the stall."

The General turned to face the man, "Safely into the stall?" he repeated slowly in a menacing tone. "That was NOT what I witnessed! If I had not intervened, you were going to inflict irreparable damage to the horse." His face lost all emotion and his eyes cleared like glass, as if he was being possessed by an evil force, "A very valuable horse... MY HORSE," he growled.

The men looked at each other in puzzlement as they still could not figure out what the General was insinuating. Suetonius clenched and unclenched his fists, the muscles in his lower jaw were very visible as he clenched and unclenched his teeth, the rage inside him starting to rise. "That horse is worth more than all of your miserable lives added together!" he exclaimed. "So, this is what is going to happen." The General paused as he strode over to a trunk, opened it and retrieved three pugio daggers. He wandered over to his desk, removed all the papers from it before placing the weapons in a row in front of the three. The General stepped back and stared hard into their faces. "I do not care who is ultimately responsible and I have no time to establish who is, so you will decide between you."

The men's faces drained as they glanced nervously at each other, the General walked over to the door, halted and turned to look at the men standing near his desk and brightly announced, "I am going to walk out of this door and close it behind me." Suetonius paused to allow the words penetrate the three soldiers' minds. "One of you will follow in my steps, the other two will be dead," he casually informed them as he turned and reached for the door handle. "If you cannot decide... You will all die!" The Generals' lips slowly rose into a sadistic smile as he opened the door. "You have five minutes," were his parting words as he left the room and slammed the door behind him, the men's cries for clemency falling on deaf ears.

Suetonius stomped out of the mess and into the rain, paused, closed his eyes, lifted his face to the sky as he took pleasure from the wet drops smashing on to his skin, the experience momentarily distracting him from his world. He took a deep breath and held it briefly before snapping back to reality, strode with purpose over to the duty officers' post and called for the officer, who quickly identified himself.

"That is my office." Suetonius explained as he pointed to his quarters, "the door will open in a few minutes and one man will appear," he continued, and he lowered his arm as blood curdling screams emanated from his room. "There will be two dead bodies inside, you are to clear the bodies and the mess immediately, do you understand?"

The smartly dressed officer pulled himself to attention, "Yes sir!" he barked.

The General nodded in the direction of his room as the screams and shouting continued. "Oh, and the one that will emerge..." he said in quite a matter-of-fact way, "is a murderer and is to be executed immediately, do I make myself clear?"

"Yes sir!" snapped the unblinking officer.

The General nodded his approval and made his way to visit Apollo, satisfying himself that his pride and joy was settled before conducting a tour of the harbour and inspecting his men as the grizzly deed was carried out.

The rain failed to cease but the winds dropped enough to enable the military to proceed with the crossing. The continuous rainfall drenched the land and penetrated clothing, soaking through to the skin in moments. The oiled leather tents of the legions afforded little protection as the water had started to flood under the tent flaps and had started to ingress through the stitching. The camp was dismantled at speed and loaded on to the various vessels, followed by the thousands of soaked legionaries, many of whom started being seasick before the boats had even left the harbour! The arduous crossing was long and rough, and on reaching firm ground the men mumbled their gratitude to their favourite deities for having survived the crossing. Their bodies continued to sway back and forward as their legs slowly readjusted from being on the rocking, pitching crafts.

One drenched individual clambered through the mud along the newly erected rows of tents, makeshift coverings, equipment and wagons. He asked several people where he could locate the General but no matter which direction he took, he just seemed to end up back where he started. Eventually he stumbled upon the tent of the Procurator and, when learning of his message, Decianus led the way through the encampment. As they approached the opening in the fencing that surrounded

Suetonius's extensive personal quarters, the messenger hurried on. He made his way past the guards and repeated his purpose several times before he was finally ushered through a thick velvet curtain, "Ave, Dux... I bring news!" The messenger stuttered as a group of bodyguards pulled their swords to protect their leader Suetonius, as he slept in his campaign cot.

The noise roused the general, "Mmmm, what?" sputtered the new Commander of the Roman campaign in Britannia as he woke, stretching his body out of its slumber as his dreams turned to reality. "Speak!" commanded Suetonius as he rubbed his eyes, swung his legs over the side of his cot and sat up.

The messenger ventured forward and dropped to his knee. "I bring news of an uprising," he said as he struggled to see the drowsy General in the poorly lit room. The oil lamps flickered and were dimming as they started to burn out. The man cleared his throat and continued, "There is news of a move against Rome, the Celts to the far north of Britannia have made attacks from the northwest and have started to push Rome into a retreat!" the messenger declared as he bowed his head.

"And?" the General growled, "You wake me for this?" he questioned as he shook his head in disbelief. "This..." he grumbled as he gesticulated wildly, "NOTHING!" The most powerful man sent by Rome struggled as he raised his body off the bed and stood up straight. He arched his back, started to stretch the sleep out of his stiff limbs and, as he rolled his head in a complete circle, called for his slave, "Boy, bring me my piss pot."

The slave rushed forward and placed it before his master, before stepping back a few steps and staring at the ground, waiting for the next order from his impetuous master.

The General confidently threw his head back and, as he continued to empty his bladder, he shouted to all within earshot, "Get me Catus Decianus... Find him at once!" The General mulled over the information, as he considered the news, a smile appeared on his face and he muttered to himself, "Mmm.... Good... Very good..." His attention suddenly returned to the domestic situation as he wandered forward and nearly fell over the messenger.

"Get out of my sight!" Suetonius growled as he raised his arm and flicked his hand towards the door indicating that the slave should leave rapidly with the recently filled jar. He barely had time to finish the rest of his ablutions when Decianus burst into his inner sanctum.

Decianus had heard the basics of the news as the messenger arrived and gathered as much detail as he could as they both rushed to Suetonius' private quarters. He had known that he would be called for at some point. The podgy Procurator panted so heavily that the guards could hear his wheezing and puffing before they could see his overweight figure stagger from the darkness, and they ushered him past without a single challenge. "Ave, Suetonius!" saluted the Procurator, nearly falling over from exhaustion as he staggered into the General's bedroom. The Procurator was the Roman government's financial agent and had been in Britannia for some time.

Suetonius looked at the man with a certain degree of repugnance before finally asking, "This Druid thing... This so-called uprising with the tribes and these bloody druids..." "The Cornovii" Decianus interjected.

The General fired a cross look at the Procurator as his train of thought was rudely interrupted. He paused, raised his right hand in the air and waved it vaguely in a circular motion as he retraced his thoughts. "Druids and the north tribe thing..." he finally repeated with a tone of dismissal and disgust in his voice. "What do we know?" Suetonius demanded.

Decianus dabbed a cloth over his purple, sweaty face as he gasped for breath. "They are being almost impossible to fight, catch or trace. These people to the North and West." The man arched his back in an effort to ease the muscles that were now burning as lactic acid started to surge through his body, "The tribes number around fifty thousand or so. We were led to believe most were farmers." The man was silently relieved that he was not forced to do route marches as he drew another deep breath, "All these tribal leaders think that they are equal to Rome and to the Emperor. These ridiculous fools think Rome is going to be easy to remove by launching attacks from nowhere and then retreating into the mist." The man paused as he gasped once more, "Our Roman predecessors suffered the same in the South but changed tactics and started to adapt to the situation by creating puppet kings. The South was such a great success, they did such a great job of winning over these barbarians they now truly believe that they are not only kings of their people," the man leaned over and steadied himself on the General's desk, "They look out from their simple mud roundhouses and truly believe they are kin with the Emperor himself!" Decianus started to laugh at the absurdity of the situation. "The Cornovii, the Deceangli and Gangani are examples." He grinned.

Suetonius looked at the man incredulously as he exploded, "They what?" He snarled, "They think what?" The General could barely believe the words he had heard. "These barbaric bastards dig around in the mud and they think they are *equal to the Emperor! A man who is the ruler of the greatest empire the world has EVER known!*" Suetonius screamed as his face turned purple with rage. "I will tell you what Rome thinks of this snivelling scum, shall I?" Suetonius closed his eyes tight and clenched his fists. "I will tell you of their position in our Empire!" he shouted as his jaw clenched and he looked for a surface to hit. "They are less worthy than the shit on the shoes of our slaves!" he raged as he brought his clenched fist down on the table before him with all his energy. He quickly turned his back on the men who had just witnessed his temper so they could not see his anger as the red mist cleared. He swung around to face them again. "I am already sick of this cesspit of a country!" he declared as his gaze focussed on Decianus and he threw his fist, his index finger outstretched, towards Decianus' face. "I am furious that you, and all who came before you, could not crush the rabble in this god-forsaken place." His rage almost made Decianus empty his bladder with fear and the colour suddenly fell from his cheeks as the General continued, "Because of your lack of control, your greed, I have been forced to come over here to this hell hole of a place, when I should be relaxing and enjoying a life of privilege in glorious Rome... And... *I* have to SORT IT OUT!" Suetonius temper was rising again as he wandered over to the Procurator. "AND YOU FIND THIS... FUNNY!" he screamed into the man's face. Wild strands of spittle exploded from the General's mouth and slapped the man in the face. The rage was burning inside Suetonius as he stood with his hands drawn into fists so tightly his knuckles were white. His face was contorted, and his jaw was clenched so hard, you could see the veins standing out around his temples. He drew himself up and moved so close to Decianus their noses almost touched and growled in his face, "I want to crush this scum... I want their land, their treasures, I want the elderly to be put to the sword, I want their lands awash with their blood, I want the fit and strong made slaves and the villages burnt to the ground. I want them erased from history. *See to it!"*

Decianus hung onto the last few words that fell from the General's mouth and silently breathed a sigh of relief that he was to see another dawn. In fact, he had been waiting for this moment, he could sense an opportunity and smell the greed. His empowerment was the break he had been patiently waiting for, the chance that could, or rather would, make him very, very rich; now he had permission from the top, he was going to take full advantage. He was going to become a very wealthy and powerful man. So rich and powerful he would never have to entertain despicable violent thugs such Suetonius or have them scream in his face in the middle of the night ever again.

Decianus almost forgot himself as his imagination ran away with him, but quickly managed to remember the etiquette of the situation as he pulled himself to attention as he heard the words, "Ave, Dux!" He managed to join in with the messenger and as he blurted out the words his clenched right hand struck his chest smartly, almost winding himself in the process. Suetonius impatiently tutted as he nodded his head, "Hail!" he mumbled as he gestured to the pair to get out of his room. Decianus turned on his heels and marched out, hardly able to hide the smirk on his face at Suetonius' words.

Suetonius ordered more oil lamps to light the room, "Rome is going to unleash hell," the words tumbled through his mind. "*I am going to unleash hell!*" He thought to himself as he sat down at his desk and started to scribble. By mid-morning he had the outlines of a plan worked out and assembled a team of the brightest officers from his most trusted cohorts.

Chapter Five

The breaking dawn had a strange feel about it. The sun was nowhere to be seen on the horizon but already the sky was becoming brighter and had a growing baby-blue hue as the darkness of night was banished by the new day. Light refracted off the clouds creating extraordinary hues of purples, oranges, pinks and reds. The sun slowly rose a little higher in the east, its bright orange light flickering through the boughs. The heavy, broad-leafed branches that twisted from thick trunks, mostly growing outwards and upwards from the myriad of sturdy trunks of various tree species. When the winter stripped them of their lush green foliage, the trunks looked like forearms and wrists pushing out of the earth, the boughs looked like bent, twisted arthritic fingers pointing and prodding at the heavens.

The sad, lonely silhouette of a huddled figure could just be made out, cloaked by the darkness in the poorly lit room. The fading shadows in the room flickered as the flames from the dying lamps threw their final death throws as the oils ran low. The shape crouched motionless and silent near the fire, just staring blankly into the void. As you moved closer the form slowly became more defined, it was that of a woman, with shoulders hunched forward as she curled over, her chin gently resting on her knees as she perched precariously on a tiny three-legged stool. A woven shawl was gently placed over her back by her daughter, who was not only concerned for her mother's well-being but consumed with grief herself. The crouched woman reached up for it with her shaking hands and when her searching fingers found the cloth her hands instinctively grabbed and closed tightly on the material, like a new-born baby clasping its hand shut on a parent's finger. Her arms moved, slowly dragging the shawl up over her back and shoulders and up to cover her head. The woman looked away from the dancing flames and caught the eye of the person who had offered the shawl. She slowly nodded her thank you to the kindly figure as the girl reached out and touched her mother's hand. Tear tracks on her cheeks briefly caught the flickering light; her eyes were red and bloodshot. The glimpsing nod was all the recognition she gave before slowly turning her face back to the fire pit, returning to her previous motionless state, lost, silent, just staring at the last of the flames of the fire in the centre of the great hall. The flames danced lower and lower against the black backdrop of darkness. Every orange flash and the reducing red glow emerging from the fire cast fewer and darker shadows in all directions on the wattle and daub walls. It gave a haunting illusion of dancing imps or fairies leaving the party and heading into the dark night to plot their next wrongdoings, mischief and harm at their next gathering, as the dying, flickering light disappeared.

The shawled figure's eyes failed to register or recognise any motion of the numerous people around her as she continued to look forward. Her body gently, rocked back and forward as she stared into the middle distance, as if in a trance. A blank expression filled her once fine features and slightly chiselled chin. The only sound that could be heard was the gentle sobbing of people grieving their loss as they slowly moved in the darkness around the large, high-roofed space and passed the trestle where the body of the King Prasutagus lay. The hunched figure was surrounded by the elders of her tribe, all paying respect to her in their own way as she was comforted by her two loving daughters. They had seated themselves on either side of her, occasionally reaching out their hands and delicately touching her shoulders. Their grieving mother reacted occasionally by reaching her hands up and placing them on her children's soft fingers for a brief moment. She was vaguely aware of their presence, as they verified their love with gentle gestures, whispering occasionally in the woman's ear and reassuring her that they loved her dearly, but she was still very, very alone with her thoughts. She was lost in her own house, even with her own family and people around her, she was still lost. She had lost her best friend, her husband, *her King*.

The lady had a fixed stare but was not seeing anything as her mind reflected lovingly on the man she had just lost. Memories of their time together tumbled through her head, the laughter, the joy, time shared with their beautiful children. Prasutagus had always carried himself with a distinguished, regal air. He had been tall and athletic in build, with striking features, which certainly made him stand out from the crowd. Swathes of blond hair, which was always immaculately brushed and braided fell over his shoulders. On special occasions his hair would be embellished with gold strands and an ornate headpiece would sit on the crown of his head and the finest clothing would adorn his fine figure. She felt a warm glow inside as she recalled his piercing blue eyes, that look he would share with her and her alone when he thought nobody else was looking. His eyes would narrow as his lips turned up and formed a slight smile that would make her heart melt and her cheeks would flush slightly. He had had a smile that could soften the coldest of hearts. The lady sighed deeply as she recollected the tones of his voice, his manner of speaking and the very slight accent which had such an extraordinary effect on people. The king had had a way about him, his character was quite compelling, and people had been subconsciously drawn to him. She had watched crowds hanging on his every word, listening to his voice which was deep, rich and silky smooth. She smiled as, in her mind's eye, she could see him playing with their daughters. The way he would carry them in one hand when they were just born, their heads resting in the large palm of his upturned hand, their tiny bodies lying the length of his forearm with their heels on either side of his elbow. He would often hold them like this when holding court, implementing plans, issuing orders, listening to the arguments between his subjects. He would lift the baby gently up and down, occasionally hushing her as she rocked to sleep while he made and passed judgements. Boudicca's mind jumped to seeing him playing with the girls as they grew, often chasing them around the grassy meadows near their dwelling, the three of them laughing so much their sides would ache and sometimes the girls laughed so uncontrollably they were simply unable to move.

Boudicca heard a single hushed word, "Mother?" The name made the hunched body suddenly jerk in response as she was snapped out of her memories and thoughts, "Mother?" the elder of the two girls, whispered quietly, as she leaned forward and put her arm around her mother and shook her gently. "Mother, it is time, we are here with you, we are both here for you." She whispered into her mother's ear before gently kissing her tear dampened cheek as the pair helped her to her feet.

As she snapped out of the trance, she breathed in deeply through her nose, filling her lungs. The heady mix of wood smoke and a pungent mixture of herbs prepared by the druid master, made her feel lightheaded, as she struggled to compose herself. She turned slowly and raised her arms, placed them softly around her offspring's waists and pulled them both close to her.

"I am fine my darling sweethearts... *We* will be just fine," she muttered in a hushed tone as she gently patted the girls' torsos. She turned her head and tried to smile, even although the pain in her chest made it feel as if her heart was being ripped out.

"You are right," murmured the younger of the two girls, "Everything *is* going to be just fine Mother," she continued reassuringly. Although she was the younger of the two, she had a very calm manner about her. "Father made sure all will be safe for us after he departed this world," she revealed, "We know that he has divided his land and wealth between us and Rome. He informed us of his wishes, and we promised to follow his requests to the last. You are to remain our Queen and your people have sworn sacred oaths to do your bidding and respect your judgement."

The recently bereaved lady looked at each of her daughters in turn, "That is what worries me my darlings, our King is dead, and we are now at the mercy of the Romans." She swallowed hard through the tears of grief that were starting to overtake her. She was very aware, that as a woman, she would not be recognised by the Romans as Queen of the Iceni, she also knew that the documents her husband Prasutagus had signed as a client King, meant that *all* the lands reverted to the Empire on his death if he had no male heirs. She, like her husband, hoped that the last will her husband had drawn up; giving half of his wealth to Emperor Nero, would pacify Rome enough to ensure that they would be left in peace.

Cloths were gently wrapped around the lifeless body by the 'bearers of the afterlife', who were ladies of the court, dressed in ceremonial bereavement clothes. As they finished, they stepped aside to allow the king's body to be lifted above the heads of six warriors. They had been specially selected and were the largest and strongest of the Iceni warriors.

The celebration of the dead king's life started near the grand entrance to the Romanesque villa where Boudicca lived. The slow, steady beat of a solitary drum was eventually accompanied by chanting from a few of the mourners. A druid priest collected the Queen and helped her to the exit of the villa. As she emerged into the daylight, the bright glare stung her eyes, making her blink hard she looked about her and was physically taken aback by the sheer number of well-wishers waiting for her. The Iceni numbers were swelled by Iceni allies and neighbouring tribes; the Corieltauvi, the Catuvellauni and especially the Trinovantes.

Many tribal kings had travelled from afar with their own courts and supporters to pay their tributes and celebrate Prasutagus' life and achievements at his funeral. It had not taken long for the tragic news to travel. Everybody who had ever had contact, either personally or professionally, with King Prasutagus had known they were in the presence of a very important, honourable, and courageous person. A man who always seemed to have his people in the forefront of his mind. Every action and decision he made was always balanced, fair and considerate. Prasutagus prided himself on the success of his family, his people and the alliances with his neighbours, as well as with the mighty Roman empire, that had ensured a period of unrivalled peace. The Romans had forcefully exercised their power and he had quickly realised life was better as part of the Empire rather than to pick fights with the invaders. Rome had proved it was a profitable partner, helping to make him and his people wealthy and had improved all their lives by making life far more peaceful and comfortable, especially if you considered the other options- which were either death or slavery!

Outside the palatial building the large, murmuring crowd of mourners started to separate and fell silent as they made way for a cow, led through the masses by a young druid apprentice. The beast was brought forward while the priests offered prayers and made choregraphed movements, designed to enthral and mesmerise the crowd. As the masses were brought to a frenzy, the head priest raised a huge, curved knife, screamed an incantation in the direction of the sun before dragging the sharp blade around the cows' throat. The opening wound started to bleed profusely before the blade was plunged deep into the animal's neck. The slaughtered animals' knees buckled as it slumped to the ground while more prayers were offered in honour of the dead king. The blood was collected into several large vessels that were passed around the crowd. Each of the mourners took a sip of the blood, a symbolic gesture in honour of the beast giving its life to support life, before passing it to the next person.

The chief priest solemnly bowed his head and led the procession of the druids and the drums, the warriors bearing the King's body, followed by Boudicca and her daughters, up the hill to the grave prepared for the king. A congregation of hundreds followed close behind, all praying to the spirits to take the king to his final resting place with his ancestors.

A druid priest, dressed in a white cloak, stepped onto a rock placed on the top of a large, rounded mound of earth. With several great dramatic gesticulations, he began the ceremony to inter the king's body into a large, prepared grave, with a grand entrance, a narrow stone-lined corridor eventually led to a stone chamber, which contained the bodies of past Iceni kings. He raised his right arm, and with a few words of prayer, reached over to his left side, grasped the handle and released from his belt an engraved and jewelled scythe. This he raised above his head and, with a few well-rehearsed words, he slashed the air, then ran the sharp blade across a fistful of herbs. This display was part of the celebration of the circle of life and demanded the spirit world accept the spirit of the dead king.

The body was carefully carried through the opened entrance to the round burial house and into the prepared grave where he was laid gently on his side; the knees brought up towards his chest into the foetal position. His shield, sword and helmet were placed beside him before the small cortege retreated and the entrance closed. As the prayers continued, a mound started to form as every person present added soil and rubble to cover the entrance. Finally, the turfs of grass were returned, and rocks were arranged on top to seal the grave. As the last rocks were being carefully placed; the crowd turned and slowly headed towards the settlement to continue the salutations, leaving Boudicca alone with her two daughters at the graveside.

The Iceni women had spent the hours of darkness preparing special breads, made from local wild grains and flavoured with wild herbs. The ingredients had taken hours and hours of sourcing, grinding, mixing, kneading, standing to allow the natural yeasts to act with the sugars, the reaction causing the dough to rise before it was 'knocked back' as the bakers kneaded the dough again. The dough was divided into small lengths and allowed to rest once more as the clay ovens were brought up to temperature and made ready to accept the white oblongs, baking them and creating a gorgeous golden-brown crust. The bread sounded hollow when tapped with a knuckle and gave a satisfying crunching, tearing sound as it was ripped apart, revealing a delightful, fragrant interior.

The men had not been idle either, they had busied themselves fermenting various brews, filling jugs with beer and mead, they had butchered several animals, prepared the meats, and erected tables with rustic benches in order that the mourners could be seated as they feasted, drank and celebrated throughout the coming days.

Boudicca was so lost in her memories that she had lost all sense of time. She still stood alone after the mourners and her daughters had retreated. She physically jumped as a hand was placed on her shoulder. The hand's owner cleared his throat before moving closer and uttering in her ear, "Boudicca, I have known your husband from when we were children and we often played together. I feel some of your loss and your pain, as I feel I have lost part of myself as well." The formidable warrior paused as a memory of the two flashed in his mind and he sighed before continuing, "I vow to be by your side, my people are at your command!" proclaimed the tall, powerfully built man.

Boudicca turned and looked Donnchad in the eye before dropping on to her left knee in front of him. "King Donnchad of the Trinovantes, I thank you for your very kind words," she murmured graciously. "My husband was very fond of you and always spoke very highly of you and your people," she continued quietly as she stared at the man's feet, "I am moved and honoured to be in your presence."

The King stretched out his right hand and placed it under Boudicca's chin making Boudicca look up at him. "Stand!" His eyes were bloodshot, and she could see his pain as he tried to smile. "Please stand, Queen Boudicca. I am your equal. I would never expect your husband to bow in front of me. Now you have taken his place as Chief of the Iceni," he murmured as he fought to remain composed, "You are Queen of the Iceni, equal to any King!" he said reassuringly with a tear in his eye.

"King Donnchad, you do realise that Rome will not recognise me as Queen, and even worse, I am afraid that Rome will no longer recognise the Iceni," Boudicca said with a wobble in her voice as she fought to keep her feelings in check.

"We have all signed the same treaty with Rome," countered Donnchad, "and we have been assured that our heirs will be recognised and our lands safe for future generations. The agreements made with the Romans are to remain if we all abide by them. I believe the Romans are honourable and will not go back on the words they have written," he informed her slowly and he nodded to affirm his words. "They are here, on our island, and are hugely outnumbered. They know, as we all do, that as long as we have the numbers, we have the advantage."

"The one thing you are overlooking is that Rome is quite clear, and always has been, that they do not recognise queens as heirs," countered Boudicca, "And I simply do not have your faith, or level of trust in these invaders."

Donnchad carefully considered her words before he continued. He felt the priority was to get the Queen through this day. "Boudicca... you must talk to them. I am sure that you will make them see sense," he smiled gently. "You are exceptional at presenting your position and getting what you want. You have a gift; you excel at making others believe that your thoughts are indeed their thoughts!" Donnchad assured her. "Come, it is time to face your people, to drink with them, eat with them and show them your strength," he advised kindly as he wrapped his large hand around her dainty fingers and squeezed them gently. "They are looking for your help and guidance while they also grieve."

Boudicca smiled slightly at the words as she looked into his eyes. Her eyes misted as tears filled them and ran down her cheeks, before the pair turned and slowly walked away from the grave and towards the largest of the roundhouses and the palace. Her daughters had waited near the entrance to the settlement and fell in behind the pair as they passed. They followed closely behind, silent in their loss and saddened as they remembered those long-lost days. As the last of the mourners wandered back, the gathering clouds released their rain, almost as if the heavens were crying too.

Chapter Six

Oliver felt strange as his head swirled; something was wrong. He had his eyes firmly closed in preparation for the bang on the back of his cranium, but it never came. His head never hit the ground with the painful thud he was expecting. To his surprise, the landing was soft as his head sank into the soft ground beneath him. As he lay there, he was even aware that the dog had stopped barking and his hands no longer seemed to be grasping the monster of a brother that he had a firm grip on. Even his surroundings smelled different, not the festering stench of sweaty socks and boys' room, his nostrils were filled with the aroma of leaf litter, bracken and ferns and he became aware of a damp, earthy smell. Oliver's senses were slowly returning, he moved and tried to sit up as he slowly opened his eyes and as he did, he was immediately thrown back into the moss by someone who was definitely not Michael.

Oliver struggled. "Get off meeeeee!" he growled, as he tried to wriggle free.

"Shhhhh!" hissed the person as he planted his hands firmly over Oliver's mouth in an effort to silence him and pinned him to the ground with the weight of his own body.

Oliver immediately froze, all his energy, awareness and comprehension were stolen from him, and his shocked body stiffened. He was almost nose to nose with the face of a stranger! As his eyes focused, he grabbed wildly at the stranger's wrists, fighting and struggling as he tried to pull them off his. The face moved to Oliver's right and positioned his mouth next to Oliver's ear.
"Stop... Shhhh!" the stranger whispered desperately. "You will get us killed if we are discovered."

Oliver stopped wriggling for a moment and tried to make sense of what was happening. He could hear talking in a strange language, the sound of metal jingling and the noise of a large number of people walking in step with each other, almost as if they were marching, and they were very close by.

As he lay motionless in the moss, Oliver caught a whiff of the person's breath and was nearly sick as his eyes watered. It was a strong smell that reminded him of garlic and poo. How can anybody eat poo, or garlic for that matter? Kiera's breath was never that bad, even if she had been licking her backside, and she did that a lot!

The voices started to fade, along with the steps, as the Roman legion marched past. Strong sunlight filtered through the trees, creating a dappled, shadowy light around the pair. The person pinning Oliver to the ground slowly released him and crouched over Oliver, peered through the bracken surrounding them, carefully checking to make sure they were alone. Oliver could make out the figure of a boy, about the same age as he was but dressed very differently.

The boy slowly turned his head backwards and forwards and he listened carefully as he looked through the fronds of the ferns around them to check the coast was clear before carefully standing up. "Who are you?" the boy whispered once he was sure they were alone, "Or rather what are you?" the scruffy lad enquired as he turned towards Oliver and stared in wonderment at the body lying in front of him.

"I... I... I'm... I'm Oliver," stuttered the shocked, still prone Oliver.

"What are you wearing?" the boy asked with a hint of bewilderment in his voice as he looked Oliver up and down and a shocked look fell across his face as he tried to recognise the colours of Oliver's clothes, "You are not from any of the tribes I know of!"

Oliver did not have the chance to answer as another bombardment of questions came at him thick and fast.

"Are you Roman? Are you spying on me? Are you from the gods?" The lad blathered out, "You must be from the gods, yes, that's it; you must be from the gods!" The boy nodded to himself as gabbled on, "I have never seen anybody like you before."

Oliver was very, very confused. This was definitely not his bedroom; he was not even in his house. Who was this person? He shook his head from side to side as he tried to make sense of it while trying to answer each of the questions being thrown at him. Perhaps he was dreaming. He hoped he was dreaming.

"I… I… I… don't know," Oliver stammered in reply. "I… I… I... really don't know." He spluttered as he rubbed his eyes then scratched his head. "Who the hell are you?" he demanded of his new companion.

The boy eagerly jumped up and down, "My name is Aiden of the Trinovantes," he enthused as he threw his head back proudly, planted his fists firmly on his waist and pushed out his chest, "and this is my land."

Oliver could now see the young lad in his full stature. He was slightly shorter than Oliver, his loose and badly fitting clothes hinted at a slim build beneath. He wore a tunic, coarsely woven from brown wool, a pair of blue and brown checked trousers and a short cloak of the same checked cloth that was fastened at his neck by an iron pin. He had a mass of long red hair, which looked like it had not seen a comb for a while, with strands of hair shooting out wildly in all directions and a braid on one side. The odd bramble was tangled in his hair as he had been running, playing, and foraging around in the undergrowth. The mass of hair draped over his shoulders and framed the owner's thin face, complementing a very pale freckled complexion, highlighted with streaks of dirt and smears of dried mud. "If ever there was a ginger nut!" Oliver thought to himself.

The figure suddenly realised that all his questions had not been answered satisfactorily. "What are you doing on my land?" demanded the vision in front of Oliver.

"This is *your* land?" Oliver whispered in a hushed, questioning, dubious tone, indicating a disbelief of the previous statement.

"Yes. It belongs to MY people," Aiden declared with a real

sense of pride, "and we *hate* the Romans."

Oliver was taken aback by the last claim. "Romans?" he scoffed, "your people?" He taunted gently.

Aiden was perplexed by the attitude of this odd stranger in his midst. "You heard me, it is MINE!" he hissed, his face twisted and contorted as he snarled, "We HATE Romans… And other strangers!"

Oliver's teasing stopped abruptly, "W..W... What?" he stumbled over the words swirling around his head as he attempted to comprehend what he was being told. "Are you Travellers?" he enquired.

Oliver was very confused and could feel a very bad headache fast coming his way. "Did you say Romans?" he pondered, "Romans?" Oliver quickly surmised that this was definitely a wind-up, and he had nearly fallen for it. "He-he-he-he... ROMANS?" Oliver started to laugh so hard he had to wrap his arms around his tummy in an effort to stop the ache, "Ha-ha-ha-ha-ha."

"What's wrong with you?" enquired the antagonised and angry looking lad, "Have you been at the Druids' mead?" quizzed Aiden.

"Mead?" Oliver retorted, "Druids' mead?" he cried as tears started to roll down his cheeks, "Ha, ha, ha, ha." Oliver had heard of mead. Miss Wallace had said something about mead in history at school. He desperately tried to remember. What was it? He could not remember. Oh, how he wished he had paid more attention.

Aiden looked up at the skies. "I have to get home; the light is starting to fade," he declared with a certain urgency as he started to stumble though the incredibly tall ferns surrounding them.

Oliver controlled his mirth, "Okay, nice to have met you Aiden." Oliver smirked as he held out his hand. His Grandad always insisted he did this when meeting a stranger for the first time, and it was now a force of habit.

"You're weird. The gods *have* sent you!" stated the young Celt as he looked at Oliver's outstretched hand with a look of distrust and wonderment.

"Me?" Oliver was still having difficulty believing what he had been told, "*Me*?" he retorted. "I am not the one who jumped on top of somebody for no reason and told them to shut up because a bunch of Romans were wandering past! I know you dress like a pagan in a history book, that is your choice, but to claim that you own this land, or at least your people do!" Oliver derided as he shook his head with a big grin on his face. "We all know the Council owns it," he grinned. "And another thing, you obviously have never seen a dentist, or even cleaned your teeth," he proclaimed bravely, "either that or you have a deep, and very worrying, taste for silage, judging by the smell of your breath, and you have the gall to call me 'weird'!"

Aiden felt a bit taken aback and confused by this seemingly unprovoked attack, an attack from a messenger from the gods of all people. "You *are* weird," he insisted. "Look at you, your clothes, your shoes, even your hair." The young Britain was losing his temper. "You started to give away your hiding place, *nobody* does that!" he retorted. "Even if you wanted to die, and believe me, you would if the Romans got hold of you," Aiden snapped. "If you want to match yourself against their gods, DON'T INVOLVE ME!" His temper was getting the better of him. "Your clothes smell odd, you look strange and have colours that not even the wise druids' wear!" he growled and he looked Oliver up and down as he struggled to think of the next insult, "and, and…your hair is cut short like I have never seen before, not even the blasted Romans have cuts as strange as that." Aiden's face went red with rage as he searched for more aggressive reasons, "and you talk funny!" Aiden harrumphed as he spun on his heels, turned his back, and crossed his arms.

Oliver stood up, dusted himself down and looked through the green bracken and swathes of ferns, but all he could see was more ferns. He jumped up on to a fallen tree trunk and peered over the top of the plants. As he scanned the horizon, panic set in as he realised very quickly, he did not recognise his surroundings at all. "Erm, Aiden, wait, hold on!" he quickly pleaded to the young lad who was fast disappearing through the greenery without him. "Stop!" he shouted out desperately, "How do I get back to Broomfield Road?"

The figure stopped dead in his tracks as he mused over the question, "Where?" a puzzled Aiden replied.

"Broomfield Road?" Oliver repeated, he could hear his voice starting to tremble.

The Celt paused before he shrugged his shoulders. "Never heard of it," Aiden stated in a matter-of-fact way. "I have heard of Watling Street, is it near there?"

"Watling Street?" Oliver could not believe what he was hearing, "What? No!" Oliver felt a shiver of panic overcome him. "That does not help!" Oliver was really scared now, "I have no idea what or where Watling Street is." He fought to keep his frustration under control. "I have no idea where I am and obviously neither do you!" Oliver screamed through gritted teeth. "You said this is your land, or at least the land of your people, and you have never heard of Broomfield Road?" Oliver angrily pointed out as he drew a shaky breath. "Next you will tell me you have never heard of Cringleford."

"No indeed," Aiden shook his head.

Oliver countered, "Norwich?"

"What witch?" Aiden puzzled.

"NORWICH!" shouted a frustrated Oliver.

"I don't know what you are talking about," Aiden was racking his brains, he honestly had never heard of any of the names Oliver seemed to be randomly spouting out.

"I think you might have lost your memory," Aiden whispered under his breath. He started to deduce that this strange boy must definitely be from the gods, purely because he could not think of any person that spoke like Oliver, dressed that way, and asked questions that had no answers. He rapidly racked his brains but could not think of any other purpose for the meeting. He deduced that this strange being could ONLY have come from the gods, and it was safer to keep him on his side and befriend him rather than anger him and incur the wrath of the gods.

After a few moments Aiden had persuaded himself that Oliver must have come from the gods, that was the only reason; and Oliver had been sent to test him. If he did not look after him, he would make the spirits very angry, that was the last thing he, or his people, would want. In fact, he was more concerned about his mother or his father finding out that he had fallen out with a messenger from the gods and what they would do to him. That thought was far scarier! In fact, if Aiden abandoned Oliver and the gods were angered, and it became known that he had done this, it would be widely believed that he was directly responsible, his life literally would not be worth living. In fact, he would be given to the druids who would offer him to the gods and his life would be extinguished as an offering to appease them. His life would be made hell before he would be drugged, bound, dispatched and his body abandoned in shallow grave. Aiden had felt the sting of his father's belt on his backside before. He also knew what it felt like to have his mother drag him by the ear to the cows' enclosure and order him to pick up cow pats for a lot less than this. He also had seen the Druids sacrifice with the victim's death ending in being garrotted and his lifeless body thrown into a bog as an offering to the gods. All of which did not appeal to Aiden at all!

Aiden quickly deduced the only course of action was to keep Oliver close, try to ensure he was safe and get him home as quickly as he could. "Come, stay close to me," Aiden demanded as he beckoned to Oliver, and he spun around on his heels and started to run into the ferns and scrub. Oliver picked himself up and tried to follow the strange boy. After all he knew he was lost and being in dark, strange woods at night was not his idea of fun.

Aiden moved through the forest with the speed of a cheetah,

bobbing beneath low branches and jumping over trees that had fallen. Oliver was running at full speed but could barely keep up with him and struggled with the pace in the fading light.

"Hey Aiden!" Oliver tried to shout as he huffed and puffed, "Wait!"

Aiden stopped dead in his tracks, turned and looked back at his newly acquired guest as he shook his head in disbelief and a flicker of annoyance. "Keep up, I have to get home," he tutted. "I don't know what I am going to do with you!" he declared, just before a smile came over his face as he had an idea flash across his mind. "I know," he teased, "We need a goat herder, and the last one home gets the job!" His taunting did not stop, "You can sleep with them, you'll love it… They all stink!" he teased as he tried to cajole Oliver into keeping up with him, hoping that Oliver did not become suspicious that Aiden had discovered who Oliver really was.

"Goats' stink!!" Oliver mocked, "I'm not sure if you know the definition of stink, but they must really smell bad if you think they smell worse than you do!"

Aiden tried to restrain his fiery temper. "You can always stay put," he snarled as he stopped and turned to face a wheezing Oliver, "And wait for the gods to reclaim your soul."

The pair stared at each other for what seemed like an eternity before Aiden lifted his left arm and playfully punched Oliver on the shoulder as a smile broke out on his face. Oliver could not help himself and started to giggle, not because it was funny but because he felt relieved and knew he would have shelter and food while he worked out what was happening here, and more importantly, how he was going to get back home. Before long, the pair started to laugh. Oliver playfully punched Aiden back, before the pair turned and started to pace along the causeway together.

Oliver glanced to his left as something caught his peripheral vision, "What's that?" he exclaimed as he pointed to a shiny object that nestled, partially hidden in the undergrowth. The pair stopped and moved closer. Oliver could see it was a metal buckle attached to a leather belt that was glinting in the dappled, late evening sunlight as it nestled in the hedgerow. Oliver tentatively reached out, grabbed the strap and gently pulled. As he tugged at it, he realised that there was something on the end. He tugged a little harder and he could see a canister of some sort. The pair looked at each other in wonderment at the find. Aiden gasped as he recognised something on the case as it emerged from the flora. "That is a Roman eagle," whispered Aiden as he pointed to an embossed symbol. "They must have dropped it when they marched past."

Oliver was half listening; Aiden's words did not register as he roughly manhandled the case, turning and rotating it as he searched for the opening.

Aiden suddenly reached out and grabbed Oliver's hands. "Stop!" he cried. His words caught Oliver's attention, making him freeze. "What are you doing?" Aiden demanded as Oliver started to twist one end.

Oliver paused, "I am going to have a look. I have never seen anything like this before." He quipped, "Don't *you* want to know what it is?"

Aiden's panic over come him, "N .... n ... n ... n ... no I don't!" he shouted. "If the Romans catch you with this, they will crucify you," Aiden said in horror.

"Don't be silly, we don't even know what it is yet," Oliver grunted in ignorance as he threw off Aiden's hands and started to strain and twist at the top. The canister eventually popped loudly as the lid parted dramatically from the casing. Oliver was exerting such force with his right hand it shot up towards the sky as it came away, tantalisingly revealing a roll of parchment inside.

Oliver could not help himself, "Look, it's a letter of some sort!" he announced as he tugged and pulled the paper free from the casing, almost dropping it as he did so. There was a weight attached to the centre of the parchment by some red coloured ribbons.

"Hey," whispered Oliver, "that is a wax seal! It looks very important," he said in a hushed voice.

His travel companion shook his head as he stared in disbelief. "I don't like this. I don't like this at all," Aiden insisted as he slowly turned pale, "Put it back and let's go!"

"No, hold on. Let's see what it says. It could be something very important. I learned about this sort of stuff at school," Oliver insisted as he tried to pull the wax from the parchment by sliding his fingernail under it with no luck.

Aiden tutted as looked on, "Use your sgian," he suggested uneasily.

Oliver glanced up, "My what?" he queried.

"Your sgian," the young Celt repeated.

Oliver shrugged his shoulders, "I have no idea what you are talking about!" he exclaimed.

Aiden stared at the lad. "Have you lost it?" he asked. "I would be in big trouble if I lost mine. My father would literally tan my hide!" he said as he reached for the sheath hanging from his belt. "Here, use mine!" Aiden chortled as he grabbed the bone handle and tugged it free from its leather sheath and passed the object towards his new friend.

Oliver was shocked as he found himself staring at a glinting blade. "A knife!" he blurted, "No, we don't carry them." He swallowed hard as he hesitated to reach out towards the sgian. "It is against the law."

"Ha-ha-ha-ha, against the law? You come from a very strange place indeed!" laughed Aiden.

"Look, it doesn't matter now, we'd better get out of here," Oliver gasped as he furtively looked around. "If this is important, whoever dropped it is bound to come back looking for it," he said as a deep frown crossed his brow.

Aiden nodded at Oliver's observation, "Come, this way!" he commanded as he grabbed at Oliver's shirt and started to drag him along.

The pair left the causeway and Aiden took the lead and broke into a trot. Oliver felt like they had been jogging for hours through the dense woodland and undergrowth, when Aiden suddenly had a spurt of speed as he scrambled and climbed his way up a large, steep mound, with Oliver in hot pursuit. Aiden reached the summit, stood up straight, took some deep breaths as he stopped and pointed, "HOME!" He declared with a proud smile on his face as Oliver followed up behind him. Oliver was very surprised to see a large clearing with seven roundhouses and various other buildings in the distance. He observed a few very strange-looking cows, nothing like the dairy cattle he was used to seeing at home. These all looked very thin, grey- brown in colour with ribs poking out, short legs and with very long horns that looked far too dangerous for his liking. Oliver's knees gave way and he fell to the ground in a heap as it registered that he really was not near his home. He looked up as it dawned on him that there were no aeroplane trails in the sky, no traffic noise what-so-ever, which had always been the background noise to his life. In fact, it was so quiet he could clearly hear his own heart thumping in his chest and the air whistling in his nostrils as he breathed, both noises starting to freak him out a little bit. Perhaps the 'Romans' were not acting, perhaps Aiden was not pretending. Oliver slowly realised that he really was lost, not only geographically, and he quickly became very aware that this boy standing next to him was definitely from a much earlier age. Somehow, Oliver seemed to have gone back in time. He buried his head in his hands. His shoulders started jerking up and down as he began to sob out loud uncontrollably.

The young Celt felt a pang of sorrow and reached out his hand and placed it gently on Oliver's shoulder, "Don't worry." Aiden said quietly, "My mother and father will be pleased to meet you, and I am sure you will be made welcome in our house." The young lad reassured him, "Father will know what to do." He heaved at Oliver's arm and tried to lift him to his feet.

"I am lost, really lost. I think I..." Oliver stopped himself. The whole idea of suddenly appearing in another time was just not feasible. He could not even get a grip of what had just happened yet alone explain it, and without a doubt there would be far more questions than he could answer. "Nothing," he mumbled as he fought to make sense of it all.

The nearer they got to the village the more uncomfortable Oliver felt as a sense of foreboding started to fill him with dread. The homestead stood on slightly raised ground in an almost circular natural clearing, ringed by woods and forests. Oliver noticed crops growing in the land all around, marked out by crude wooden fences. The roundhouses had reed-thatched roofs that looked to be perched precariously on top of mud walls. The entrance was a simple door hole with a hide curtain being the only barrier separating the outside and inside worlds. As they got closer Oliver could make out handprints on the outer mud walls, where a mixture of mud and straw had been smeared over, and pressed into, a wicker frame. Some of the smudged prints were large and some so small they looked like children's hands; it looked as if the whole family helped and was involved in the creation of their homes.

Various animals slowly came into view. Oliver could certainly smell the livestock, well the remnants of their bowel movements before he could visually identify them! He could hear pigs grunting as they snuffled about, their snouts pressed into the ground as they eagerly hunted worms, roots, acorns, anything they could get into their mouths and crush using their incredibly strong jaw muscles. With their large tusks, the pigs did not seem to be too fussy about their diet! Oliver noted a couple of small, raised hutches to the left. Chickens wandered freely up and down the ramps as well as meandering between the stilts of their houses and between the buildings. They pecked incessantly at the ground and were gently clucking under the watchful eye of an impressive looking cockerel, which looked as if he could be an unpredictable, vicious, brute as he meaningfully strutted up and down the hutch roof.

Oliver observed smoke leeching through some of the reed thatch, as the smell of bonfire smoke overcame the smell of manure and of sulphur from stale urine. Before them lay a web of rustic-looking cobble pathways where stones had been roughly thrown down on the ground to allow feet to rise above the mass of mud that surrounded each dwelling. The stones and pebbles had obviously been placed there deliberately as they criss-crossed the land and seemed to connect every doorway with the others in the small hamlet. There was one path though that did not lead to a door but to a small shelter covering a pit. Oliver surmised that it must obviously be the rubbish tip, or the toilet and judging by the stink coming from it, both!

Aiden stopped for a moment, "What do you think is on the parchment?" Aiden asked as he looked up to the skies, pulling faces as he considered his own question. "Perhaps it is a magic potion?" he declared with an alarming confidence in his deduction.

A puzzled look flashed across Oliver's face as he looked incredulously at his companion. "I don't think so," he replied as he shook his head. "I don't think the Romans write magic potions on parchments, seal it with a wax seal and then place it in a fine embossed leather cylinder for careful transportation!" Oliver stated as he racked his brains for all he was worth, trying desperately hard to work out what it could possibly be. "Perhaps it is a list, or it's some kind of order?" Oliver concluded as he stared at his new friend.

"A list of what?" enquired his young companion before helpfully suggesting, "Gifts?"

The pair stared at each other, each desperate to read the minds of the other before Oliver shrugged his shoulders. "No idea!" Oliver exclaimed as the two erupted into a fit of laughter for no apparent reason.

"My father will know." Aiden giggled, *"*Father knows *everything!"*

"My father *thinks* he knows everything!" laughed Oliver.

"We'd better get a move on," Aiden said. "I am starving," he announced as he started to run towards one of the larger huts. "Aren't you?" Aiden shouted over his shoulder.

Oliver was not going to be left behind and sprinted to catch Aiden, "Do you think your parents will mind me staying with you?" Oliver shouted at Aiden with an air of uncertainty.

"Naaah, any friend of mine is a friend of theirs," Aiden cried out, "Well, that is what they keep saying to me!" The young Celt shrugged, "Let's show them our find and get some food. I'm almost fainting with hunger!" And the pair picked up the pace.

They charged through one of the oat fields, leaving two parallel lines in their wake, much to the annoyance of the men tending the fields. "Father, Father!" Aiden yelled out as they got closer to the buildings, Aiden ran around one of the houses as he followed his father's response. He quickly changed direction and disappeared round the back of one of the huts. Oliver was in hot pursuit but stopped dead in his tracks at the sight that greeted him as he ran around the hut. He was shocked to see the body of a deer on the ground with a figure crouching over it, shouting his hellos as he went about butchering the carcass. The ground was covered with blood as the entrails were pulled from the dead beast.

"We have had a bit of luck today!" the figure bellowed without looking up. "Mind you, not so lucky for this one, or the one your father is working on Aiden!"

Oliver could feel his stomach start to turn and had to look away quickly before he threw up where he stood. He had seen a film of a pigs and cows hanging in a slaughterhouse, but that was after the beasts had been butchered and skinned. However, he was intrigued, so he swallowed hard and determined to make himself watch as curiosity got the better of him.

"Where's my father?" Aiden called to the figure. The man turned, nodded and pointed to one of the larger roundhouses.

The pair ran through the large arch and stopped dead in their tracks. "Father? Father?" Aiden puffed as they peered into the smoky darkness.

"What is it lad?" came a voice from the dim interior. "And who's this?" the figure asked. Oliver peered into the gloom but could not see anybody in the darkness as the voice continued, "Where does he come from dressed like that?" the man enquired, "He's not from a tribe I know."

"Father, this is Oliver!" Aiden announced. "He has been sent by the gods," he proudly exclaimed. "We found this, look!" he revealed. "Well Oliver found it and gave it to me," he declared. "It is the gods giving us help," Aiden continued as he offered the leather cylinder.

Aiden's father looked over from pulling the rope that disappeared up into the rafters. He was busy suspending joints of a second deer into the roof space to smoke the meat and preserve it. The smoke from the fire in the centre of the room was drawn up towards the roof and hung about the rafters before gradually making its way out through a small hole in the centre of the reed thatch and out into the outside world. The smoke did have its uses in preserving the flesh of skinned animals, as long as they were hung high enough in the smoke cloud to dry out without insects or rot setting in. Oliver could see the man tie the end of the rope to one of the wooden uprights before he turned to the boys, wiping the blood from his hands with a cloth as he did so.

"Oliver?" he nodded his head in acknowledgement at the new arrival, "Welcome, you can call me Jannon." The man smiled at Oliver and gestured towards the canister. "Give it to me, Aiden, so I can see it properly lad." He took it in his hands, held it up and stopped dead in his tracks. Jannon stared silently at the item in hands, he gently turned the scroll in his fists as he spotted the eagle emblem. "Oh no!" he mumbled as the colour in his face drained. "Where did you find this?" Jannon's hands started to tremble as he realised that he could be holding Imperial Roman orders.

"We were on the other side of the woods. There were hundreds of Romans marching in file. I... I think they dropped it, Father," Aiden replied shakily as he watched his father physically start to shake.

"They will be back for it, that is sure, and we had better not get caught with it!" Aiden's father mumbled as he shook his head slowly.

"It opens and there is a parchment with writing on it," ventured Oliver. "And a wax seal," he commented as he pointed to it.

"That's it!" Jannon declared with a sense of purpose. "We will have to take it to the one man who will know what to do. Boys, we had better get going at once. We don't want to get caught with this in our possession." The man paused as he thought about everything, they would need to take with them, "Aiden give Oliver some of your clothes, we don't want him to stand out any more than he does already. This messenger from the gods had better try to blend in!" Jannon swallowed hard and cleared his throat, "We don't want to attract any unwanted attention."

Aiden beckoned Oliver to follow him further inside the hut and headed over to one side of the roundhouse as his father pulled the leather door curtain across the entrance behind them. The dim light was now so poor that Oliver thought he had suddenly become blind. Aiden threw more wood on the fire in the centre of the room, giving the space some welcome illumination as it flared up. He wandered over to his mother, who was busy grinding spelt wheat on a big stone on the floor. He threw his arms around her shoulders and planted a big kiss on her cheek before eagerly explaining about Oliver. He continued to recount the brief adventure as he went over to a small wicker chest pressed up against the wall. The lid creaked as he lifted it, and Oliver could see Aiden holding the top open with his head as he busily rifled through it. Aiden pulled out a rough woollen top along with a very basically designed pair of trousers and passed them over to Oliver, who pulled the smelly, scratchy jumper over his tee shirt and climbed into the trousers. Aiden was considerably shorter than Oliver, a fact verified by the large gap between the trouser bottoms and the floor.

"Where are we going Aiden?" Oliver asked as he stared at his exposed ankles.

Aiden rushed around the room collecting various items. "To a wise man who will be able to tell us what the writing says," Aiden informed Oliver in a matter-of-fact way. "We are going to see the wise man, King Donnchad. He lives a couple of days journey from us, so you will need these," he informed a startled Oliver as he passed numerous items to his companion. "After all we will be sleeping outside, and it is cold at night," Aiden informed Oliver as he rolled up some deer skins and passed them over for Oliver to carry.

Aiden's father explained to his wife that they needed to take the scroll to King Donnchad, and she stood up and started gathering food together and prepared a parcel of dried meats, bread and cheese. She fetched a number of goatskins that had been sewn and sealed to make containers for liquid and filled them with mead. Meanwhile his father cut some chunks of flesh from the deer carcass and placed them in bags for the journey. Jannon also packed some wool and dry tinder with pieces of flint, so that they could make a fire to keep them warm and safe on the journey.

"Okay, boys, eat this bread, meat and cheese, drink your mead, then get some rest, we must be ready to leave at first light."

Aiden's father stepped out of the house and strode over to his brother's roundhouse. He called a greeting as he lifted the hide door and casually wandered in. Oliver and Aiden walked past to the toilet trench as they heard Jannon explain, "I have to go on an urgent trip to visit King Donnchad. I can't tell you why, but I ask you to watch over my family in my absence," he said. His voice became quieter as he walked further into the hut. "I am not sure how long I will be, but I will be back as soon as I can. Six or seven days at most."

Chapter Seven

"Does it do nothing but rain in this cold, damp, miserable godforsaken place?" grumbled the leather-shoed centurion. "The skies are constantly angry and wet on this island, as if the gods have abandoned all that is here." The Roman had a mood almost as black as the sky over his head. "And this stinking mud clings to you like a young child cling to its mother. This clay cakes everything it touches!" he whined as the cohort of Roman soldiers marched relentlessly on in a tight formation through the wild British countryside. "Most of all I hate the way these tunics smell of wet dog and stale piss when they get wet!"

"That is because they use different wools and then use urine to stop the colour from running when it gets wet," Marcus casually informed the disgruntled warrior, with an air of authority.

"Whenever I am issued with a new tunic, I always sprinkle perfume on it to try and stop the stench," Cato added in a matter-of-fact way.

Aelianus shot a look of surprise at Cato. "What?" he exclaimed loudly, "Why the hell would you do that?" He asked incredulously, "Are you hoping these crazed barbarians will not kill you because you smell like a girl?"

"No, it is because his darling wife will not allow it in the house!" Decimus laughed out loud.

Their companion, Lucanus, the oldest member of the eight-man contubernium piped up, "What are you moaning about now?" He smiled as he arched his back, threw his head back and took a deep breath through his nose with a big, exaggerated sniff. "This is my fourth tour of this lovely land they call Britannia, and I know the weather well!" He looked over to his left and called out to the man at the end of the line they were marching in, "Hey Festus! How is the rain falling? Is it vertical or horizontal?" "Vertical," came the sharp reply.

"Ahhh, then we can all relax my dear friends, for we find ourselves here in summer!" The comment made his marching companions groan at the attempted humour.

"Stop the talking, keep marching, or I will have you eight on first watch duties!" barked Albus, a large Sicilian who was the decanus – an experienced soldier in charge of a contubernium, a group of eight less-experienced soldiers who shared the same tent.

The freezing hail and rain lashed down from the ever-darkening skies, briefly illuminated with flashes of lightning, followed closely with the boom of thunder. The rain quickly soaking every man in the legion to the skin. The hailstones stung any exposed flesh. As the Romans pushed on, the ground very quickly turned to deep mud under the hob-nailed, sandalled feet of the two thousand strong task force. They had almost half of their own body weight of equipment arranged about their bodies, as well as a long train of carts following closely behind them, carrying the essentials needed when a force was moving into the unknown.

"Hey Cato!" Decimus called out, "With you being the fount of knowledge... Did you know that our illustrious boss Albus tried to join the cavalry once?"

"Really?" Cato replied quizzically, "No, I did not know that particular nugget of information," Cato paused, "Why did they not take him and stop him from making our lives so unbearable?"

"Well... My fine African friend, they have a simple rule," Decimus tried to stifle a laugh as he continued, unaware that Albus was marching just behind them and could hear every word being spoken, "In order to be considered to join the cavalry, first you have to be brighter than the animal you're supposed to be riding!" The inevitable punchline made the band of eight laugh uncontrollably.

"Right, that's it! I have had it with you shits. Sentry duty for all of you for three nights!" Albus shouted, although he could hardly be heard over the sudden bursts of thunder and almost deafening noise of the heavy rain beating against the soldiers' helmets and armour.

Cato grinned, "Sounds like the gods do not agree with our industrious leader!"

Festus glanced towards Albus before looking over to the African, "Shhh!" he hissed, "You will get us killed, you bloody fool!" And the rain soaked though their woollen cloaks and doubled the weight of their clothing.

As punishment went in the Roman army, extra sentry duty was not as bad as it could have been. In fact, Albus was very fond of his team, but he was always careful not to let them know that, as he was very aware that familiarity with the men under his command would breed contempt. He had seen it for himself. A team could turn very quickly if not kept in their place. If a team started to question orders the natural order of command could be broken, and the men would become uncontrollable and refuse to obey the simplest of commands. It could give rise to insubordination and even mutiny. It was well known that if the lower ranks started to question orders, the discipline would disintegrate and once it was lost it would be impossible to regain their respect. This could ultimately result in them all losing their lives, either at the hand of the enemy or at the hand of Rome itself. Rome would not shy away from spilling the blood of its own troops to maintain high levels of discipline. One example of this was 'decimation' and was known to be carried out if a legion lost a battle. The men would be forced to line up and every tenth man would be stabbed to death by the man next to him. The purpose was to ensure that every soldier understood that losing in battle was not acceptable nor would be forgiven. These soldiers had all worked hard and well over the years, gelling as one unit, despite their differing backgrounds, experience, and the years of service they all had. They worked together, they trained together, spent their down time together. They cooked, ate, bathed and slept together. Each trusted the others implicitly and they moved as one, each one complementing the others' strengths and weaknesses.

Laenus pondered as they marched on, "Now here is an idea. Why the hell are we walking when we could all be on horseback?" he queried.

Lucanus glimpsed over, "Laenus," he said in a matter-of-fact way, "You have taken the Emperor's three gold coins, and you signed up for twenty-five years of service, as we all have... As *infantry* and not just any infantry but the Ninth – THE GLORIOUS NINTH!"

"Who are we?" he shouted aloud.

Without hesitation the reply echoed up and down the ranks, "The Ninth!" As the declaration rang out every man felt proud to be in Rome's most famous and revered legion.

"WHO ARE WE?" he bellowed.

"THE NINTH!"

"WHO ARE WE?" he cried again at the top of his voice.

"THE NINTH. THE NINTH. THE GLORIOUS NINTH!" The chant grew louder and louder with each round.

"GLORY TO THE NINTH AND DEATH TO OUR ENEMIES!" was the scream from the cohorts as they reached a deafening crescendo.

No comfy life and security for these men for a while as they marched relentlessly on, not that that was the case generally. Being in the legion meant every day was a hard day, and for good reason, as the military commanders knew only too well. The ranks all needed to pull together, they needed to live as one, to move as one, to fight as one. If they fought as one, they stood a high chance of survival and ultimate victory with the wealth and glory that came with it. The Ninth Legion was a crack force of highly trained troops with a fearsome reputation that went before them and echoed around the whole empire, they were hard and fearless. All had an unwavering and absolute faith in their fellow combatants and in the legion itself.

Every legionary trained hard, and Rome ensured he was at the peak of both mental and physical fitness. Each man was issued with the best equipment, the best rations and were held in the highest admiration by the whole of Rome. The officers worked very closely with their men and fought alongside the regular soldiers. They witnessed at first hand the bravery of the men they commanded and as a result they earned the respect and trust of every man under their command. The eight friends bunked down together, whether they were at the garrison or on campaign. As in all contubernia, each man trusted the others with his life. This was the way of the Roman soldier. The training was harsh, but it had to be so that the men reacted to orders without thinking or questioning. When not on campaign the day would generally start around daybreak. The first task was to get the fires relit, especially when the weather was cold, which was no easy task! Cato always made the fire roar, he seemed to have a magic touch. Each man would take a share of the grain rations, add water with a bit of salt to create a porridge, and warm it on the open fire. Breakfast was usually a quick affair. If the weather was warm, bread and cheese would be the food of the day, not that it ever seemed to be warm in Britannia!

After ablutions, each of the eight would check the equipment of the man to his left. The eight always did this. It meant that when inspections happened, every piece of their belongings was in the best state. All eight men had received company punishment recently because Lucanus had forgotten to clean one of his bowls. Although he had a hard time from the other seven, they all vowed it would never happen again. By doing each other's kit check, they lessened the chance of failing the inspection. If they did, it would be because they all messed up. The punishment would be deserved by all and that made it more bearable.

When the men were ensconced in the garrison, the legion would be ordered every day to gather all their belongings and dress in full armour. They would complete a route march of eighteen miles, with a mixture of running and marching. The target time for completion was four hours. If you failed, well...

punishment followed.

On returning from the route march, they would have a short amount of free time, before being issued with heavily weighted training equipment - a short sword and a shield. These would be more than double the weight of the standard issue gladius and scutum, and hand-to-hand combat would be practised. The result was a force that had built, and deserved, a reputation for being so tough, so frightening, so violent, that they were perceived as almost uncontrollable. Such a formidable force were they, that you would be glad they were on your side. If they were not on your side, you would give them a very wide berth if you had any sense.

The Roman-built road that had made the march more bearable had ended 30,000 steps ago. To make things worse, they were heading towards prime ambush country. The road had fast become more of a muddy path, and trees were growing closer and closer to the track. Bushes and tall ferns filled the area between each trunk in the woodland. It was the perfect cover to allow your enemies to get really, really close without being seen. This meant you could be taken by complete surprise. It was an ideal place for an ambush and Lucanus knew this.

He had been in Germania four years before, when the Barbarians launched themselves from the bushes at the unprepared troops. The Barbarians had hidden themselves and lain in wait on either side of the long and narrow pathway. It had a natural banking on both sides, topped with pine trees and bushes, offering ideal natural cover for the ferocious tribe. Every single one of the horde of Barbarians had been raised in the forest, and their lives were inextricably part of the green lands that provided all their needs. The Germanic tribes believed that even their heathen gods lived and breathed around them, providing prosperity, as long as they were appeased.

As the legion made its way along the ever-narrowing roadway, they were being watched. Hundreds of pairs of eyes were trained on the cloaked, and lightly armed, force. Every step that was taken was one step nearer death. As the last man passed a creaking, curved, silver birch tree, a shrill scream echoed around the valley. The huge birch fell, blocking any chance of escape, separating the light infantry from its wagon support, and more importantly from its cavalry support. That is when the savages sprang into action. The legion heard a few deft chops from expertly wielded axes as ropes were severed, and then they heard the creaking, crunching noise of tree trunks rolling freely down the steep sides of the ravine, and crashing into the bodies of the troops below.

The Barbarians were close behind the rolling trunks. Shrieking, axe-wielding, blood-thirsty savages, they slashed at the bloodied Romans, and despatched them effortlessly into the underworld. Some of the axes hit flesh with such force, that the wielder could not pull it free to kill another, so it was left in situ. The Barbarian then drew a double-edged sword ready to strike at the next Roman. The attack happened so fast, and the Romans were caught by such surprise that they were in complete disarray. They had no chance to regroup and make a stand, or even defend themselves properly.

The attack was over as quickly as it had started. The shrill blood-curdling shouting of the attacking horde was replaced by the screaming of the injured and the moaning of the half-dead. Blood stained everything. It covered hands, arms, legs, bodies and the faces of the few legionaries left standing upright. The ground could not absorb all the gore, and pools of blood had formed all around. The scene was one of complete devastation.

Lucanus survived and had helped fallen men around him to their feet, pointing them back towards the comparative safety of the wagons. As one man struggled to stand, Lucanus reached out and took hold of the man's arm, only to be greeted by an agonised scream before the man passed out and fell to the ground, leaving Lucanus holding a severed limb. It had been hacked off just above the elbow, and only held on by a single strip of skin. He could not help himself, his knees buckled, as bile and vomit exploded forward from his mouth and nostrils.

The memory of that attack made his blood run cold, and a shiver ran down his spine. "I don't like this. I don't like this at all. I have a bad, bad feeling." Lucanus muttered.

The tall African rolled his eyes. "No! Not the Germania story," Cato tutted out loud.

Lucanus was oblivious to the comment, "It was the third," he began in earnest, but only managed to get four words out before the sentence was recited by a myriad of voices

"Week of the campaign, and we led the column!" they all joined in, doing poor imitations of his nasally voice as they did so, before falling about with laughter.

"You don't know..." Lucanus retorted.

"...You weren't there!" They all jeered in unison at the increasingly enraged man.

As their cohort of five hundred men marched through the wooded copse, Lucanus felt all his senses heighten as he looked up to see the grey-washed sky slowly disappear, replaced by the boughs of the different trees surrounding them. All of the leaves seemed to combine, entwining and cutting out the light. The result made him shudder as the temperature fell away. The wagons followed close behind, each pulled by plodding mules and every man knew the day was far from done. The military always kept the men busy and occupied. When on a march, resting up for the night meant first building a camp, not just a few tents thrown up, more like a fort, complete with defensive ditches, fences made up of pilum muralis (sharpened wooden stakes) and look-out posts.

The Romans had been attacked in the dark hours, as men slept, on more than one occasion and they had learned the hard way. Most of the soldiers had lost their lives before they could rise, slaughtered in their beds. The new style of camp was perfectly designed to create security. It meant that the men would sleep behind the defences in their leather or oil-soaked cloth tents, and the space inside the defences could also accommodate a large, tented headquarters, animals and wagons as well as all the camp followers.

"Not far to go now boys, I can feel it in my waters," quipped Marcus optimistically.

Decimus rolled his eyes, "Oh no," he snapped, "I get a bad feeling every time you say that. Never mind Lucanus and his dark and bloody woods, the last time you said that we ended up digging latrines for six long weeks."

Marcus shot a cross, dirty look at his companion, "Well, how the hell was I to know it was the bosses' food we ate!" he replied huffily.

"How the hell were *you* to know it was the bosses' food you *stole*!" wailed Maxetius.

Festus could feel his temper darken, "Yes... and you were lucky," he paused as the memory flooded back, "Well, we were all bloody lucky the man believed it was an honest mistake!" he eagerly reminded the group, "or he would have had you put to the sword, and I would hate to think what would have happened to the rest of us!" he growled.

"Enough!" barked Cato. "We all agreed. It is forgotten," he reminded them.

Albus caught up with his eight charges; and with a big sarcastic smile he announced, "I hope you morons have your shovels at hand. I have arranged a treat for you eight when we start to camp in around three thousand steps."

The men all looked at each other, shaking their heads. They knew what was coming.

Their boss smirked at the dejected faces to his left. "Aw don't look like that! You won't be digging poo holes all night this time!" he said with an air of reassurance, "You will be filling them in tomorrow too!" He laughed sarcastically. "Oh... And don't worry, you won't have to dig all night." The boss snarled, "Festus, Lucanus, Cato, Marcus, I have arranged for you to take second watch," Albus grinned as he turned to walk away.

"Ha, ha, ha, at least we get some sleep." Maxetius sniggered as he pointed a finger at the four dejected souls, but it proved to be a premature gesture.

Albus spun on his heels and looked hard at the band of men, "Maxetius, you are on the third watch. Decimus, Aelianus, Laenus …you are on the third watch as well!" he smirked sarcastically, "Sleep tight tonight ladies!" Albus' face dropped into a sinister grimace. "Not so funny now, eh?" he growled, "What do you have to say to that?"

"Thank you, sir!" the eight snapped back in reply. They knew that if they failed to acknowledge the command, they might have to deal with a lot worse!

Albus took a deep breath as he tried to control his temper, "Now stop this blasted chatter and tomorrow march like proud members of this magnificent army," he bellowed as his face turned purple with rage.

Now only a thousand steps, then we can rest, Marcus thought to himself. His mind started to wander and imagine dinner, feet up, a nice bath, off to a warm comfy bed for a deep, deep sleep. He was rudely snapped out of his daydream by Albus screaming, "Right, you nasty vermin!"

Marcus shook his head "Damn! I almost forgot where I was," he thought to himself before muttering, "I have another ten years of this. *Ten years!* My gods are not looking fondly on me."

The man to his right, Decimus, heard Marcus mumbling. "What?" he enquired enthusiastically, intrigued by the noise tumbling from Marcus's lips.

"Mmm?" Marcus mumbled with a quizzical look as he turned his head in Decimus's direction, as the words finally penetrated his brain. He had not realised his brain and mouth had been connected as the grumbling thoughts bounced around his conscious mind, "Oh, I was just wondering what I had done to anger my gods. I have another ten years of this!"

"Ten years, I would say that's a blessing," Decimus smiled.

The tall African caught the chatter "Yes, you could be dead!" he grinned satirically, "and still have another ten years left to do!" laughed Cato.

Festus overheard the banter, "Are we lucky to be here then?" he enquired, "because I don't feel very lucky.

Their gossiping was interrupted once more. "Don't forget to collect the trenching tools when we stop, LADIES!" snapped Albus, who was in no mood to hear the insignificant chatter.

The eight friends looked at each other, "NO, SIR!" they all barked in unison as they snapped their heads to the front and stared hard at the shiny-helmeted heads of the men before them.

It was the humour that kept the men going, especially when things got tough, dangerous or morbid, and bonded them as a team. Some characters tried not to get too attached, which made them appear aloof and untrustworthy. Others found solace in the company of others as the real threat of death was ever present. Life could be lost in the blink of an eye and that made lasting friendships very difficult to cultivate. It didn't help that they were in a strange land, with very different weather. The cold chilled them to their bones, which never left them, resulting in most longing for the warm Roman sun on their bodies. Without a doubt they were well fed, and their bodies were kept in the best of shape, but the soldiers never really relaxed and were always on their guard. Not everybody was pleased to see the eagle standard of Rome cast its shadow on the land. They lived in a very violent time. Life was hard, short, and sometimes bloody. Although a Roman soldier signed up for twenty-five years, it was very unlikely that he would reach his retirement! Mind you if he did, he was entitled to land and a pension from a grateful Empire. When each man signed, they were promised that they would see the world, and have more adventures than any young person could imagine.
"Look on the bright side my boys," grinned Aelianus, "with all this rain, at least the ground will be soft and easy to dig!"

The Ninth legion was under the command of Quintus Petillius Cerialis, a strikingly handsome career officer and a seasoned campaign general, who drove his men hard and was deemed a man to stay well clear of. His temper was very short, his punishments could be extremely harsh, so everyone kept their heads down. It was better to face a quick death at the hands of the enemy than to be the recipient of the general's displeasure, which would ultimately end in death, but a very slow, drawn-out, and painful one. He was the man responsible for making the Ninth the feared killing machine that it had become and he had received the Eagle standard personally from Caesar himself. The standard was a statue of a golden eagle on top of a golden wreath of laurel leaves. The leaves of the evergreen laurel represented the eternity of Rome. Beneath the wreath were metal banners proclaiming and recording the victories achieved by the Ninth. All the honours and recorded victories were mounted on a long pole, so that it could be held aloft and seen by every man in the column and enforce the memories of the battles and the men who had fallen in the struggle to create the legend that was the Ninth. It was used to remind the common soldier of why he was fighting - for honour and to protect the legend. The Eagle standard was to be defended to the death, as it was a great honour bestowed to all in the regiment, much to the envy of other regiments. Eagle regiments could always be identified by the standard, which was carried and defended by the aquilifer, who wore a wolfskin draped over his shoulders, the head of the wolf used as a hood in the belief the spirit of the wolf would enter the soul of the bearer. The guard of honour around the standard was made up of a cohort of seven hundred of the bravest, most experienced, and ruthless men of the whole army, hand-picked to guard the standard, rather than the usual five hundred men of other legions.

Petillius was easily identified by his richly decorated armour and fine red cloak which covered his back and flowed over the rump of his horse. His horse was no ordinary beast either, but a fine, tall, white stallion that stood at least a hand above the rest of the horses. The General always took great pride in his appearance and set a fine example to his men. He always surrounded himself with his centurions. These men, who each led a century of eighty to a hundred men, were hand-picked, battle-hardened, cut-throats and were not afraid to kill, maim or murder men, women or children, all in the name of the glory of Rome. All done without question, as the following of orders was primary and of vital importance up and down the ranks. All these men had one thing in common though, they all respected Petillius Cerialis. Each followed to the letter every command that he issued for he was Rome in their eyes. In turn he relied on, and had to trust them with his life.

The reason was simple, if Petillius lost a battle or campaign he would have Rome baying for his blood. He could run the risk of his officers turning on him and his senior officers might well rise up against him if he did not keep them in check. Enemies would be easily made if his instructions were to be questioned. It would be quite easy for him to be murdered by the soldiers beneath him, under the instruction of a political enemy, who would fill his position as well as claim his riches, land and power. All of which was very, very attractive, so Petillius had to stay one step ahead of any perceived threat to keep his power, and his life.

One of the centurions in charge of the friends' cohort was a miserable little man, a Spaniard, by the name of Septimus, who did not carry as much favour as his contemporaries. The result being that he and ultimately the men below him in rank, was given more than his fair share of the dangerous tasks. He was a clumsy fellow who walked with a limping gait and had a tendency to stutter, but he was quick-minded and very sharp-witted. He had suffered quite a serious injury, which affected him deeply, when his horse was killed under him in Spain. The pair had been riding together for nearly fifteen years and the man had a little more faith in the beast than he perhaps should have had. Septimus took the loss quite badly, but finally decided that he should purchase a young colt stallion as a replacement. The four-year-old horse had differing ideas to Septimus on being a military beast and would regularly try to unseat his rider, much to the amusement of his immediate peers!

As the cohorts reached the chosen resting site the men fell out from the column and went about their duties setting up the camp. It was done with efficiency as it was a practice that happened most days, and the men went about the work with the minimum of instruction from their superiors. The friends who found themselves on latrine detail wandered over to the wagons, liberated the digging tools from the piles of neatly stacked tools and implements and set about the trench making.

The mounted Septimus had completed a mission to transport orders and distribute them among the officers of the Ninth. He pulled the reins hard and brought his reticent steed to an abrupt halt and grabbed around behind him. His fingers searched the basic saddle and blanket desperately for the orders given to him earlier by Petillius Cerialis. They had been fastened by two buckles to his saddle. Well, they *should* have been fastened to his saddle. "Shit!" he thought, as he frenziedly checked again, "Shit! Shit! Shit!" The buckles had been ripped away and, in his panic, he drew his gladius from its sheath and pointed it at various decanii.

"You, you and you!" he bellowed, "Fall your men in, NOW!"

The men jumped to attention in ranks as commanded.

"Pay attention!" he screamed, and the rows of men obediently fell silent. "We are re-tracking our movements and we will find a scroll container with the legion's seal on it. If you fail, you will fail me and you will fail ROME. If you fail Rome, I will order *decimation*. I will make sure that all of you will kill every tenth man. Do you understand?"

"Hail!" was the response as they all brought themselves to attention and raised their right arms in salute.

"Poor souls," Festus whispered to Laenus as the eight friends temporarily stopped digging and looked at the sorrowful sight unfolding in front of them, their attention grabbed by the shouting and the screaming Septimus, whose face was purple with rage.

"I hope for their sakes they find whatever has been lost," mumbled Lucanus.

"I hope they use swords rather than clubs for the decimation if they don't!" whispered Festus as they watched the soldiers march out.

Maxetius glanced at his companions, "Would you be able to kill me?" he asked his friends as they solemnly watched the men start to head away from the camp.

"If it was a choice between you and me, then I would gladly send you to Elysium!" replied Aelianus without taking his eyes off the departing group.

"That's charming that is. Thank you very much," Maxetius tutted as he looked along the line towards the others and was a bit surprised to see them all nodding in agreement.

Laenus tutted and shook his head, "I would even blunt my gladius especially for you. Give you something else to moan about!" he chipped in cheerfully.

The band of friends sniggered as they turned back to the ditch and set about their digging duties once again, before they were spotted and accused of slacking.

Chapter Eight

The boys could hardly keep up with Jannon as he stomped through the ever-darkening forest. The air was damp with a strong smell of rotting leaves and dank ferns filling the air. They could see the light was fading as the sun was slowly setting. Oliver could feel the temperature starting to drop, even though the sun could not be seen through the canopy overhead. The entwined boughs of the mighty trees all perpetually fought to capture every beam of light on their leaves. As Oliver looked up, the branches reminded him of twisted arthritic fingers laced together as he peered towards the ever-darkening sky. His attention was grabbed by the voice of Aiden's father who was aware of the sun dropping over the horizon and he searched for a good place to set camp. "Aiden, we will camp here!" Jannon declared as he pointed to a small clearing. "Take Oliver and find some kindling and some firewood. I will find some materials to make a shelter. I have the two sheets of oiled cloth, so we should be dry enough if it really pours. We will certainly need the warmth of the flames tonight as there is very little cloud in the sky." He called out cheerily as he busied himself looking for suitable branches.

"And to keep the wolves away Father," replied Aiden.

Jannon was amused by the flippant comment, "Of course son!" he smirked as he nodded and smiled in agreement.

Oliver's face dropped, "WOLVES?" he gulped.

Jannon stopped in his tracks and glared at the young guest, "Yes!" he replied in all seriousness, "To keep the wolves away." He could see the look of fear flash over Oliver's face and could not help himself as the colour drained from the boy's face. "Just be glad we have not seen any traces of bears for a while!" Jannon countered, trying hard not to let his voice quiver as the internal fits of laughter bubbled inside him.

Oliver gulped and swallowed hard. He had never realised or even considered that the pack hunting animals were going to be around. After all, as far as he knew, they had been extinct in the wild for over four centuries but after that revelation Oliver made sure he stayed very, very close to Aiden.

"You have wolves here?" Oliver queried as he glanced all around nervously, his voice wavering with fear.

His young companion nodded. "Of course," Aiden replied. "Did you not see the paw prints over there?" he continued matter of factly as he pointed to some marks in the mud.

Oliver gingerly wandered over to where Aiden had pointed and stared hard at the numerous marks in the mud, "Ohhh... They look like large dog prints," he gulped. "How do you know they are wolf?" he asked as his voice raised a couple of octaves with fright.

"Simple," shrugged his companion, "Because they move in packs, and there are many together," he replied proudly as he gladly imparted his knowledge. "They tend to follow each other in single file through these paths if they are not hunting." Aiden folded his arms, pulled himself up to his full height, raised his chin and asked with an air of authority, "Can you not smell their scent and the stink of their poo in the air?" He paused for a moment before he declared incredulously, "I think that is why we have not seen bears, not in my lifetime anyway!" Aiden carried on collecting small pieces of twigs and sticks for the fire before casually revealing, "Wolves have taken our goats before." He stood and looked up as recounted the last time it happened. "They are always silent until they have their prize. There is a moment of panic from the livestock then a silence before they start to howl, and I mean really howl. It is as if they are sending a chilling 'thank you' when they all join in. Stealthy, clever and loyal to each other, they are," Aiden exclaimed with admiration.

"D... D... Do you think they are near now?" stuttered Oliver as he glanced anxiously around the glade, spooked by every little movement in the undergrowth. He started to tremble, his eyes widened, and the slightest sound immediately drew his attention and made his hair stand on end.

Aiden looked up to see the fear on Oliver's face. He could not believe Oliver could react in such a way and decided to play upon it a bit. "Could be," he muttered mischievously, "They stay and hunt in packs you know." The boy looked around furtively. "And this is perfect for them," he added as he tried not to laugh. "All this bracken and fern gives them plenty of cover. They tread so carefully, crouch low and as they get nearer, they start to crawl, ready to pounce. At the opportune moment, they pounce and take you by the throat. The muzzle and jaw close so tightly on your windpipe. You don't have time to shout." Aiden reached up with his hands and wrapped his hands around his throat, "Death is quite quick, if you are lucky!... They then violently shake their heads from side to side." He shook his head from side to side as he spoke. "The force simply snaps your neck!" Aiden explained as he turned to Oliver, trying desperately hard to stifle his laughter, "Mind you, if they don't snap your neck, they just keep a grip on your windpipe as the life slowly ebbs away from you." Aiden tried hard to stop his shoulders jerking up and down as a fit of the giggles nearly over came him. It would not have mattered; Oliver was far too preoccupied searching the bracken for the beasts to have seen him. Aiden took a few deep breaths and regained his composure before continuing, "Mind you, they could be right on top of us, and we would never know!" Aiden exclaimed as bent over and picked up a handful of dead leaves from the forest floor. "Shhh!" Aiden put his finger to lips. "There..." he whispered as he pointed to a bush. "Can you see it?" as he started to slowly retreat.

"See what?" whispered Oliver as he slowly turned his head in the direction that Aiden was pointing, narrowed his eyes and he squinted and strained to see what Aiden was pointing at. He peered into the darkening shadows, desperate to see what Aiden was pointing to and identify any danger.

"There," Aiden hushed as he moved his pointed finger backwards and forwards at a clump of brambles.

Oliver moved slowly nearer to Aiden, mainly for protection. "Where?" he whispered as his head moved closer to Aiden's head.

"WOLF!" Aiden screamed as he threw the leaves into his companion's face.

"AAAARRRGHHH" Oliver screamed, as he turned and ran away in fright.

Aiden's body folded in half. "Hahahahahahaha..." he cried as his hands grasped his knees. "Hahahahaha! Your face... Hahahaha... WOLF! Hahahahaha!"

"Oh yes. Very funny," humphed an angry, but relieved Oliver as he crossed his arms. "I bow to the world's *greatest* comedian," he continued as he bent forward in a mock bow. "If you stop wetting yourself for a moment, it's my turn to show you something." Oliver exclaimed as he looked around, "Have you ever been a parachutist?" he asked with an air of authority.

Aiden fought to regain his composure, "A what?" he asked with a puzzled look on his face as he tried to make sense of the strange word that Oliver had just spurted out.

Oliver spotted exactly what he was looking for, "Follow me!" he commanded as he turned and ran into the undergrowth, Aiden in hot pursuit. Oliver dodged around gorse and low hanging branches as he sprinted towards a silver birch, it had to be right, between four and five metres tall would be ideal. He found just what he was looking for and scrambled up the narrow trunk until he got near the top. With both hands he stretched up as far as he could reach, then he threw his weight away from the tree's trunk. "Woooooooo!" he screamed as the tree started to bend and lowered him gently to the ground. Aiden had never seen anything like it! He took to his heels as he could not find his own tree quickly enough. It had to be one taller than Oliver's – obviously – "Over there," Oliver called as he pointed to an ideal target. Aiden scrambled up and did the same as Oliver had done. "Whhoooooppp!" he screamed as the tree bent and delivered him to the ground. The pair scrambled up their respective trees and this time counted to three and both leaned out at the same time, the roars of laughter rippled throughout the forest.

"Hey! You boys sound busy!" called Jannon from the darkening distance. "Hope you are finding plenty of tinder and wood. We need to get this fire lit now!"

The pair suddenly halted in their tracks. They had forgotten their task. "Sorry Father, we are working on it!" giggled Aiden as he and Oliver urgently started to gather more bits of twig, and dried leaves. "We need as much as we can carry," Aiden instructed his newfound best friend. "We want to have a good strong fire tonight, and we'd better hurry up as we also need to gather some ferns to help make a roof and to make a bed with."

When the boys got back to the clearing, Jannon had two straight thick branches leaning against a couple of trees, and was busy lashing thinner lengths of wood horizontally, from the ground up, onto the leaning lengths. He glanced up to see two huge bundles of tinder waddling towards him "Well done lads, that's enough to start," Jannon conceded. "Now can you gather some ferns? We need them to make a roof on the lean-to to give us some cover."

Jannon had made these lean-to camps thousands of times, and every time Aiden witnessed him doing it filled Aiden with wonderment at the speed his father worked. Jannon had arranged the simple roof against the coming breeze, knowing that it would give plenty of protection to the three of them, and once the fire was going, it would fill the shelter with heat from it, making it quite cosy, and perhaps giving them the chance to get a decent night's sleep.

Jannon greeted the boys as they tottered back with armfuls of fronds. "Keep going boys, that's not nearly enough," he said as they piled the ferns in front of the lean-to. "The more you get, the better you will sleep," he urged as they turned on their heels and disappeared once more.

The slightly built man busied himself, weaving the fronds in between the horizontal lengths before laying more material over the top to give them plenty of insulation and then spread the oiled cloth over it all. "At least we have some provisions, so we won't need to go hunting tonight!" he thought to himself.

Jannon looked over to see two big bundles of greenery trudging wearily towards him, "Right. One more load should do it boys," he said as the pair dropped the loads, turned and trudged off once again. He filled in the sides before taking a step back to view his handiwork and nodded to himself as he admired the shelter. The boys soon returned, and the last load of ferns was spread out on the floor as bedding. Jannon rooted around in one of the leather bags, "Right lads, lay your skins out on top of the ferns while I get the fire going," and he produced a handful of sheep's wool from the dark recesses of his bag.

"What's he doing?" whispered Oliver as he watched intently.

Aiden threw a puzzled look at his friend, "Are you kidding? Father's making a fire!"

"What?" puzzled Oliver, "I thought he would start by rubbing two sticks together?"

Aiden glared at him, "Two sticks? What are you talking about?"
"Well, don't you rub them together to make fire through friction?" enquired Oliver. He had seen indigenous people on the television drilling two sticks with a bow to create red glowing embers. They blew on these as they added dry leaves and before you knew what was happening there was a raging fire.

Aiden wondered what Oliver meant by friction for a moment, he had never heard the word before. "Rub two sticks together? Is that what *you* do?" giggled the young chap as he spread the skins out on the ferns.

"No! Don't be stupid!" replied an indignant Oliver.

Aiden glanced up, "Me being stupid? I am not the one talking about two sticks," he laughed at the preposterous suggestion. "So how do you get a fire started where you come from?"

Oliver shrugged his shoulders and blurted, "Easy, we use matches or a lighter."

Aiden had never heard of such items and just stared at Oliver with a puzzled expression.

Oliver glanced up and caught the look that Aiden fired over and felt compelled to explain. "Matches come in a box with sandpaper on the side. The match is a small piece of wood with a head on one end, and when you strike it on the sandpaper it bursts into flame," Oliver smiled. "It is a bit easier than that looks," he said as he nodded towards Aiden's father, who was kneeling on the ground, hunched over with his nose almost on the ground. In one hand he held a piece of metal, and in the other was a piece of flint. Jannon smacked the metal length into the flint, sending sparks into the mixture of wool and very small strips of wood and bark. After a few strikes sparks reached the intended target, Jannon spotted the result and gently lifted the mass in his hands and pulled it up to his mouth. He drew in a deep breath, pursed his lips and gently, slowly, he released the contents of his lungs in a controlled steady flow at the centre of the bundle. He turned his head to one side and took a deep breath of fresh air before turning his face back to the mixture in his hands, pursed his lips once more and let out another long-controlled breath, causing the tight ball to smoke heavily. The third breath and the ball burst into flames, Jannon laid it gently on a few carefully placed sticks, before placing numerous sticks indiscriminately on top followed by a few handfuls of leaves. As the mixture burst into life, Jannon carefully placed larger and larger sticks on the growing pile.

Very soon the three travellers were contentedly sitting on logs and staring into the flames, munching some of the sourdough flat bread while Jannon used his sgian knife to whittle some lengths of green twigs from a hazel tree into points. He peeled back the bark before he threaded some of the deer meat he had brought on to the sticks and passed one each to the boys, Oliver copied Aiden, he leaned forward and held the meat skewers over the red-hot embers. He watched his meat turn from dark red to light brown as the pair twisted and turned the skewers as the meat gently cooked through. Oliver was salivating as the aroma of the cooked meat reached his nostrils. He was unsure if he would like deer meat and could not remember if his mum had ever cooked it before, but Aiden was chomping merrily into his share.

Oliver tentatively nibbled at a bit. The succulent meat had a deep smoky flavour and a texture that took him by surprise. The taste of the deer was exquisite, the strip of venison simply melted in his mouth as he chewed slowly, savouring every moment. This was so unlike his Mum's cooked meat, which you could break your teeth on! The combination of the preserving method of a little salt before being hung in the roof to lightly smoke had really enhanced the meat. When Oliver placed it in his mouth the taste made him go, "Mmmmmm," out loud. The smoky lean meat also took on a hint of the flavour from the wood skewers. Washed down with mouthfuls of mead from a goatskin bottle that they all shared, only added to the flavours. Oliver could honestly say it was a truly gastronomic experience.

The mead was a strange taste to Oliver, it had a sweet smell, but the first taste was a bit bitter. The brew was made from honey fermented with water and juniper berries, which gave a peculiar mix of sweet and sour as it washed over different taste buds in his mouth, the mixture making his tongue feel a bit prickly as he swilled it around his mouth. As he swallowed it left a warm glow as it went down. After a few minutes, his head felt quite light and he just started giggling to himself, as his eyes no longer could focus properly.

Jannon moved around the boys as they cooked more meat, placing logs on the fire and threading more strips on the green twigs, "Tell me more about where you are from, Oliver," Jannon enquired as he worked.

The boy fidgeted as he tried to answer without sounding strange, the mead was having a strange effect on him. "I am not sure," he replied slowly, trying to give himself time to get his story straight. "I live at 17 Fountain Street, but I don't know where it is, or where I am now!" he finally blurted.

The inquisitor did not understand the answer and probed a little bit to try and establish some details. "Is it in the sky?" he ventured, "You know, at night is it near the stars?"

"I'd... d... d... don't know where that isssh," Oliver mumbled as the effect of the mead alcohol started making his lips numb, making talking quite difficult. What he did know was that he was suddenly very tired, and just wanted to lie down.

Jannon was not finished with his questioning, although he was unsure if he should be asking the question in case it upset the guest, who could bring the gods' displeasure upon him, but he had to know. "Did the gods send you to protect us from these Romans?" enquired Jannon as they all sat staring into the dancing flames, daring not to look at the boy to his right.

Oliver giggled as his head started to spin a little, "No... *No!* A bloody monster, hic," Oliver belched before he continued to slur, "It... it ishh a pain in my arsh. It jumped on me... I opened my wardrobe and now..."

Jannon had no idea what Oliver was gabbling on about, He had never heard of a wardrobe, or cupboard for that matter. What he did hear was that the monster attacked him, and now he was here. Oliver *must* have been sent by the gods, that was the only explanation.

The two boys clumsily stood up and stumbled off to have a pee. Both were exhausted from the efforts of the day and the effect of the mead, and they lay down next to each other on their fern and skin beds. Oliver was asleep before his head touched the ground.

A snap of a twig jolted Oliver awake, his body froze as he tentatively opened one eye and listened. He heard some movement and thought he recognised the shape, so he sat up. It was Jannon adding a log to the fire. As he turned to reach for more wood from the small pile, he noticed Oliver out of the corner of his eye. "Put your head down, we have an hour or so before the light will come. We have a long walk ahead of us tomorrow, so rest as much as you can," he whispered.

Oliver relaxed and dropped his head back down, but sleep was simply not going to happen, no matter how hard he tried. The flames died to embers, the black night slowly gave way to the blue-grey light of the dawn, Jannon gently placed his hand on Aiden's shoulder and then on Oliver's, "Come on boys, time to rise, we need to break camp and make a start on the day."

The two new friends both sat up, yawned and rubbed their eyes. As they did so, Oliver arched his back and stretched his arms out as far as he could. He relaxed and went to stand and as he did so, he accidently let go of the loudest, longest fart ever. Oliver had never blushed so much in his entire life, the violent expulsion resulted in the pair bursting into a fit of laughter, Aiden scrambling to get out of range of the obnoxious gas before it could reach him!

"I am warming some bread before we extinguish the fire, so I suggest you go over there, behind that tree," Jannon lifted his right arm and pointed in the direction of some large trees. "I have scraped a hole, and there is some moss there to wipe your bums when you have finished," he declared in a matter-of-fact way.

Oliver went crimson with embarrassment. Not only had he let one rip in front of relative strangers, but he could not remember the last time somebody was so candid about bodily functions. He hurried to get behind the tree.

The bright day went quickly as the three paced through the woodland, Oliver occasionally looked up beyond the tree canopy to see the sky was a clear blue without a cloud to be seen. The boys talked almost the whole way without stopping, which was good, as it meant they had something to occupy their minds. It also distracted them from the fact that they needed to travel about twenty miles before they could stop again for the night. Jannon was conscious that they needed to reach Donnchad, the King of his tribe, the Trinovantes, and present the parchment with the utmost haste.

The afternoon stretched on, and the boys looked more and more as if they were ready to drop. Jannon ensured the boys kept drinking and that they had plenty of short breaks to snack on their supplies to keep their energy up. As the day wore on the breaks became more frequent as fatigue started to overcome them. He found another ideal resting place to stop and sent the boys to fetch wood and ferns as he made a fire. That night was very different. The boys dragged themselves around, and hardly a word was said. Jannon lit the fire, skewered some more deer for them all but they barely kept their eyes open long enough to finish their food. Jannon turned to pass some mead, but he was the only one sampling the nectar from the gods. The boys had passed out from exhaustion on their deer skins.

The following dawn Jannon was up quickly, warmed and snacked on some bread and cheese for his breakfast and extinguished the fire, before he started to break the camp once more. He had let the boys sleep for as long as he dared. He knew the boys were tired, but they needed to reach Donnchad with the utmost urgency. He was starting to think that bringing the boys was a bad mistake as he could move so much quicker on his own. But Mardina, his wife, was right. If the parchment was important, then their son should be recognised and celebrated for his discovery and Oliver was far too important to be left behind. He had the devil's own job rousing the two young companions, but eventually Jannon succeeded in waking the pair. They both moaned and complained bitterly as they stretched, rubbed their eyes and really struggled to raise themselves from their warm comfy beds. The enthusiasm of the previous morning was definitely not present, in fact they barely munched on their breakfast.

"Right boys, we are nearly there," Jannon informed them cheerily as he clapped his hands and rubbed his palms together. He continued, "By this afternoon you will be in front of the King." He nodded with pride at the thought, "Our King!" He looked at the two rather unimpressed faces before him. "I know you are tired, but you can rest when we reach Braughing."

The three picked up their skins and other pieces of kit. Jannon threw the straps of various bags that contained their dwindling supplies over his shoulder as they strode out of the clearing and along the winding pathway. They were all putting in a little extra effort. As the pace picked up Oliver started wishing that he had spent a little less time in front of his computer and the TV, and more time exercising!

Chapter Nine

The sense of excitement was palpable as the Roman teams were briefed and prepared for their task. The cohort under the command of Decianus Catus moved out swiftly, a force made up of legionaries, auxiliaries, and slaves. It was not unusual for slaves to be conscripted into covert operations such as this, but they were not soldiers. They were personal servants, perhaps clerks if they could read and write, or personal servants to the officers, and they also led the mule carts carrying supplies, helped erect tents and the setting up of the cooking and bathing areas.

The journey would take the cohort a couple of days, so they had taken a few carts, and, when no one was looking, some extra goodies were liberated from the kitchens along with a few flagons of wine in order make the journey a little more comfortable. Not that they carried a lot of equipment, the carts would be used for carrying the booty that they were about to remove from the Iceni!

The assault force had camped just out of sight of their target and, on the fateful morning of the attack, was primed and eager to begin, with the element of surprise firmly in their favour. Their camp had been broken down and they were champing at the bit to get underway just before daybreak. The plan was to catch all the Iceni warriors still sleeping in their beds before they had time to arm themselves. The team would take premium livestock and goods. Collection of as much booty as possible was the main objective. All jewellery and valuables were now the property of Rome and were to be confiscated. A few of the pieces would be redistributed between the men once the main job was completed. Some of the fittest fit men and women were to be captured and dragged into slavery. They would be sold to the highest bidder, providing some more revenue for the captors. Those who resisted would be put to the sword.

The gods seemed to be with the raiding party, gentle sunshine warmed the ground below their feet as they approached. The upbeat mood heightened as they marched along the track heading further into the land belonging to the Iceni. Well...it had belonged to them, up that point. The orders issued from General Suetonius Paulinus were very straightforward and basic: 'Strip Queen Boudicca of the Iceni of all her belongings and lands, as they now belong to Rome. Because of the inconvenience she is causing to Rome, I demand she be discredited and punished in front of her tribe. If there are any objections it is to be met with maximum force.'

On the morning of the third day the scouts reported that their target was close by, and the cohort prepared themselves. The instruments of Rome went into automatic mode as the training took over. Each man dressed himself meticulously starting with braccae woollen trousers over his subligaria underpants and tunic. On top, fastened around the waist was the thick leather pteruges, a skirt of leather strips designed to protect the thighs. Lastly was a scarf, called a focale, which stopped the armour chain mail and breastplates from chafing and rubbing their necks. The men placed the sharpened blades of their gladius swords and pugio daggers in sheaths hanging from sword belts. All adjustments were made carefully as occasional banter bounced backwards and forwards among the hardened soldiers. They all made sure the deadly tools of their profession were readily at hand as they would be needed very soon.

The force approached Boudicca's stronghold in absolute silence as the last of the night fires died away and the horizon to the east slowly gave way to a new day. The sky gradually passed from black to dark blue as the sun started to make its presence known. As the sky lightened to an inky blue and snoring became the prominent human noise, the Romans took their cue and split into three blocks. The centre block, containing most of the armoured raiders, and the two flanking sides that were made up of armoured auxiliaries, all made their way into the still dark morning. The centre block spread into a crescent shape as the two flanks disappeared towards the back of the settlement. There was a rear entrance through the high fence, much to the relief of the flanking men. These two smaller flanks went in first. Their job was to flush out the drowsy inhabitants and drive any resistance towards the centre block where they would face death or surrender. The main objective though was to find the Queen and present Boudicca to the officer in charge.

The sun had risen just enough to allow the occasional beam of faint light to break through the forest on the left of the settlement, catching some of the low mist that was hovering over the field of crops. It illuminated some of the protagonists who silently manoeuvred to their starting positions and waited for the moment to attack. The quick, shrill blast of a horn sang out, and the signal to attack was obeyed by all the force in unison. With blood curdling yells the attackers ran into the compound and charged into each house in turn. Coupled with screams from the terrified victims inside the buildings the noise should have been enough to waken the gods.

Into roundhouse after roundhouse the attackers stormed in, wielding their gladii in their right hands and forcing men, women and children in various states of dress, out of the roundhouses and towards the centre of the settlement. If any resisted or tried to defend themselves, they were struck down indiscriminately. The noise alerted others, women grabbed babies and children by the hands and tried to get to the safety of the trees. Some were hit with arrows, crossbow bolts or spears that rained down on them as they tried to run. The warriors grabbed any weapons they could and in a desperate rush charged outside their houses and did their best to overcome the invaders, but the effort was futile. The Roman aggressors were too organised, the defending warriors were far too outnumbered and disorganised to put up any real resistance. Many quickly realised the fight was done and took flight into the surrounding fields, some managed to slip past the Romans and carried on running without looking back. Not out of fear, but in order to reach the neighbouring villages of the Iceni people as fast as they could to raise the alarm.

The invaders quickly reached the centre of the settlement and the Roman-styled palace that the late king had constructed. As some of the invaders smashed through the front doors and hastily made their way through the building room by room, others herded the captives into the open ground in front of the palace. The very fact the palace was made up of separate rooms was very unusual for a Celtic village, but King Prasutagus had considered himself a Roman ally and had built the palace on the designs of the buildings erected by earlier victors who had come under the eagle standard of Rome. He had incorporated very basic mosaics and had frescos painted on the walls, just as Romans did. Prasutagus always portrayed himself as the king of his people and claimed he was always approachable, but he had demanded and enjoyed privacy for himself, his wife and daughters, limited as it was.

The Romans crashed through the various rooms as they hunted their quarry. Each room was filled with a heavy, heady odour. Potions derived from various plants had been prepared by Druid Priests to help ease the pain of Boudicca's broken heart, and these emanated from smoking perfume burners. The concoctions had been specially prepared to blur the line between reality and dreams, and they also believed it would be a link to the spirit world and aid the spirit of the recently deceased king to join his forefathers. The clanking of the raiders' metal armour was clearly heard as they continued to smash through each door before they finally stumbled over their prize. Boudicca herself. She was on her knees, head bowed in front of a posy of wood and wildflowers praying to her late husband and the gods, begging them to give her strength to deal with what had happened, and more importantly, to face what was about to come.

The word soon reached the Roman officer, Decianus, that she had been captured. He mounted his horse and rode up to the settlement boundaries. He kicked his horse forward and wandered through the devastation. He stopped briefly to survey his bounty, as it was being loaded onto carts. As he made his way forward, he barked, "Make sure every man, woman and child that is still alive is rounded up and brought to the palace of this jumped-up bitch!"

Decianus brought his steed to a stop outside the palace, swung his right foot over the neck of his mount and slid to the ground. As he did so, he proclaimed at the top of voice, "Bring me the woman who claims to front this rabble, I want her bowing to me and hear her worship the might of the glorious Roman Empire!"

Boudicca was dragged into the light, her arms bound behind her with a leather tether just above the elbows, her strawberry blonde locks falling loosely over her shoulders and down to her waist. Her facial features could only just be made out through the strands of hair that covered it, but the look of fierce defiance in her eyes was clearly visible.

"Kneel before the might of the Roman army and proclaim allegiance then you, and your people, might just live to see the end of this day!"

Boudicca remained silent and resilient as she stood before the Officer, staring him in the eye as she tried to keep her temper. Her rage would not help her at this moment in time.

"Perhaps you might want to think over my words very carefully..." the Roman Procurator snarled.

Boudicca raised herself to her full height, tilted her head back and looked down her nose at the man in front of her. Her silence was deafening as she magnificently demonstrated her defiance.

Decianus nodded and beckoned to some of the auxiliaries standing at the doorway of the Roman-style palace doors. Without a word they slipped inside and shortly terrible screams from her two girls could be heard. Boudicca stood resolute and still on the spot as the screaming continued. Then there was a sudden silence as she witnessed her two darling girls being dragged by their hair like criminals rather than the princesses that they were. They were dragged into the light. The pair had had their clothes ripped off, exposing their naked forms as they were thrown towards the back of a cart, trying desperately hard to cover their flesh from the stunned, silent crowd. Roman soldiers jumped on to the open cart and grabbed the wrists of each girl, pulling them bodily up on to the cart's wooden floor, and then tying their wrists to the sides of the cart.

The cruel, sadistic Roman wandered around his victims, "I order you to kneel before the might of Rome!" Decianus snarled at Boudicca as he held out his right hand and pointed to the ground just in front of her.

Boudicca stood firm and resolute as she stared at the horizon, refusing to acknowledge any instructions or orders from the invader before her.

The Roman was tired of her behaviour and his patience was starting to run thin. "Kneel to the might of Rome!" the Procurator repeated.

Boudicca threw her head back, "I will NEVER bow to the cowards who attack defenceless girls... You underestimate me... You underestimate the Iceni!" she proudly declared.

"Very well," the Procurator sighed as he glanced at three legionaries to his left and nodded. The soldiers grabbed Boudicca and dragged her to a post that the Romans had hastily erected in the centre of the square. Her arms were released temporarily before her tunic was torn from her, stripping her to the waist. Her wrists were bound with a leather thong in front of her, a rope was threaded through this and fastened to the top of the wooden post and pulled tight, forcing her body to press up against the wood.

"How dare you touch a Queen and treat her like this..." Boudicca growled through her gritted teeth. "I will see that your Emperor puts your head on a spike!" she screamed in rage.

The Procurator signalled the legionary with the whip, who raised his hand above his head, summoned all his strength, and brought his hand down with such velocity and violence the whip cracked as it rapidly changed direction before he smashed it into Boudicca's bare flesh.

Decianus stepped over to the bare-backed Boudicca, leaned towards her head and snarled, "The Emperor that you threaten me with is the very Emperor who sent me!" He grinned before retreating and signalling for the next blow.

Boudicca's legs nearly buckled as the whip landed, she was grateful the post was there to keep her standing. Her jaw clenched, her eyes closed tightly, and she drew in a deep lungfull of air as the pain ripped through her. "I have borne children... I won't cry!" her inner voice repeated over and over in her head.

The whip smacked into her a third time, again her face screwed up and contorted with the pain as she fought to remain upright. "I won't scream... I won't give them the satisfaction," the inner voice screamed in her head.

Decianus leaned in towards her face. "Who owns your land and your people now?" the man snarled. "You or Rome?" he taunted sarcastically.

The Procurator stood back once more and nodded to the soldier. Again, the whip was heaved back before being thrashed forward, forcing a loud crack as the ends rapidly changed direction, the knots streaking through the air before they smashed across her back. Boudicca was unaware of the blood running down her back and soaking into her skirt. In fact, she could feel nothing except the intense stinging pain, and she struggled to stay upright on her trembling legs. "Not Rome!" she barely gurgled through the agony.

He nodded again, and the whip ripped at her again and again until Boudicca almost lost consciousness. The Procurator ordered her daughters to be thrown in front of Boudicca. He wanted her to see the bruised and blood-streaked bodies of her girls as he grabbed Boudicca's hair and drew her head back, declaring loudly to the gathered mass as he did so, "THIS IS YOUR QUEEN!... SEE HOW SHE BLEEDS?... THIS IS A NOBODY!" He looked around at the shocked faces of the horde gathered in front of him. "This is what happens when you disrespect Rome..." he raged. "This is how Rome will destroy you..." Decianus continued as he slowly paced in front of them. "This is what happens if you defy Rome!" he barked, before smartly marching over to the officers and issuing more orders. "Men, we will have no more trouble from this scum..." he paused before turning and addressing the crowd, "Those who oppose Rome again will be removed from here and placed in slavery, all those who are fit and strong enough to work. You will fetch a decent price and be useful for our farmers, who will work you until you drop in our fields, tending our grain for us..." he warned as he slowly walked around Boudicca and her daughters. "As slaves of Rome," he taunted, his face starting to turn colour with rage as he drew a breath and screamed, "I will remind you; your life is cheap!"

His men all let out a loud cheer and ran into the palace to strip it of all its wealth. The carts were brought around and loaded up. Furniture was stacked high, sacks of grain, baskets of bread and meat, piles of furs, all was taken, as Decianus grabbed all the jewellery he could find for himself, nothing was to be left. Ten of the fittest warriors and some of the women were tied in a line behind one of the loaded carts and prodded forward at spearpoint.

The Roman Procurator mounted his horse and signalled for the retreat as he kicked his stallion forward. The crowd of Iceni watched all their valuable possessions leave as they waited for the last Roman to disappear out of sight before charging to their Queen and her children. The three were released from their bindings and gently carried into the palace, so they could be tended to and have their wounds treated.

Two of the house-guards flanked their queen and supported her weight as she was cut down from the post. "I will spill the blood of EVERY last Roman..." she murmured as she opened her eyes and stared into the face of the person who released her from her bonds. "I will cut them open and walk on their entrails," muttered the Queen before passing out with the pain.

The Iceni who had managed to escape to hide in the forest gradually returned to the settlement as people from nearby villages started to appear and swelled their numbers. A senior house-guard to Boudicca shouted orders and gathered a selection of men together. "I want all of you to raise the alarm with every Iceni settlement and gather all the fighting men you can find!" He then turned and pointed to three of the men and ordered them in turn, "You go the Corieltauvi... You go to the Catuvellauni... You go to the Trinovantes..." He paused briefly to gather his thoughts before continuing, "Tell them what has happened, remind them of the allegiance they swore to King Prasutagus and Queen Boudicca." He nodded at each to seek their acknowledgment then he continued to speak, "Tell them to raise their fighting men and join us here at the next new moon." He smiled briefly to himself. "Remind them that if they are not keen, they will be next if we fail to take a stand. "GO! GO!" he ordered as he ushered them to leave.

Chapter Ten

By mid-afternoon Oliver could see that the trees were becoming thinner, smaller, and more light was starting to filter through the thinning canopy, the aroma of leaf litter was slowly being replaced with various grasses and tree pollen which started to make him sneeze. He caught a faint whiff of firewood burning as they moved nearer and nearer their destination. The path they were following became wider and stretched upwards as they moved on, and became more solid underfoot as they climbed higher. Oliver could see that there were two definite paths running parallel; these were cart tracks for sure. It was not long before Oliver, Aiden and Jannon cleared the woodland and could see a large bustling settlement spreading out below them. Houses and huts sprawled out from the centre in an almost haphazard way. In the centre was an impressive large building, the main dwelling of King Donnchad, and it was definitely a house fit for a chief.

"That is where we need to be heading," Jannon stated as he pointed down into the town and toward the large rectangular-shaped construction. "The palace of Donnchad!" he exclaimed proudly as they all stood together, absorbing the sights below them for a moment before they moved forward almost as one. The approach was so steep they almost started running as gravity pulled them down the hill and closer to their journey's end. The three finally passed the outer boundaries and made their way through the narrow streets, flanked on either side by roundhouses. Some had large openings where forges burned, the air filled with the banging of hammers crashing and clanging on to large anvils as blacksmiths went about their business. Others had tables with merchandise arranged around them selling everything from bread, meat, fish, clothing and materials to jewellery. Interspersed between the houses were pens containing various livestock. Oliver found the noise created by people talking over each other and the animals crowing, neighing, grunting, and snuffling was almost deafening after the last three days of comparative silence. The smells emanating from numerous piles of rubbish and offal combined with the animal manure that had been churned and mixed with mud under hundreds of feet, hooves and wheels made the street nauseating. Oliver could not believe that rubbish was just thrown into heaps, and no one was cleaning the streets.

Jannon and his young charges wound through the lanes before they eventually found themselves at the chief's door. Jannon announced himself to one of the house-guards, explained that he needed to speak with King Donnchad with the utmost urgency, and that he had with him a parchment that needed to be seen by the King. The guard instructed the trio to wait and he disappeared inside. After a few minutes the guard returned and instructed them to leave all their weapons with him. Jannon took Aiden's sgian and held out his open, upturned hand to Oliver, "It's alright, give me your sgian Oliver."

"I... I don't have one!" Oliver replied.

Jannon was surprised at the reply, "Don't have one?" he repeated slowly, "Have you lost it? You will be in trouble!" Jannon tutted and smiled.

Oliver glanced at the guard and then at Jannon, "No, I... I... I guess so, I mean I have never had one," replied the very tired and rather nervous Oliver.

The guard stared hard at Oliver for what felt like ages before he gave a small nod at Oliver's response, relieved Jannon of the blades, ordered them to follow him and led them into the Great Hall.

They were marched into the large room where a booming voice announced their entrance to the chamber. "Jannon son of Hertbod, Tribe Trinovantes!" bellowed a large ginger-haired man. An imposing brown-haired man leaned forward from a tall chair raised on a platform in the centre of the dim room and beckoned them to approach.

The three slowly stepped forward. "Greetings, my King," said Jannon as he bowed his head and placed his hand on Aiden's shoulder. "This is my son Aiden." He then placed his hand on

Oliver's shoulder, "and this lad is called Oliver. He is the one who found this …" Jannon held out the leather canister to Donnchad. "Evidence, my lord, that he has been sent to help us."

Donnchad glanced over to the boys in front of him and the silence was broken. "W… W… We have found this, and inside is a sealed parchment, y… y… your majesty," stammered Oliver, who was in complete awe of the vision in front of him. He had never met a king before and was surprised how the man in front of him looked like the tribal chieftains he had seen on various television programmes and films. The man had a booming voice, a mass of greying strawberry-blonde hair with an impressive beard to match. The King was a large, broad-shouldered man, and he towered over everyone else when he stood up. He took a step towards the three, reached out a massive hand and took the leather receptacle from Jannon, turning the object in his hands as he admired the craftmanship. He grasped the cylinder with his left hand and wrapped his right hand tightly over one end and deftly twisted and pulled the top. Donnchad cracked the canister open, and an audible pop rang out as the two parts separated. He rammed his sausage-like fingers in and rooted around before withdrawing them with the parchment firmly in his grasp and pulled it free of the casing. He carelessly cast the cylinder aside and it dropped onto the floor. The contents were far more important and interesting than the vessel. He took his sgian and slipped it under the seal, with a quick twist the wax was separated from the paper and the letter unravelled. Donnchad held the top of the letter in his left hand and unrolled it with his right. Wrapping his fingers around the bottom, he pulled it tight and began to scan the letters. After a few moments he cleared his throat and exclaimed, "It is indeed Roman; the writing is in Latin." The King then fell silent as he read the contents. The three travellers watched the King's face as his eyes moved left to right, absorbing every written word. Donnchad breathed in deeply as he cast his eyes up to the ceiling every now and again as he understood the words.

The silence that had been interrupted occasionally with the odd tut from the learned man was finally broken, "Thank you, my friends, this is indeed a very important find. I know you have travelled with the utmost speed and must be exhausted." The great man paused as he gathered his thoughts. Donnchad realised he had to make moves to attend the Iceni as soon as possible and he called for the captain of his house-guards. On the officers' arrival Donnchad wasted no time in describing the situation, "According to this scroll, Boudicca is going to be in real trouble with Rome. We have a crisis of conscience here. We have pledged allegiance to Rome, but I have affirmed our loyalty to Boudicca, wife of my dear friend when I attended the late King's funeral." Donnchad thought for a moment and ordered his captain to prepare his armies and cavalry to be on full alert and ready to move at a moment's notice. He simply could not abandon her to the fate Rome obviously had in mind.

"Your timing is more than fortuitous, it is fate. I know many tribal nobles who attended the funeral with me and made the same pledge." Donnchad barked some orders to his attendants to get things organised. "We have a little time before we have to move out, so please rest here and regain your strength, you will be coming with us." Donnchad smiled at the three. "Join me tonight when we eat." The King bowed his head towards the young traveller, "Oliver, I believe you have truly been sent to deliver us and I will be honoured if you will all join me as my guests at my table for dinner. In the meantime, please rest." He declared as he turned to a house-guard, "See that our friends are looked after."

Oliver and his fellow companions were pleased their journey was not in vain. "Thank you, my lord," The three said as they bowed before the King, who nodded his acknowledgment in return before turning to his left and calling to his second-in-command.

"Garaint, gather the Council at once!" Donnchad bellowed as he signalled the three to leave his presence.

They were led out of the room by a serf, who walked briskly in front of them as they followed down a corridor and were shown to a room, where there were fresh clothes waiting for them, and bowls of hot water for washing were brought through. Once they all had chance to recover and rest for a few hours, a servant tapped lightly on the door before he opened it slightly and poked his head round. He informed them that he had been told to summon them and escort them to the King's table. As they made their way to the Great Hall the servant talked incessantly about how they were honoured to be seated at Donnchad's table. No sooner were the three seated than the mead started to flow, food was passed around, the chatter grew louder and more raucous. The King turned to Jannon. "Tell me man... You say the messenger from the gods claimed to have found this message and handed this scroll to you?" he enquired as he filled his mouth with venison and looked hard at Jannon. He chewed the flesh and washed it down with a big gulp of mead before turning his head towards Aiden's father and looked hard into his eyes, "How can you be sure we can trust this boy?" he asked as he studied the man carefully, watching Jannon's reaction. The King prided himself on being able to know a man's thoughts through the way he moved his body and the expressions that subconsciously flashed across the face.

Jannon hesitated as he considered the question. "Sir, he has been in my care for a short while, but I believe him to be sound," he declared with all honesty. "I think I am a good judge of character. I know boys in general, and I know he could not act so convincingly for so long without giving clues away." Jannon looked up to the ceiling as his brain rapidly searched through his memory of the recent events, "He really does have a sense of wonderment at everything around him, truly as if he had never seen many of these things before."

The King listened intently as he watched Jannon before diverting his attention to Oliver, who was laughing and joking with Aiden. "How long exactly was this?" enquired Donnchad as he watched the two boys.

Jannon lowered the drinking vessel he had just raised to his lips before he could take a mouthful of mead, "This would have been for five days sir."

"Very well," the King declared as he sat back in his chair and demanded more mead from a nearby servant, before signalling to the men flanking him on either side to move closer so they could hear what he had to say. The men obediently moved in and listened intently as their lord spoke. Donnchad went over the details with them and explained how the scroll had come into his possession as he explained. "The details written in the letter we have intercepted are very important, in fact so important that they will change the purpose of our people and could even change our country forever." The king paused as he took a big swig from his goblet before continuing, "The points detailed in this document completely changes our relationship with Rome. It verifies that we are all under threat." The King leaned back and took a deep breath as his cheeks flushed and he closed his eyes tightly, the reaction being the result of slamming food and mead down his throat down too quickly. After fidgeting in his seat, he slammed his clenched fist into his chest and forced a belch so loud it instantly stopped all conversations in the room.

As the evening went on the King became more and more enraged as the alcohol increased in his blood levels, until he could not contain it any further and slammed his fists on to the table causing plates, jugs, food and implements to jump. "I knew I could never really trust the change of Emperors," he screamed. "And I was right!" he declared. He looked at the shocked faces gathered around him as he shouted, "What it says is that Queen Boudicca of the Iceni is not to be recognised as Queen on the death of her husband; and that the lands of the Iceni will now belong to Rome, as well as all the wealth the tribe owns!" He stood up, "As we all now know the Iceni King has died, this means Boudicca and the Iceni are in trouble… Big trouble." An audible sigh and gasps echoed the news as Donnchad sat back down and contemplated the words on the document.

The chatter started again as Donnchad signalled for the two boys to come over to him and stand before him. The pair dutifully left their places and rushed forward at the King's request. Donnchad fidgeted and perched on the lip of his throne, leaned forward, and spoke directly to the pair, "I, and our people, are very grateful to you for bringing us the news contained in this letter and you will be handsomely rewarded." He looked beyond the two as he loudly addressed the rest of the room, "In the meantime, we MUST stand by our brethren. We must leave as soon as we can. Raise the alarm and muster all the fighting men we can." The King looked back at the boys, "That includes you two, I am afraid to say that you are not heading home very soon!" The mead took effect as he raised his goblet aloft and screamed at the top of his voice. "To the Trinovantes!" The people in the hall all stood up, raised their goblets repeated the toast and emptied their drinking vessels in single gulps before banging them down hard on the tables.

Donnchad called for his house-guards and issued orders for some to ride out among the villages and settlements and call all of fighting age to arms. Every able man was to arm himself, make himself ready to fight and to attend the King at his palace before they moved all together. He turned in the direction of Aiden and Oliver and beckoned to them to move closer to his table. Donnchad needed to watch Oliver's expressions and reactions for himself in order to determine and satisfy himself, whether Oliver really was a messenger from the gods, or a spy sent by Rome. He idly stroked his beard as he smiled at the two young lads, both unaware of the look of suspicion that flared in his eyes as he spoke, "You young men have done a great deed. I am very proud of you both, and I want you to remain here as my guests." He affirmed, "Tomorrow you will train with my house-guards and start to learn how to fight like the brave men you are destined to become."

Aiden and Oliver looked at each other, Aiden had a huge smile on his face and looked as if he was about to burst with pride. Oliver grinned but did not grasp the enormity of the offer. Aiden could see the uncertainty in his friend's face and nodded to him in an act to try to reassure his companion and mouthed, 'That's brilliant!' before the pair turned to face the King.

Aiden could not contain his joy, "Thank you my Lord!" he grinned.

Oliver followed suit, "Thank you," he beamed, "my Lord!" and he bowed.

Donnchad nodded regally at the pair, before he turned to his right and mumbled his orders to his guard, "Inform Garaint that he will have two new apprentices to join the men training tomorrow." He narrowed his eyes as he whispered, "And tell him to watch the pair very carefully, I want a full report."

Turning back to the boys, the King raised his hand. "Both the pleasure and gratitude are all mine," he purred. "Enjoy the rest of the evening and do not be late in the morning!" were his parting words as he dismissed them by waving them away.

The two boys took two steps backwards before turning smartly and walking back to their places at the table. With the excitement of the news, they did not sleep much that night! The dawn could not come quickly enough for the pair, who chattered and gabled the night away. The two eager pupils were up and out of their dorm before the servant finished tapping on their door, almost knocking him flying as they barrelled down the corridor, keen to get into some action.

Oliver and Aiden stood in line with the other house-guards, who had gathered on the training ground and were busy chatting and discussing how the day might go with some of the men, when the side door opened. The Commander of the Guard marched smartly towards them and snapped at the men to 'Come to!' The men all jumped to attention at the command. Oliver and Aiden followed suit, although slightly out of step, and tried to stand like the men around them, feet together, arms by their side with thumbs pointing to the ground, they arched their backs, pushed their chest out and raised their chins. Oliver felt important, and very proud to be standing to attention with his friend and the other brave fighting men.

The Commander slowly walked past the men, looking them up and down in turn, subconsciously nodding to himself as he did so. As he reached the end he spun around smartly, took a deep breath and roared in a deep, gravelly voice, "As you know, fitness is our goal. Fitness keeps us alive. Fitness KILLS

ENEMIES! When you fall out, collect your shields, swords and equipment... You will be delighted to know we have a treat for you all, we are going to run six miles before breakfast," he grinned at the shocked faces of the motionless teams. "House-guards... to your duties. Fall out.!" he yelled as he pointed to the entrance to the grounds. The group turned and filed through the gates with Oliver and Aiden bringing up the rear. The thought of a six-mile run had certainly stopped the chatter between them, although they were excused carrying the equipment! The guards set a hard pace, Oliver found it very difficult to keep up, but the house-guards all kept encouraging him.

"Bloody Michael... Bloody Spinks, I will kick your arse," was all he kept saying to himself over and over in an effort to drive himself on. "I will be the one clipping your ears!" The thoughts stopped him thinking of the pain in his legs as the lactic acid built up and his breathing became more laboured. "I will be so strong you will be afraid to even look at me." Oliver kept thinking, although all his body wanted to do was stop and lie down.

The house-guards cajoled and encouraged the boys as they finally stumbled back to the settlement and into the barracks to be greeted with a hot breakfast of oats and bacon, which smelled divine to Oliver and Aiden. The pair wolfed it down as if they had never eaten before. After filling their faces, they were allowed a brief rest before they were tasked to clear the men's utensils before joining the soldiers outside, who were busy battle training. The Commander and senior officers were only too aware the guests were still too young to be put through all the punishing regime the soldiers went through on a regular basis. As the two friends emerged from the quarters and joined the regiment of men, they were both issued with a wooden sword. They pair glanced briefly at each other before they started to hit each other while laughing like a couple of loons. The game suddenly stopped as the Commander screamed at them to 'stand to' and pay attention if they wanted to learn how to fight properly like men and to learn the most efficient way to hit their opponent. To learn the vital areas to hit to create the lethal blow against their opponent. They were told to watch the men as they initiated blocking tactics and deflection of the blows that would be coming at them. The Commander told them that they would be expected to replicate what they had watched and demonstrate what they had leaned. Oliver and Aiden were transfixed as they watched in awe at the sure-footed and well-practised footwork of the soldiers. They appeared to dance as they kept their balance, always keeping weight on the dominant foot so that the maximum force could be administered through the body and the arms. The boys started off by learning how to react defensively to protect themselves and then attack with the swords. First Aiden would strike at Oliver, who would block the sword strike with the shield and deflect it, trying to open Aiden's side for a counter strike or blow as he moved. The boys did this in slow motion under the instruction of the senior house-guard before being allowed to do the moves faster and faster, all under the careful observation of the Commander who watched from the side-lines, making mental notes as he silently monitored the action. They then reversed roles, getting quicker with every turn. Once they had mastered this first move, they moved to second and third moves, swapping roles after every sequence ended. The training ended with another six-mile run.

The boys joined the men in drinking as much water as they could before they set off. They had all worked up a huge thirst before the run. "This is sooooo much better than my computer games!" Oliver said aloud without thinking.

Aiden heard him. "What are you talking about?" his young companion queried. "What is a computer game?"

Oliver tightly closed his eyes as he regretted not thinking before he spoke, "Never mind Aiden, just believe me, this is way more fun!" Oliver laughed as he tried to deflect the question. "Let's get running!" And he charged after the house-guards.

The training continued over the following days, as Donnchad waited impatiently for the tribe to gather. Oliver was positive he could feel every muscle in his body grow and both boys started to feel like real warriors. The trained fighters had really taken to the pair because of their willingness to learn how to move, advance, retreat, attack, defend as a group, and the speed at which they learned sword skills.

After the fourth day, King Donnchad had completed most of the preparations to mobilise his armies towards the lands of the Iceni. As part of the preparations, he made an unexpected appearance at the training ground to watch the men in action before he called for his chief house-guard.

Donnchad nonchalantly wandered over to the Commander. "Have you been watching the boys?" he asked in a hushed tone.

The chief house-guard did not avert his gaze from the action going on around him, "Yes my Lord."

The King nodded at the news. "Good, let's take a walk," he continued, "Tell me of the one called Oliver?"

The soldier paused for a moment as he compiled his assessment in his head. "He is different but eager to learn." He paused as he pondered his next revelation, "He speaks in a tongue unlike ours, but he uses the same words, and he talks of things and places I do not know or understand. I have been watching him very carefully. He is agile, fights well and handles the practice swords competently. He always calls out to others and jumps into the fight. He is very keen, and he has a lot of promise"

Donnchad hung on every word, "It is claimed he has been sent by the gods." The King revealed as he stopped and faced the house-guard, "What do you say?" asked the King.

The man was taken aback by this revelation and considered the kings' words. "I ...I agree," nodded the chief house-guard. "There is something different about him," he continued slowly as he was trying to piece the information together in his mind. "He is not from…" The thought that Oliver had been sent by the gods was difficult to accept, but then he was being told by his chief, so it must be right. "He is not from here, of that I am sure, but he has spirit and a good true heart and never retreats from the fight."

Donnchad listened intently to the man's report. The edges of his lips started to turn up and a grin exposed his teeth at the news, which conveniently mirrored his own thoughts as they wandered back to the mass of exercising troops. The house-guard bellowed at the melee to break from their activities and form into rows. When they had done so, he called them to stand to attention. Donnchad nodded at the Commander and stepped forward. "Tonight, we will celebrate, tomorrow we prepare to show our support to the Iceni!" he declared with the air of authority worthy of a seasoned king.

The feast that night was a celebration to be remembered for generations. The priests were presented with a cow, which they duly sacrificed, slitting its stomach open and reading its entrails as they spilled onto the ground. With great theatrics the priests threw their hands to the skies and declared in unison, "The omens are good, the gods say you will all be victorious!"

The news was received with a huge cheer from the crowd as large jugs filled with mead were passed around and voices grew louder as the festivities got into in full swing. Donnchad climbed up onto his chair, held his hands up and called for silence. As the hush fell across the gathered masses, he asked for Aiden and Oliver to be brought to him. As they approached, he cleared his throat and addressed the horde in front of him. "People of the Trinovantes," he began, "We have two very brave and special young men in our midst." He raised both arms into the air. "I have been watching these young warriors fighting with our house-guards; unbeknown to them," he stated as he looked at faces in the crowd, pausing for dramatic effect. "They have demonstrated they are fearless." The King looked at the young pair that had been pushed to the front of the gathering. "Aiden, Oliver come forward and salute your King!" he demanded as he climbed down from his chair. The boys took a few steps towards him and knelt at his feet. "Having proved their bravery and loyalty I have a special reward," he informed the boys as the audience listened intently. "As a mark of my trust and respect for you," he declared as a guard joined him, holding objects on a wooden tray in front of him. Donnchad looked down at the two bowed heads. "Stand!" he ordered. As the boys rose to their feet he explained, "These sgians are made of the finest metal, the handles are from a stag that I took when the sun was cooling and the days shortening. The scabbard sheath is made from the hide of the regal stag." He continued, as he picked up one of the knives, "Oliver, take this as a mark of my appreciation." He handed the object over and proceeded to reach over to the tray and picked up a silver and gold stylised brooch, "Here is my mark, all members of my household wear these as a symbol of recognition." Oliver stared at the item with amazement. Donnchad leaned in towards Oliver and informed him it was to be pinned on his left breast, over his heart. The King stood back and signalled the crowd to cheer. As the roar subsided, he continued, "Aiden, take this as mark of my appreciation." As the young lad reached out his shaking hand, his eyes opened wide, and his mouth fell open as he gazed at the object briefly before temporarily tucking it in his waist band as he eagerly awaited the coveted brooch to be presented. The pair looked at each other as big grins filled their faces. They looked back at Donnchad as he continued, "May they serve you well and keep you safe." As he nodded sagely, he signalled to the lads to hold the gifts up for the whole gathering to view. The two boys glanced at each other as they did so and turned to face the hushed crowd, who gave a huge roar of approval on the King's cue. The eruption of noise as he lifted his hands reverberated around the buildings and echoed into the dark night. Donnchad let the cheers continues for several minutes before he lifted his arms to shoulder height and waved his hands, calling for quiet. As the volume dropped, he called out, "Friends, I have another announcement. Step forward Jannon son of Hertbod."

The shocked father looked to his left and then to his right to make sure his King was asking for him in person. When nobody else seemed to take a step, he marched over to Donnchad, dropped down on his left knee and bowed his head.

Donnchad looked down at the figure in front of him, "Jannon

of the Trinovantes," he proclaimed as he reached for the tray once more and retrieved a third brooch, "I appoint you 'Master of Deity'. You are to steward the special guest among us and are charged to keep him safe and near." As he finished the last word, he threw his hands up once more, to be greeted by another deafening roar of approval.

Oliver felt as if his heart was going to burst out of his chest with pride as the celebration continued around him. "I wish Mum was here to see this, she would be so proud," he thought to himself. As the words ran through his mind a single thought suddenly ripped through him, melancholy and fear flooded his thoughts, upsetting him to the core, He had not thought about home properly until that point. A lump came to his throat and his eyes started to fill with tears. Would he ever see her again? He could not bear to be in company; he wanted to be on his own as he did not want his friend to see his tears. Oliver jumped up and ran out of the celebrations. He sprinted through the corridor and into his room where he dived on to his bed, buried his face in the fur cover and started to cry uncontrollably.

Donnchad had a rude awakening from his deep, mead-induced, slumber by his house-guard commander. "My lord!" the man murmured as he approached the snoring mass of flesh, blankets, and fur. He coughed and cleared his throat, "SIRE!" he called out, "SIRE! we have word from the Iceni, it is bad."

The King slowly came to as the words penetrated his blurred mind, a mix of dream and reality suddenly cleared at the news. Donnchad sat bolt upright, "WHAT?" he demanded loudly as he rubbed his eyes. Donnchad splashed water on his face and threw on some clothes. Then he went through to the Hall and sat down heavily on his throne.

The Commander ushered in the Iceni house guard, who made his report. The shock of the news, the barbarity of the attack on Boudicca and her daughters stunned the hardened warrior King for a few moments and he sat motionless. Then Donnchad jumped up in rage and screamed for his Captains and barked orders for all the gathered men to move out and attend Boudicca as soon as possible.

The lad was shaken awake by Aiden, "Oliver, come on. We are all moving out this morning."

Oliver sat up and rubbed his eyes, he had not even realised that he had been asleep.

As the boys went outside, Oliver immediately became very aware of the sudden increase in noise. People were busy with preparations. Everybody moved around with a sense of purpose, carrying supplies of food and weapons, breaking down temporary accommodation around them and loading these onto the many carts that lined the courtyards and roadways. Not much was said, but the sense of urgency was very apparent as groups of women, children and old people gathered in groups around the vehicles while the fighting warriors assembled around the meeting stone, a large pillar of granite that had stood in the centre of the Trinovantes' town for generations.

Once Donnchad was ready to leave, he led his house-guards out of their barracks and filed into the town. Donnchad held up his hand as they reached the meeting stone. The army halted on his command, and he stepped up onto the riding platform of his war chariot. His groom had waited patiently, holding the pair of decorated ponies until the King arrived. The warriors all fell in behind the professional militia and formed one long column.

The King looked back proudly at the army behind him and paused for a moment before sharply facing forward, taking the reins in his hands and slapping his ponies forward. The men marched behind him and the carts carrying provisions and equipment brought up the rear. The women and children followed behind, hitching lifts on the back of the carts as they passed. The Iceni settlement was a few days' journey away, so another adventure was ahead of the boys and for Jannon, who had been joined by his brother, their spouses and children. Oliver was pleased with the thought of riding in the cart, which was pulled by two mules. Although the two boys really wanted to march with the house-guards, having a cart to rest on occasionally on would certainly be a relief for their aching, growing bodies.

Chapter Eleven

There had been a strong feeling of unease growing among the inhabitants of Colchester, or Camulodunum as the Romans called it. The place had always seemed to have a negative atmosphere and never truly felt warm, even in the hot summer days as the sun baked the ground around the city. Perhaps it was caused by the bad feeling and vibes from the Trinovantes tribe, the local tribe that had been displaced by the Romans. The local tribe who believed that the level, tree-felled lands with the proximity of rivers and springs, providing fresh and well stocked waters, was a perfect site for them, a sacred site provided by the gods.

The place had once been the main town of the Trinovantes, who believed the site to be magical, the home of their guardian spirits, before they were dislodged by the Romans. The Empire that had torn down their homes and replaced them with buildings set out in the recognised and identifiable grid pattern of a Roman town. The Romans had not only built houses, but shops, inns, bath houses and temples and an amphitheatre to entertain the masses. Even the Trinovantes King's dwelling had been torn down, its treasures stolen by the Governor, much to the anger of the ousted King of the Trinovantes. Rome had plundered the tribe repeatedly, the goods and monies they had stolen funded the building of the walled garrison, the fitted sewage systems and even paid for a grand temple to be constructed in honour of the Emperor Claudius.

Camulodunum was the main town for the Roman occupation of Britannia, the central hub for all its administration and military force in Britain. The city's main temple, complete with an underground crypt, was a sight to be seen, the opulent décor, the giant statues of the Emperor and the deities watched over by an army of priests, priestesses, and vestal virgins, all paid for out of the kindness of the Trinovantes. Well by the taxes the Romans had forced on the people, plus the goods the Romans had stolen! The Roman population was mainly made up of Roman veterans with their wives, several of whom had been from local tribes. Many relationships had been fostered to show the willingness of the Romans to make an uneasy peace, some had been the result of romance, but plenty were individuals who had been taken by force. Some of the inhabitants were originally locals who had been made free citizens of Rome, but the largest proportion were military and administration personnel. Most of the accommodation in the town was occupied by service wives and families, all contributing to the prosperity of the merchants and the town itself.

Although the financial mainstay were the administrators, the town was the financial hub for Britannia. The main employer of the town was obviously the military garrison. The garrison should have been at full strength, but Gaius Suetonius Paulinus had issued orders to the garrison master to move the main force north. He intended to invade the mysterious lands of the Druids and put them to death, a violent move designed to break and destroy the Druids once and for all. This peculiar race of people seemed to have a mysterious hold over the Celtic tribes. The hold was more than religious, the Druids administered medicines and enforced a legal system that the Romans simply could not fathom. Suetonius was following the broad instructions issued by Nero, and *nobody* failed Nero, not if they wanted to remain alive and their families to be left in peace. That is why Festus, Lucanus, Cato, Laenus, Maxetius, Aelianus, Decimus and Marcus found themselves marching with the 9th Legion as part of the Eagle Cohort. An army slave led the mules that were weighed down with the tent and equipment for the close group.

In fact, there was literally only a handful of soldiers left to guard the Camulodunum garrison itself and they were on very clear orders to defend the fort, and only the fort. The veterans were too few and far too old to give any effective defence and protection to the rest of the population that was made up of traders, shop keepers, innkeepers, women, and children. Although they all lived in an uncertain and violent era, none of them had any idea of the real threat and danger that was fast approaching them, an uprising of the tribes bent on revenge.

The Corieltauvi, Catuvellauni and the Trinovantes tribes had all learned of the violent punishment inflicted on Boudicca from the Iceni house guard messengers. After years of being downtrodden, bullied and treated more and more like slaves, enduring ever increasingly harsh terms dictated by Rome, their hatred of the Romans was being slowly intensified over the years. Loan interests were being increased or recalled for no apparent reason, along with the very real threat of losing their citizenship rights and being thrown into slavery. The very real threat of being stripped of wealth and lands, just as the Iceni had been after the death of their King, created a growing distrust and fuelled rebellion in them. All had reached the same conclusion, the time for rebellion had come. The three Kings had gathered their own forces and arrived to show solidarity with the Iceni over the course of the preceding weeks, pledging allegiance to the Queen as they did so. Their house guards and all their warriors in attendance followed suit, causing the army numbers to swell rapidly. Every man understood that life would be changed forever, and the security of their loved ones was at stake as they swore to fight to the death. In that one moment all four kingdoms had united and created a colossal, combined force. They all had the motivation... They had the belief... They had the leader... Boudicca … and her formidable army was soon to be on the march.

Colchester was the first and obvious target for the combined attack. Boudicca was aware that the Roman garrison had been given its orders and had made its move towards the Island of Mona in the north-west, to wipe out the Druids. She also knew this meant the garrison would be poorly defended and so it would be easier to take. Boudicca had requested the presence of the Kings and the captains of the house guards and gathered them around a large table. As the group fell silent, she looked at each in turn and cleared her throat, "This is our time," Boudicca began as she drew their attention to the plan laid out before them. "Our first target is Camulodunum," she revealed as she pointed vaguely to a sketch of the town's street layout. "We will strike the fear of our forefathers into the heart of every Roman and of the Roman Empire, as we raze it to the ground."

The gathered crowd all cheered and roared their approval in unison as Boudicca continued, pointing once more to the drawing laid out before her, "This is the city... As we all know, it is walled."

A voice chipped in as Boudicca paused for breath. "Anybody would think they did not want us in!" Donnchad interjected, his comment causing chortles among his fellow leaders.

"Absolutely," Boudicca smirked as she drew their attention back to the drawings, "and as we all are aware, the best way to take a guarded gate, or a bridge, is from both sides." She continued, "so throughout the day we will send carts in through the gates with weapons concealed among the goods and about the wagons. The Romans are not expecting us, so will not be checking the carts in any detail." The Queen paused and looked at the faces around her, checking that all were following her plan. "Your men are to pass through unarmed and mingle with the town's folk into the evening. Under the cover of darkness, they are to retrieve their weapons and prepare to take the gates from the inside. We are to coordinate our attack and commence at the same time, causing confusion among the defenders." Boudicca paused once more and double checked her plans in her head before continuing, "In the meantime, the wagons with your women folk are to remain here, in the woodland surrounding the city. Once our forces are inside the walls, we are to move methodically through the various buildings." Boudicca paused as she looked at the faces around her and she slowly growled, *"No one is to be left alive in our wake!"* She glanced back at the sketch and commenced once more, "The element of surprise, and the dark, are our friends. The main gate is situated on the West side. This will need the biggest proportion of our forces, naturally, being the biggest gate, it will allow more of us through!" Boudicca had no time for polite manners as the details of the plan were the key to success. "I will need to have a quarter of all your house guards under my command in order to take the main gateway," she ordered and looked up at each king in turn expecting their approval of her demands before progressing. "Make sure your forces have ladders and are prepared to scale the walls at these points and take and hold these ramparts!"

The men all stared intently at the finger as it dramatically banged the sketch at various points then Boudicca began to speak once more. "We know the garrison buildings are at these points. When the alarm is raised, they will be swarming like angry bees but will not be expecting us to be attacking them from the ramparts above them!" Boudicca paused to allow the details to sink in with her co-conspirators. "The signal for the main attack to begin will be flaming arrows launched high into the sky and fired at the gates and. Make sure your men are in position and ready to scale the wall defences when you see those arrows."

Boudicca looked round and asked for any questions from the men. All shook their heads, so she continued. "Good!" She smiled, "Once we have forced our way in, we will take and hold the gates, making sure that nobody leaves and raises the alarm. As I start our attack on the main gate, Addedomaros, you take the North gate." Boudicca glanced at the smiling chieftain and acknowledged him with a nod as she informed him of his task. "You are to leave a patrol on the gate and push your way to the right and join me here," she said as she pointed to a corner of the map. "Here is the garrison, you are to take it and set it ablaze."

The Queen looked up once more and looked for one her closest allies. "Brawley," she exclaimed, "you take your Catuvellauni through the North Gate!" She glanced at a second tribal chief, "Volisios lead your Corieltauvi through the South Gate and Donnchad," Boudicca reached up and placed her hand on the man next to her, "You take the East gate with your Trinovantes!" She let her hand drop to her side as she stood up straight and looked around the room. "Each of you are also to leave a handful of warriors to guard and hold the gates. Once you are in, you are to make your way towards the centre."

Boudicca looked down at the map once she was sure all the group were up to speed with her plans before she pointed to the middle of the map. "Here you will find the main Temple," she exclaimed as she tapped the map, "You are to make your way here and wait for us to join you." Boudicca raised her head to the ceiling and rolled her head in a full circle as the muscles in her neck had begun to knot tightly. She drew a breath and shuddered before returning her attention to the drawing. "As you make your way to this point, you are to raid EVERY house. Nobody is to be left alive, is that understood?" She paused to give all gathered an opportunity to 'buy into' the plan and vocalise their agreement. All began nodding and mumbling their approval as she continued, "And I mean nobody!" Boudicca started to growl as the hate swelled inside her, "No women. No children. No slaves, NOBODY! I want the streets to run with the blood of these Romans. All the goods and valuables you find are yours to keep." Boudicca took a deep breath and tried to calm her anger before continuing, "I want nothing left behind. Remember, we are all to regroup at the main market square in front of the Temple of Claudius. Once there we will sack their precious sanctuary. When that is done, we leave; nothing will be left but a smouldering ghost town."

All those surrounding the table had eagerly nodded as the plan was explained to them once more, muttering at various stages as they each mulled the plan over in their heads.
"Does anybody have any questions?" enquired the Queen as she examined the faces in front of her. "No…?" she ventured as the audience shook their heads. "Good, choose your men to go into the city and load wagons with their weapons. Then ready your main torces, we attack at midnight, so give the orders to move out then."

The gathering slowly dispersed. The house-guards were the first to leave, making their way to the gathering points to spread the word. Donnchad made his way out of the building to be greeted by his advisors, Jannon and his young charges being among the number. Various conversations and questions were being raised. Boudicca was close on Donnchad's heels and was intrigued by some of his entourage. As she casually wandered past, she noticed Oliver and Aiden, their brooches gleaming in the light. The glint caught her eye and made her pause. She observed the royal regalia and jumped to a reasonable conclusion. She placed her hand on the King's shoulder, "Donnchad, I was unaware that you have two striking sons."

The man glanced over his shoulder at the Iceni queen with a quizzical look. "Sorry?" he blurted as he looked in the direction of her gaze. A broad grin stretched across his face at the mistaken assumption, and he started to laugh. "My dear Boudicca, I am honoured that you should think these fine, striking young men could possibly be my sons, but alas it is not true, proud though I would be if they were," he commented as he slightly bowed his head and raised his right hand towards one of the lads. "Your majesty, I would like to introduce Aiden son of Jannon." The boy bowed dutifully, and he blushed at the introduction as his King declared, "This fine young warrior is the lad who helped find the scroll which lays out the Roman plan we shared with you." Donnchad looked back at Aiden with a sense of pride. "And he has a bright future ahead of him." The King dropped his arm and turned slightly to his right before raising his arm towards Aiden's companion. As he did so he continued, "And this young chap is called Oliver." Donnchad paused as he was not too sure how to describe Oliver to Boudicca. "Oliver has been sent by the powers that govern us all to protect us. It has been foretold that he is a talisman of good fortune for our endeavours, and he delivered the warning that Rome is rising against us."

Boudicca moved closer to the boy to get a closer look. Her eyes studied him closely as she looked down to his feet and back up to his head before slowly reaching out and touching him on the shoulder. She closed her hand over Oliver's shoulder and gripped his muscles, gently squeezing them, confirming for herself that he was indeed real. As she did so she nodded gently and smiled, "Oliver, I am pleased to meet you." Her eyes softened as she spoke, "I understand you have been sent to bring us good fortune, it is pleasing that the gods are with us."

Oliver was completely dumb struck. He was being addressed directly by one of the most famous and revered characters in British history. He struggled to speak but only managed to spurt out, "Thank you Your Majesty." He could feel himself blush as his head started to spin.

Boudicca turned to her faithful ally, "Donnchad, I trust you have made provisions to keep these two important characters safe?"

The Trinovantes' King was a little shocked at the question, "Of course," he reassured her as he introduced Aiden's father. "This is my appointed steward for the two lads, Jannon son of Hertbod, from the Trinovantes."

Boudicca nodded regally before she took Donnchad's arm and pulled him away. "Can you trust this man with such a valuable talisman?" she quizzed in a rather concerned tone.

Donnchad laughed loudly at the question, "I hope so, he is Aiden's father!"

Jannon came into the roundhouse with Cleland, the Iceni owner who had been requested by Boudicca to open his door to Jannon and his family, although Oliver's identity had been kept secret. The following morning the word was given to be ready to move out.

An animated Jannon almost ran through the door, barely able to hide his excitement, "Mardina, ready the cart... I will find the boys and ask my brother to join us." He turned to his host, "Cleland, thank you my friend," he cheerfully exclaimed. "May the gods look down and protect you and yours." He smiled as he reached out for his friend's arm.

Cleland smiled as their hands clasped each other's wrists, "And you my friend, my brother in arms, may our gods keep you safe."

"Where are we going?" asked Mardina as she started to busy herself with the packing.

"Camulodunum!" they replied simultaneously as they smiled to each other.

Mardina stopped in her tracks at the news. "Camulodunum? But that's the biggest city in the country," she gasped. "It is the Roman capital." Mardina's mind was tumbling as she tried to think of a reason. "Why are we going there?" she finally asked.

The warriors looked at each other and grinned, "We are going to strike at Rome and where best to do it?" Jannon reasoned as he shrugged his shoulders.

"But... But... But it is full of Romans. We will be murdered!" stuttered a very worried Mardina. "They have a garrison, and there are many legions there."

Cleland shook his head and reassuringly informed her "No, the legions are not there, they have gone north. That is why we are to attack the city. The gods are helping us. The moment has come! We attack at midnight of the first quarter moon!"

After several hard days of marching, the four tribes set up the final camp before the raid and prepared themselves for the attack.

Boudicca called a council of her leaders. "Tonight, we will take Camulodunum. We will lie up two miles from the city using the woods as cover. When night comes you will gather your men." Boudicca paused before she addressed the kings individually, "Volisios, you will be on my right, Brawley you will be on my left," The men nodded their agreement before she continued, "and Donnchad, you will be on the other side of Brawley coming in from the east. You will keep your men moving and come around in a wide loop until you are facing me on the other side of the city." Boudicca then addressed the room, "When the quarter moon is at its highest, we attack. You are to approach in absolute silence, so make sure all your men know the plans. You are to tell everybody, and I mean *everybody*, that there are to be no cooking fires. We don't want to alert the enemy, or give our position away... Does everybody understand what they are doing?" The question was answered with a loud "Aye," and a sea of nodding heads, as they all began to leave to go about their duties and final preparations.

As the light faded, the men readied themselves, saying silent prayers as they picked up their shields, bows, spears, and swords, kissed their loved ones' goodbye and started to assemble on the edges of the woodland overlooking the city target.

Jannon looked at his son and his friend. "This is no place for you yet my son, I need you to look after your mother until I get back," he instructed as he placed his hands on either side of Aiden's face, pulled him towards him and kissed his forehead. He turned to Oliver, "Oliver, the King has requested you join him, he needs the gods on his side." Jannon revealed as he placed his hand on Oliver's shoulder.

Oliver looked worried, and turned to Aiden, "But... S... Sir... I cannot go on my own... I need Aiden with me."

Aiden's face broke into a huge smile at the prospect of joining the fight.

Jannon looked at his wife. "If the gods want my son …, who are we to stand in the way?" sobbed Mardina as the tears rolled down her cheeks. She grasped the boy to her chest and gently kissed his forehead and gave her blessing.

Every man took up his hiding place at the edge of the woodland cover and waited for the moment to advance. Night fell, and the signal was given for the force to move in on the targets. Silently the mass moved forward. Boudicca and the kings were leading from the front, followed by the house guards and then the warriors. They all filed towards the gates and waited in silence. Jannon joined several picked men and was issued with a ladder as he headed towards the east wall. He was to move forward with one of the ladders before the battle commenced and hide up against the city walls. "When you reach your positions, you men are to keep your heads down, lie with the ladders against the walls and wait for the signal. Once signalled you are to stand up and hold the ladder in place, brace your backs against the wall and hold on tight." The house guard muttered to the men gathered around him, "The house guards will run at the ladders and will follow each other up. There will be a lot of weight on those things, so hold firm!" the house guard concluded.

The ladder carriers moved dutifully to the front of the columns as the instructions were given. With ropes slung over their shoulders and ladders in hand they crouched low and slowly edged towards their places to lie in wait.

Jannon saw a few burning arrows rip through the night sky, quickly followed by the screams of the marauding force. He leapt up from the ground and positioned the ladder up against the wall as he had been instructed, as spears and burning arrows found their targets. Men had scrambled up from their hiding places at the signal and charged at the ladders. Jannon did as he was told and braced himself against the wall. Sure enough, no sooner had the ladder touched the wall than a multitude of feet disappeared up the rungs and jumped onto the defences above.

A horde of the invaders cleared the turrets and ramparts of the city as its defenders ran towards the gates without a chance of putting up a fight. The retreating men left the ramparts defenceless in their wake as they desperately tried to regroup into a defensive position and repel the huge numbers bearing down on them. The attack was so quick, Boudicca's army had taken two of the gates before the alarm of an attack was even raised.

Shouts and blood-curdling screams could be heard as the house guard forces started to attack the Roman defenders. The house guards moved in complete silence, slashing, and parrying their swords with such force, the razor-sharp blades separated limbs and in one case decapitated one Roman before he could lift his gladius to block the sideways stroke. His headless body staggered forward a couple of steps before dropping to his knees and then falling on his front. The invaders quickly overran the gates, the heavy cross timbers were removed, and the doors flung open for the rest of the force to charge in, led by Donnchad with Oliver and Aiden close by his side.

The same thing was going on at the other three gates, and Boudicca herself was quickly inside.

Leading the charge, she led her men left along the inside of the city wall and towards Brawley's force. She pointed to a door with her sword hand, then dramatically dragged her other hand across her throat. Two house guards kicked the door off its hinges and ran in with three more close behind. A woman started to scream, but the sound stopped abruptly, as did the cries of a child. The five men soon appeared with blood splatters on their faces and clothing.

This continued house after house as Boudicca made her way to the rendezvous point at the garrison entrance. The Commander of the fort had been alerted by this time and had scrambled his depleted force from their slumber. The defenders grabbed what weapons they could and tried charges at strategic points in an effort to resist the invading force, but to no avail. The house guards and warriors quickly stormed through the gate and met the Romans head on. The sheer number of the invaders soon overcame the battling Romans, who had retreated to the garrison compound. As Boudicca had predicted, they were not expecting to be attacked from the city walls above them. Their Commander was wounded by an arrow that punctured the flesh of his right thigh. He tried to continue fighting but was quickly overcome. His gladius was forcefully removed by two house guards, who then restrained him and made him watch as his men were struck down and butchered where they stood.

Boudicca was leading the slaughter as she navigated the streets, her rage and pure hatred gave her the strength of ten men. She fought like an enraged beast as her blade relentlessly struck and slashed over, and over again at her victims. The violence of the attack subsided almost as quickly as it had started as the defenders' numbers dwindled and Boudicca's opponents stopped coming forward. Boudicca dropped her sword down by her side and viewed the bloody mess before her as she approached the garrison entrance.

Donnchad shouted at his men to stop as they approached the rendezvous point and ordered his captains to reveal their losses. The figure was very light, convincing the King that Oliver's presence had meant the gods protected them. Oliver had demonstrated that he really was a talisman sent from them.

Oliver could not believe his eyes, or his ears as he gasped. He followed Donnchad into the garrison only to see and hear Boudicca. He had read about her savagery, but this was surely not the kindly figure he had been introduced to. What he was about to witness would change his mind forever. Here she was, the Warrior Queen, walking and talking in all her glory... Right in front of him!

Boudicca's men had triumphantly taken the garrison very quickly. Again, the Romans were defeated with little loss to the Queen's force. A man had stormed out of the main building. He just had time to clamber into his gold-adorned breastplate as the Iceni burst through the garrison gates, but he was quickly overcome. Boudicca surveyed the partly dressed Roman dead around her with a sense of revilement. "YOU!" she screamed at the Commander, as she spied the character being held by two house guards. She marched over to them and pointed her sword at the man's throat, "What's your name?"

The prisoner stared at Boudicca in a defiant silence. Boudicca slowly walked up to him, pointing her sword at the man as she screamed again, "WHAT'S YOUR NAME?"

Again, the man just stared. Boudicca looked at the few remaining Roman soldiers who had surrendered and had been made to kneel in a line facing the Commander.

"I AM BOUDICCA, AND THIS IS MY ARMY!" she screamed as she held her arms up and slowly turned full circle, pointing her sword towards her warriors as she did so. "I WILL NOT STOP UNTIL ALL OF ROME SCREAMS MY NAME!"

She turned and walked towards one of the kneeling Romans. "WHAT'S MY NAME?" she shrieked at the prisoner.

"Boudicca," he stammered as he looked at the ground.

"SCREAM MY NAME!" she demanded.

The prisoner looked up at the enraged figure. "BOUDICCA!" he screamed just before she lunged forward and plunged her blade into his stomach. She stared into his eyes as she forced the blade hard to the right causing his intestines to spill out of his body. She glared with a look of pure hatred into his eyes as the life ebbed out of her victim. The lifeless body slumped to the floor as she withdrew her weapon.

Oliver could not help himself. The sound of the blade slicing through human flesh and the sight of all the blood and shiny grey intestines falling out; combined with the smell that hit him with almost physical force, made him throw up, he had never witnessed such violence in his life. It was nothing like the computer games some of his friends played. His body turned to jelly, and his knees buckled as he slumped to the floor.

Boudicca turned once more to the Commander. "WHATS YOUR NAME?" she bellowed.

The demand was again met with an insolent silence from the Commander. The lack of compliance made Boudicca turn and walk to another prisoner. The trembling figure kneeling before her tried not to cry as she screamed at him, "WHATS MY NAME?"

The prisoner could not speak, fear had taken his voice.

Boudicca moved nearer to the prisoner. She was so close she could feel the crown of his head against her knees. She grabbed the scalp and pulled it back, "WHATS MY NAME?" she screamed into the man's face. The spittle from her mouth splattered him in the face, his bowels opened causing urine and faeces to run down his thighs.

"B… B… Boudicca," he stammered, trying not to look at her.

She let go of the hair and arched her back and threw her chin up. "HAHAHAHA!.. THE MIGHTY ROME! ...SEE HOW IT SHITS ITSELF AT MY NAME!" she proclaimed as she swung her head back, causing her ginger hair to swish freely over her shoulders.

"I AM BOUDICCA!" she screamed as she plunged her sword into the man's chest. With one swift move she pulled her blade out, causing blood to course into his throat. "BOUDICCA IS THE LAST PERSON YOU SEE AS YOU DIE!" she screamed, holding his eyes open as he slowly drowned in his own blood. As the lifeless body lurched forward, Boudicca spun towards the prisoner once again. "WHATS YOUR NAME?" she cried as she moved ever closer towards the Commander.

The man finally found his voice and he pulled himself upright as he proudly declared, "Octavius Julian Augustus, Commander and Governor of Camulodunum."

Boudicca spoke over the top of the man as he spoke. "Strip him!" she demanded, his words failing to register any reaction from her, "And lash him to that post!"

The warrior Queen wandered menacingly around the figure as his arms were lashed together. A rope was thrown over the top of the tall post, tied around his wrists and pulled, causing the man to shout in pain as he was almost pulled off the ground. "Your name is of no consequence to me," she proclaimed. "I won't remember your name, which is no surprise..." she snarled, "History will not remember you either!" She hissed in his ear as she dragged her blade across his left thigh, cutting the flesh wide open as she did so. "What's my name?" Boudicca growled as she toyed with him.

"Boudicca!" The Commander groaned as she reached down and grabbed his testicles, squeezing them tightly as she did so, causing the prisoner to grimace in agony. With her other hand she pulled her sword towards her, dragging the blade across his buttocks, cutting a huge slice into him as she did so.

"Again," she demanded.

"Arrgggh... BOUDICCA, BOUDICCA... BOUDICCA!" he screamed.

The response was met with a pleasing nod, "GOOD... NOW YOU CAN WATCH YOUR MEN DIE!" She laughed as she nodded at the house guards, who were standing behind the remaining few legionaries. One by one the prisoners fell forward as their throats were cut.

Boudicca watched the last soldier fall as she sadistically turned her attention back to the strung-up figure. "I am done with you," she tutted, "but you can save your family." The Queen looked at the dust around her feet and playfully moved each foot in turn, creating circles. As she did so, her voice dropped to an almost submissive purr, "if you tell me where they are, I will see they are kept safe."

The Commander looked hard at the figure that was taunting him. He wondered if she was telling the truth. Could or would she really save his wife and three children?

The woman spoke softly as she continued lightly doodling with her feet in the dry soil. "I am Boudicca... A Queen... A wife... A mother... I will not take the life of innocents," she calmly avowed as she stopped and stared at the man with a look of sincerity on her face, "so... Where are your family? There is no need to send them to your Elysium before their time. I beg you, let me help them and keep them safe, she requested. "This is not their battle."

The Commander capitulated, hoping that his information was not too late. "The third house on the west facing street, XI on the door," he revealed with a sense of relief.

Boudicca nodded sagely, "There, that was not hard now, was it?" She smiled as she turned towards her house-guards, her whole demeanour altering in a flash as she screamed, "FIND THE MOTHER AND THE SPAWN OF THIS SCUM AND...

BRING ME THEIR HEADS TO SHOW THIS IDIOT!" She turned and started to walk away with a demonic glaze in her eyes.

Her increased blood lust was infecting all around her. The frenzy was overcoming everybody. No Roman was spared as the invaders kicked in door after door as Boudicca continued inflicting cuts to the Commander's body, revelling in his tortured screams.

Three warriors hurriedly approached Boudicca, in their clenched fists were the scalps and heads of a woman and three children. They threw them unceremoniously on the ground in front of the Commander. He turned his head away as wails of grief exploded from his lips.

Boudicca slashed wildly at his body, before stabbing the left side of his chest, missing his heart. His demise was not to be a quick one as she enacted an appalling revenge on her persecutors. She pulled her blade out before she turned and walked away. "Cut him down," she ordered. An horrific idea flashed across her mind as she glanced at the sturdy wooden barricade surrounding them, "And crucify him over there." She demanded as she pointed to the walls.

She watched impassively the Commander's agonising demise. Once satisfied he had expired, Boudicca turned her attention to more pressing matters. "CHECK NOBODY IS LEFT ALIVE AND BURN THE PLACE DOWN!" she ordered a handful of warriors. They dutifully spread out and carried out the order. The rest of her force followed her as she headed towards the centre of the town. No house was left intact, and no person was alive, in the wake of the force.

Boudicca eventually reached the Temple and was greeted by Brawley, Donnchad and Volisios. They had all accomplished their tasks and assured her nobody had been spared.

"We have tracked the surviving inhabitants down to here. We know there are families and priests in the temple... But I fear our gods may be angry if we attack on a god's ground!" ventured a nervous Brawley.

Boudicca heard what he said, tutted, turned and marched brazenly up to the front door. "These are not OUR gods Brawley!" she hissed at him.

The Warrior Queen lifted her sword and banged the pommel hard against the thick wooden planks that made up the formidable, closed door. "I AM BOUDICCA QUEEN OF THE ICENI AND LEADER OF THIS ARMY... COME OUT AND YOU WILL BE SPARED!" She yelled as she did so. After waiting for what seemed an eternity she screamed again. "I AM BOUDICCA, COME OUT AND I WILL NOT HURT YOU!"

An old priest approached the closed door from inside and loudly spoke out, "Dear Lady, we are peace making people. We are defenceless with women and children among us," he spluttered through the fastened door. "We are of no threat to you, please extend us mercy," he ventured hopefully.

"How many of you are there?" Boudicca gently enquired, hoping to gain the priest's trust.

"Around two hundred of us, can you offer us safe passage?" the old man begged.

"We can indeed," the Queen replied, trying to mask her sarcasm. "But we will need payment to keep the mob at bay for you." The men around her gasped at her words, making her place her index finger on her lips as a signal for them to be silent as she continued, "What money or jewels do you have to offer?" Boudicca solemnly requested, "So I can protect you all?"

The priest swallowed hard as he stammered that he was unaware of any such riches, causing Boudicca to change tactics.

"It matters not, whatever you do have stashed away in there will soon be mine," she grinned. "Either open the door or I will smash it down! The choice is yours; I don't care which!" Boudicca called out in a matter-of-fact manner, pausing for a few seconds to give the inhabitants a chance to open the doors before she signalled the warriors to smash the door in, using a large length of timber that they had removed from one of the wooden defences.

Once inside Boudicca chased down the priest and grabbed him as she screamed, "This place is built from the wealth and sweat of our people. If I let you go, it means Romans are still on our land." She stopped and stared hard into the man's eyes, "And I don't think I can let that happen!"

Boudicca turned on her heels, and as she walked away, she shouted to the house guards, "BURN IT DOWN!"

"Stop!" cried the priest, "there are women and innocents in the crypts."

Boudicca froze for a moment before she calmly approached the man and coldly announced, "Today they die!" The man did not see her blade coming as she struck it hard into his body, "and so do you!"

Chapter Twelve

The hardened soldiers making up the various Legions proudly marched their way north with one sole purpose, to attack and exterminate the Druids. Rome recognised the Druids as an obstruction. They were the glue that bonded the Celtic and Pictish tribes, and Suetonius was fully aware that the extermination of the Druids was the key to the successful domination of Britain. These mysterious people were not only recognised as religious leaders or priests, the link between the living, the forefathers and the spirit world; they also administered medicines and ruled on points of law.

The feral Celts and Picts had to be brought under the control of Rome, their lands to be absorbed into the Empire. This was simply not going to happen whilst the Druids and their beliefs hampered Rome's final goal. The Druids had to be eliminated, their lands, possessions and peoples had to be seized.

The columns slowly worked their way north. Every day was a very real struggle, starting with breaking down the defences and equipment from the camp, route marching for hours before erecting the camp once more. The encampment always had a perimeter wall that was patrolled throughout the night. Although this seemed excessive, the Roman army had suffered huge losses on more than one occasion, when a resting legion's camp was attacked, and the men slaughtered as they slept. It was a tough lesson and a situation that the military was determined would never happen again. Five weeks into the patrol, the highly trained and experienced men were getting restless, itching to get stuck into some real fighting. The Celts raged an almost continuous guerrilla warfare campaign upon them, becoming a real irritation to the Romans. The heathens would attack swiftly, normally from the rear, picking off a few men and disappear before the Romans could retaliate. The attacks and attempted raids were designed to whittle down the force numbers, but more importantly, to erode the Romans' morale.

Despite the constant forays, the chilling weather and continuous wet as they pushed north, the men battled to keep their spirits high. The more dire the situation seemed to become, the more the banter and ribbing increased.

"Look out!" Festus casually mentioned, as he nodded his head towards a cavalry man who cantered past him and continued up the line on his steed, "Here comes some news by the look of it."

Albus, the gang's boss, was summoned to join a group of centurions as they gathered around the scout, all desperate for news.

Maxetius glanced over, "Here we go boys!" he declared as he eagerly rubbed his hands together. "fFnally some poor Druid is going to meet his gods or wherever it is they go!"

"Hope they have made their peace!" Laenus joined in gleefully.

Decimus chuckled out loud at Laenus as he called out, "Hope you have made your peace, your luck is bound to run out sometime soon!"

His close friend shot a glance over his shoulder, "I don't need to... I have led a blameless life!" he retorted with a large, sly grin on his face.

The group all burst into laughter as a lone voice in the crowd cried out, "How did you get all those scars then?"

Laenus lifted his head and turned it to his right, "Self-defence!" he shouted so those behind could hear clearly.

Festus could not resist the challenge. "What about that bloke at Festoria?" he scoffed, "You know, the one that you took particular offence at!"

Laenus rolled his eyes, he knew full well where the questioning was leading, "Well, he spilled my wine!" he cheerfully exclaimed.

A voice in the distance shouted out, "The man apparently

ended up with your gladius buried in his chest, for the love of the gods!"

Laenus recalled the murky details in his mind. "He fell on it!" he shrugged

"Fell on it?" Decimus queried before he exclaimed loudly, "How could he?" He started to laugh, "He was on the floor, flat on his back!"

"Well," Laenus reasoned plausibly, "He jumped up so quickly he impaled himself on it!"

The five rows of infantry that were in earshot of the banter all burst into a fit of laughter at the explanation.

One of his oldest companions, Decimus, almost stopped dead in his tracks. "Oh, very funny!" he exclaimed.

Aelianus was watching the melee ahead and threw his arm up in the air "Hold on, Albus is not looking his usual happy self!" he murmured. He was right.

Numerous figures sprinted past the column, desperate to reach their individual squads.

An instantly recognisable, but traumatised, voice shouted out, "Pay attention!" Albus cried out as he ran towards the gang. "Terrible news, Camulodunum has been sacked!" He slid to a halt in the heavy mud. "They have suffered an attack from a horde of locals, from what we can assess." The boss fought to speak as he panted heavily from the sprint to return to his men, "There is no news on numbers, or the extent of damage or loss of life, so we are sending a legion back to find out what has happened and to quench this uprising."

"Any other news than that?" spluttered a shocked Maxetius, as the news permeated his brain. "Our families are there."

The boss shook his head, "None, but just remember, the local lords are beholden to Rome." Albus also had a wife in the city and silently prayed for her safety as he searched for some reassuring words, "So it is likely the attack must be from more distant tribes. Whoever they are, they are *not* Roman." The man needed to ensure he could give his men some positives as he now had everybody's attention. "They will be badly equipped, poorly trained and each will be crucified for their detestable attack on Rome." The man nodded at the troops, reinforcing his words, "Remember, an attack any outpost of Rome is an attack on Rome herself."

All were desperate to learn more about loved ones, their friends, families, parents, wives and children.

Laenus looked to the sky. "I should be back training at the garrison, not on this bloody foolhardy, ridiculous excursion," he declared without thinking. "The barbarian bastards would still be cowering in their little hovels!"

"Hey!" shouted Cato. "Now, now," he reassured Laenus. "You know what talk like that could lead to if you are overheard."

The men fell silent as thoughts slammed and crashed through their minds. A voice morosely mumbled, "Just think of those poor souls who came back without those lost papers a couple of weeks ago."

Another filled the silence. "That was a dreadful way to go!"

Festus, angry with the unthoughtful and blandness of the quips screamed out, "Well let's make sure it does not happen to us then!"

A stunned silence fell briefly over the men at the shock of Festus's sudden outburst. He took a deep breath and gathered his composure, "Let's get our act together. We all have family back there, and we do not yet know what has happened. So, let's keep our heads and do the job Rome pays us for. Follow our orders, wipe the scum of the earth away, and get back to the arms of our loved ones."

Albus could not help himself, "Or our wives!" he quipped, but the flippant remark fell on deaf ears.

The legion collected up all their kit and formed back into neat marching lines.

"Move out!" was the order given, and the thousands of men all

moved together, as if they were one being.

It was not long before it all happened again. A scout came galloping back, this time the Centurion officers surrounded the messenger.

"Right, you miserable lot, this is it, the enemy is near. Dig deep in those cases. Thirty denarii per man. Let's have it," ordered Albus.

"How do we know if this really goes to our widows if we die?" asked Decimus

"Well, why don't I run you through with my javelin, and your spirit can visit your 'loved one' and you can ask her if she is now RICH?" screamed Albus into his face. "Now check your equipment and make ready!"

The army continued to march forward for another two miles before being given the order to halt. The next order from Suetonius was to form three columns, the friends found themselves at the front of the line. The front column was given the order to move forward and stop. The remaining two columns were given the order to form ranks of ten men deep in two lines, making two rectangle shapes one on the left side and one on the right side of the first column. The centre column was ordered to form a triangle, with the point heading straight towards where the foe was believed to be. The reason for this set up was to enable the Romans to smash through the enemy. As the front wedge engaged the enemy, the two flanking sides moved in, trapping the enemy between them. The Romans would surround the enemy, slaughtering everyone in their way.

One of the reasons that the Roman military were so successful was the equipment they carried. The scutum or shield was the most versatile. It was almost as high and as wide as the man carrying it. When tight formation was ordered, the men in the second row lifted their shields aloft and gave cover from missiles coming from above to both the shield-bearer and the man in front. They formed what looked like a giant tortoise, hence the name testudo by the Romans, which is Latin for tortoise.

One of the men glanced over his shoulder, "Hey Cato, why are you always right behind me?" shouted Festus as they formed up.

The tall African burst into laughter, "Because my friend, you are so short, you would not be able to hold your shield high enough to protect me when we move into the testudo."

"Yeah, I have noticed that, when we march forward in file, Festus has trouble seeing where he is going!" laughed Marcus.

"Oh ha-ha-ha, bloody ha," Festus replied sarcastically, before moaning, "Just you make sure you don't get hit by a stray arrow and fall, exposing me from the hell that could be raining down from above!"

Cato could not help himself, "No problem. I can see everything coming." He smirked, "Because you are so short your head is never obscuring my view!" The tall black man guffawed, "Let's face it, if you were in *my* place, your shield would be in the correct position, but your feet would not reach the ground!"

The banter flowed easily, a distant voice cried out, "Well, at least his mother loved him!" countered Aelianus.

Festus tutted and pretended to be hurt by the comment as he snapped, "Well at least I knew my mother!"

The insults just kept flowing and Maxetius merrily joined in, "Shame your mother never knew your father's name!"

A groan rumbled around the group as Aelianus retorted, "I heard you were such an ugly baby, Maxetius, that the midwife got up and slapped your mother instead of your backside!" He grinned.

The friends all burst into laughter, with spirits raised, they all felt invincible.

A mounted officer raised his right arm in the air, causing the conversation to stop abruptly as every man listened for commands.

"Ninth Legion!" An officer shouted from his mount.

They replied in unison with a loud *"Huh!"* as they all brought themselves to attention.

"Ninth Legion pace forward!" the officer commanded.

The Legion had some artillery, who had brought a few ballistae with them, the crossbow-type of machines that could fire javelin-like darts a greater distance than a man could throw. The order was given to fire the crossbows from behind the legions, the whooshing noise from the missiles speeding through the air made them look up to see the large darts shooting over their heads.

The rhythmic beat of numerous drums rung out as every man started to march, right foot first.

"Here we go boys. See you on the other side... or in Elysium!" cried Albus.

Every man smacked his javelin on the back of his shield with each step, emphasizing the sound of every foot hitting the ground to cause fear and dread in the enemy that dared to face them.

The front shields would provide an almost impenetrable wall as they pushed forward in unison.

"*Ninth Legion… Javelins… THROW!*" the officer commanded.

A wall of iron-tipped javelins was hurled at the enemy as an unordered rabble emerged from the tree line and ran out into the open ground before them, many of them knocked off their feet as the Roman weapons rained down.

"I am so glad the tips on those things bend on contact. At least we won't see them coming back at us!" thought Lucanus.

The Druids had known the Romans were on the way with the specific intention of destroying them. The wise sages had enlisted the men from two local tribes to rebuke the foreign invaders. The horde of Celts broke cover, and ran towards the red shield wall, screaming at the top of their lungs and with madness in their eyes.

"Ninth Legion… Shields ready... Testudo!" came the order as the painted horde broke into a sprint, screaming towards the soldiers with axes and swords glinting and flashing as they committed themselves to the battle.

Without stopping, the men from the second row lifted their shields high over their heads, protecting themselves, and the men in front of them from flying objects. The men on the sides moved their shields to their exposed sides, as they did so the men bunched closer together, creating an impenetrable armoured shell.

The commanding officer bellowed loud and clear, *"On my command.... EEE."* On hearing the command every man moved his left foot forward, and all chanted "*EEE*" as the foot hit the ground and they pushed forward. Then the right foot moved a half step. All waited for the next command to move forward. The command was given, the resulting push was done in a choreographed rhythm. The left foot moved again, once more the right foot took a step and was brought forward. The force of the shield wall was such that it would push through any enemy in front of it. The sheer mass and strength meant that the enemy quite often could not retreat as the rear of the force kept moving forward as the front stopped, causing the enemy to become compacted. The opposition ended up so tightly packed they simply were unable to raise their hands and strike out with their weapons. A perfect situation for the Romans who kept moving forward, stabbing, and jabbing swords and javelins from behind their shield walls. The number of men building up in front of the Roman wall quickly increased, unable to turn or move. The Roman gladius sword was a deadly weapon, designed for close action stabbing and was perfect in this situation. The enemy fighters who were unfortunate enough to fall would be stamped on and trampled to death by the Romans as they simply walked over them, thrusting weapons down into the flesh of the wounded as they stepped on and over them.

The Romans could smell the unwashed bodies of the Celts as they charged and threw themselves at the shield wall. Every one of the marauding forces, made up of men and women, had blue spirals painted on their faces and bodies. Their unkempt hair was pulled back and either plaited or held by twine, keeping it out of their faces as they attacked. Many rubbed mud or white lime into their hair to make it stand up in spikes and make them look taller and more fearsome. They would just keep attacking, literally throwing themselves at the Roman shields in a desperate bid to smash through, but the majority were cut down and butchered by the short stabbing swords as the Romans thrust out from behind their shields. The bodies of the fallen were trampled underfoot by the stud-booted Ninth Legion.

All senses were heightened as the adrenaline pumped through Roman veins. The sound of the screams from the fallen as the weapons struck home; feeling the resistance through the blade as it sank deep into flesh; feeling the muscle and flesh slowing the blade before it jarred as it struck bone, these were the experiences of battle.

The air was filled with the smell of blood, the stench of vomit, and faeces as bowels were slashed open. Time almost stood still for the eight friends, as the battle raged. The roar of the attacking Celts soon turned to screams as limbs were slashed and cut off by the slashing gladii. Throats were cut, and ribcages broken, exposing lung tissue to the daylight. If they were lucky, death would take them instantly. Those not so lucky ended up on the ground, trampled by the Imperial forces and either slaughtered where they lay or left to a slow painful death.

The sound of Celtic horns cut through the air signalling those who had not been cut down to retreat and run back to the cover of the trees.

"*Halt!*" The order rang out across the field. *"Ninth Legion… Shields… Down!*" roared the officers as they could see the skirmish was done.

The legionaries stopped, the men holding the shields aloft brought them down and rested them on the ground. The soldiers surveyed the bloodied and butchered bodies strewn across the battleground around them as they fought hard to catch their breaths. The sweat poured down their faces and bodies as they recovered from the exertion of battle. The sheer savagery of the battle was evident around them as they all surveyed the human devastation.

"*Ninth Legion... Clean the field!*" commanded the mounted officer.

This was the order that ensured none of the enemy survived. Each man checked the bodies of the Celts as they lay on the ground. The trinkets, jewellery and any usable weapons now belonged to the victors and were taken as booty and souvenirs. If a body showed any sign of life, the soldier would use his gladius and ram it into the chest or cut the throat. Nobody was to be left alive.

"These dirty scum stink," Lucanus groaned. "I don't know why they just don't accept their way is the wrong way and life with us is far better," he paused, "even as a slave," Lucanus muttered as he checked the bodies around him.

The soldier to his right heard him, "I don't know how they manage to breed," puzzled Maxetius. "Look... This one has boobs, so must be a woman, but just look at the state of it." He tutted, "It if looks this bad after death, it must have been really rough when it was alive!"

Cato looked up from the mass of blood, limbs, and entrails, "Albus would have tried to marry it!" He scoffed, "it is definitely a step up from his wife." He grinned, "At least it was sort of human!"

The group chortled as they waded through the corpses, making sure all were dead, and double-checking if the dead had anything of value on them. The crew managed to acquire quite a lot of ritual metalwork from the bodies. Some were made of precious metals, but most were made of copper and iron. Occasionally as they searched, the victors came across the odd pouch that contained a few Roman coins.

Marcus stumbled across such a pouch and ripped it open to reveal some gold and silver coins. "This will come in handy at the taverns back in camp when we get home." He grinned and he clenched the pouch tightly as they finished clearing the battlefield and prepared to move out.

The Romans checked themselves and each other for wounds. Adrenaline acts as a very effective painkiller, so you could be hurt and not realise it. If any slashes were found, the soldier was sent to the surgeon to be cleaned and stitched up. There were no anaesthetics, so the pain of the surgeon inserting the needle, and pulling the thread through was excruciating. A wound dressing containing herbs and a tiny amount of silver, would then be applied to keep the wound clean and let it heal without infection. The surgeons did not know why silver kept wounds clean, it was knowledge adopted from the Greeks and seemed to work quite well. The affluent Romans and the Greeks also had fruit platters made from silver because it kept fruit fresh for longer. It would be a further two millennia before the reason was proven and confirmed, silver has great antibacterial properties.

Albus approached them heavy footed from the struggle, "I see, once again, that you are all still alive. I guess you will all have your pensions returned to you." The boss announced with a resonance of disappointment in his voice, "Which is a shame." He grinned slyly, "I was looking forward to meeting your grieving widows and comforting them as they wept on my shoulder!"

"Yes," Festus sighed. "We are all fit, all except Cato." He reported, "He is being tended by the surgeon. He was struck on the leg by a blade," he continued as he nodded his head in the direction of the surgeon's tent. "No real damage. I think it will be a few stitches, and a couple of weeks of limping!"

Albus nodded as he listened to the report, before informing the group, "We are marching south, and setting up camp three miles from here." He smiled, revealing the numerous gaps where teeth had once been, "Aren't you lucky my boys, more trenches to dig, more latrines to cover, more poo to shift! Mmmm... Just imagine the fun, and the smell!" He grinned as he drew a deep breath in through his nose. "Gather your equipment and be ready to march in fifteen minutes. The Celts have disappeared, and it looks like you have all been spared for me to torment."

The friends picked up all their equipment and the bounty they had taken from the dead Celts and deposited the loot carefully among the equipment strapped to their mules and carts.

Lucanus placed both hands at the base of his torso and arched his back, "I can't wait to get back to the civilisation of the garrison and spending hours in the luxury of the baths," he exclaimed.

The words made Decimus stop the daydream he was having, "Ah... A bath! Now that is a luxury I am looking forward to!" he exclaimed slowly.

Aelianus threw some wooden poles on to the wagon, stopped and looked longingly into the distance, "Oh what hell!" His face lit up as he followed suit and daydreamed, "Decent grub, a sleep in a real bed, in a room with windows," he purred, "Now *that's* luxury, mmm." He took a deep breath and sighed, "and to take a nice relaxing long *shit...* I don't even mind if you six are sitting around me!" He quipped as he looked at his close companions. "I would gladly pass my sponge so you too can wipe your arses... But *only* after I have finished with it!"

Laenus wandered past and caught the last sentence. "Oh I get it!" he exclaimed, "Thank you, thank you very much." He growled, "I think of you as my brother after all we have been through, and you would gladly give me the shitty end of your stick!" he declared in a deadpan tone.

"You can keep dreaming of home," smirked Albus. "The Ninth has received orders to push on to the south." He looked the band of men up and down, "But we are to remain with the forces here!"

Chapter Thirteen

Boudicca was full of energy and excitement. She was ecstatic that her attack on Camulodunum had gone just as she had envisaged. They had the first resounding major victory in her dream of ridding the land of the Romans. She knew that word would be spreading; the army under her control now had a definite blood lust, every man wanted to kill and kill again. As she wallowed in the pleasure of striking out against Rome and winning, she became aware of a rider approaching fast. He galloped through the camp and approached Boudicca's inner sanctum at speed. Several house guards recognised the rider and directed him towards the victorious Queen's position.

The bareback rider slid off the animal and dropped down on to one knee in front of Boudicca. "My Queen," he proclaimed, "Romans are marching on the road towards Camulodunum. They must have been advised of the attack and are coming to protect the town."

Boudicca's mood immediately changed. "How many?" she demanded, "and from which direction?"

The man stood up but continued to avert his gaze as he divulged his information, "They are heading this way from the north, about five day's march away. The column is about two and a half furlongs in length."

Boudicca dismissed the messenger, instructing one of her staff to reward the man with some coins liberated during the raid, and immediately ordered the kings to attend her. The kings arrived one by one and were handed a flask of ale each as they assembled. They were not detained for long, Boudicca swept in and casually addressed the group, "Gentlemen, we have visitors coming to defend Camulodunum!" she gleefully reported. "They are a bit late for the party, but I am glad they are making the effort to attend!" The Queen spun on her heels and faced the gathering, "My report says the column is about two and a half furlongs in length, and at one man every yard, four men abreast, twenty-two yards to a chain, ten chains to a furlong, that means the guard could be about two thousand strong including support," she announced as she glanced towards the roof as she completed the mental arithmetic. "That is how much they underestimate us!" Boudicca deduced with a sly grin.

"Mm… There is a question," interjected Brawley. "Obviously we must attack, but do we destroy them before they reach Camulodunum and discover a pile of ashes?" he wondered. "Or do we let them see what has happened to their city and the remnants of their families first?" asked Brawley as he idly rubbed his bearded chin.

Boudicca paused for a moment as she considered the question. "We attack them before they reach Colchester. They are in formation and do not expect an attack. As we all know surprise is our biggest weapon, and while they are in formation, they are neatly packed together and lightly armed." The warrior in her took over her consciousness. "If they reach Colchester unhindered, they may well be able to send word and thwart the rest of our plans," she stated firmly. "They would also have the opportunity to spread out and defend themselves properly. We could end up losing more men than we need to," Boudicca advised the assembled kings and their commanders, who all nodded in agreement.

"Brawley, they are approaching your lands, I trust you and your men know it well, so we will be led by you. Where would you consider a good place to take them?" Boudicca enquired.

The King closed his eyes and took a deep breath as he visualised his lands and searched for the ideal position in his mind's eye. "The road they are traveling on leads through acres of woodland." He divulged with certainty, "The road has a major dip in one part and is steeply banked on either side, creating a natural 'V'." He opened his eyes and stared directly at Boudicca as he continued, "It is perfect for an ambush. The sides mean we have the advantage attacking downhill and trapping the enemy. It is three days hard march from here and we will arrive ahead of the Romans. The woodland is flanked with high bracken at the moment, which will give excellent cover. We also have another advantage; we will be attacking downhill and into the side of the Roman columns."

Boudicca smiled and nodded as she absorbed the valuable local knowledge. "Good!" she slowly murmured as a plan started to form in her mind. "All of you, have your men brought to arms and have light support ready to move out immediately," Boudicca instructed the assembly.

Jannon sat motionless as he reflected on the horror he had observed. He was shocked at the level of violence the tribes had unleashed. He had been in battle before and had witnessed the depravity and sheer violence that one man can inflict during hand-to-hand combat. But the unrivalled slaughter of defenceless women and children, that was a memory that he would struggle with and would haunt him for the rest of his life.

His adoring wife approached him slowly, reached her hands out and placed them on his shoulders. "Are you alright my love?" Mardina asked gently as Jannon stared with an expressionlessly at the flames bursting out from the open fire.

"W... W... What? Sorry my darling... I was miles away," the traumatised man stammered.

"I asked if you were alright?" she asked softly again as she lightly stroked Jannon's hair.

The man arched his back, "Umm... Yes, yes... Fine... I was just thinking," he mumbled as he raised his hand to his shoulder and placed it on hers.

"Of what?" Mardina asked attentively.

He tried desperately to think of a believable reason, he did not want to burden his beautiful wife with the truth. "Ohh... Err... I... I was... Umm... Nothing." Jannon was relieved to have their attention taken by one of the house-guards, who was marching around the various fires.

"All fighting men, pick up your weapons and gather on the north side of the camp," the burly warrior announced as he went on his way.

Jannon tutted as he pretended to be upset by the interruption. "Sorry my darling… I must go," he said calmly, without taking his eyes off the house guard, afraid to look at his confused and concerned wife. "Boys, we are being called," he shouted out with an unexpected air of relief, as he looked up. Jannon jumped up, swivelled around and kissed Mardina gently on the lips as he wound his arms around her waist and pulled her closely towards him. "I will be back soon, I promise," he whispered.

"I love you," she whispered back.

Jannon released his grip and turned without replying. He retrieved his sword and his shield from the back of the wagon and marched off to the edge of the camp.

The massing numbers gathered, and the house-guards ran through plans with the various groups, so they all were aware of the plot for the coming battle. Oliver looked up to see a mounted Boudicca glide past him on her war chariot and was sure she smiled at him as she swept majestically past him. The war chariot was pulled by two gleaming ponies. There was room on board for two, one to control the ponies and the second was the mobile warrior. The sides of the chariot were formed from two hoops made of hazel twigs. This strong arch was designed so the warrior could wedge his or her knees against it to keep them stable. From the mobile platform their hands were free so they could throw javelins, fire arrows from a bow or slash at the enemy with swords or axes. The two wheels skidded in the loose dirt as the chariot slid round, doing an impressive turn on the spot as Boudicca brought the two ponies to a stop in front of the men. She raised herself to her full height in front of them, standing proudly on the floor of the chariot, and shouted at the top of her voice so all could hear,

"MEN OF OUR LAND... WE HAVE STARTED ON A JOURNEY TO RID OUR LANDS OF THIS IMPERIALIST SCUM... CAMULODUNUM HAS BEEN WIPED OFF THE FACE OF THE EARTH... A NEW TOWN WILL EMERGE FROM THE SMOULDERING EMBERS... A NEW LAND WILL EMERGE!' Boudicca paused for dramatic effect as she looked at the faces in front of her, "OUR NEW LAND!"

The surrounding army raised a huge cheer at her words. Men and women jumped up and fists punched the air. Boudicca signalled for the warriors to quieten before she continued, "Our fight to rid us of this plague of Romans has just begun. THE GODS HAVE DEMONSTRATED THAT THEY ARE ON OUR SIDE!" Boudicca had been practiced in the art of speech making from a young child and she brought that knowledge to the fore as she continued dramatically, "We have a fight to take to the invaders. I WANT OUR LAND FREE FOR OUR CHILDREN AND THEIR CHILDREN!" She paused to let the words do their work in rousing her audience, "FREE TO LIVE OUR LIVES AS WE SEE FIT!" She could see a sea of nodding heads as she delivered the final punch, "ARE YOU WITH ME?" Boudicca shouted, as she threw her arm in the air, sword clenched firmly in her hand.

"AYE!" the warriors replied, throwing fists into the air.

"ARE YOU WITH ME?" she repeated throwing her arm up again.

"AYYYEE!" chanted the horde, punching the air with their fists, all becoming more excited and animated with every word.

"ARE YOU WITH ME?" she screamed, this time throwing both arms in the air.

"AAAYYYYEEE!" screamed the gathering as fists, weapons and several shields were lifted high in front of her.

Boudicca became very emotional and fired up at the response, "LETS MAKE OUR FORE-FATHERS PROUD!" she screamed over the noise, before turning with theatrical exaggeration, grabbing the reins of the ponies, and whipping the pair into life. As she moved off the gathered warriors all fell into line and dutifully followed.

Donnchad grabbed the boys by the shoulders as they were about to leave with the crowd.

"Wait, don't be so eager!'" the King called out. "This is not our fight today." The bearded man smiled, "The Trinovantes have been stood down for this one."

Oliver was relieved, but also very disappointed that he, and Aiden, would not witness the scrap after hearing Boudicca's stimulating speech.

The trap was set. Boudicca would be smashing a nut with a sledgehammer. She did not tell her force how many Romans they would be facing. Most of her men could not count, so if she said there could be as many as two thousand, they would think it was a large number, and that there was no way they could win. Boudicca was very aware how important positive thinking was, the huge advantage of self-belief. She could not afford there to be any doubt in the heads of her army, especially on the back of the huge resounding victory they now had under their belts. The victorious Queen was looking for another, decisive win. Besides, she knew the thousands of warriors she was taking with her for this battle would easily destroy the Roman soldiers. Their numbers alone would surely secure victory. After all, the odds were stacked in her favour, so, factor in the element of surprise and victory would be hers.

Orders were issued. The mounted force was to attack with the chariots at the front and rear of the column and charge the Romans down. The house guards dutifully divided the infantry force into groups, two smaller groups that would conceal themselves at either end of the ambush site and were to follow in behind the chariots. The main infantry force was split in four. Two groups hid in the deep cover that covered the steep banks on either side of the road. They lay just far enough over the brow of the hill so they could not be seen and give the plot away, with the foot soldiers well hidden in the tall bracken and ferns.

Another group was led to the far end of the valley and hidden well back. They were to wait until the entire Roman column had passed, then block the road. Their orders were to kill anybody trying to get away. The remaining infantry was placed at the head of the deadly trap. Their job was to wait until the column had passed the rear group; the moment they had passed a signal would be sent. The front group were then to jump out from the undergrowth in front of the Romans and fire four rapid flights of arrows into the front ranks before dispersing quickly into the woods. The Romans would be so busy concentrating on the attack ahead they would not notice the attack bearing down on them from both sides until it was too late. The warriors took up their places and waited silently, hidden away among the tall green ferns that grew on either side of the roadway, giving even more cover.

Most of the Celts lay down on the moss among the ferns, some knelt behind trees, all held their breaths as the Romans came into sight. The trap was set. The Celts were primed, poised, ready for the fight as the long line of soldiers appeared. It seemed to go on and on as they marched past; all marching in step, the armour of each man banging in time, glinting in the dappled light as the sun's rays filtered through the leafy canopy of the trees.

The front row had reached the incline when it happened. A signal went up and a screaming Boudicca charged over the brow of the hill towards the shocked Roman battalion, who froze at the unexpected and terrifying vision. The Warrior Queen charged her ponies at full gallop, with huge blades extending from the hubs of her chariot wheels that spun so quickly you could hear them hum and buzz as she ploughed into the column. The razor-sharp blades smashed into the shins and lower limbs of the close ranks of men as they desperately tried to dive for cover. She was followed closely by her chariots and mounted warriors. The chariots were three abreast, with the mounted warriors riding between them, screaming at the top of their voices and all at full gallop. They were pumped up with rage, anger and blood lust as the adrenaline surged through their veins, eagerly searching out the fight as they wielded their deadly battle axes and swords, sun light flashing on the bright metal as blood curdling screams rang out, the attack was on.

The Romans had no time to prepare for the onslaught that was bearing down on them. They had no chance to repel, or even step aside to avoid the wheeled attackers, who rode directly into the front row of foot soldiers, scattering bodies as they went. The attack was so quick the front rows were temporarily paralysed with the shock at the sight of what was speeding towards them. The strong glint of the sun being reflected off the weapons and the round shields, mounted on the front of the chariots, only added to the confusion. The Roman shields were no defence, as the ponies and chariots ploughed directly into them. The wheels breaking limbs as they rode through, and over, the Emperor's army.

With the front ranks being knocked to the ground, the Celts concealed in the ferns and bushes sprang from their hiding positions and stormed into the sides of the cohorts, screaming, and brandishing their weapons as they sprinted into the middle ranks, the speed of the sprint downhill intensified each blow from their weapons. Their shields slammed into the faces and chests of those in front of them, as the axes and swords were brought to bear. The Romans barely had time to draw their gladii, as the attackers' blades slashed and axes were brought down on them with such force that limbs were cleanly sliced and bodies torn apart, the blood of the Roman invaders spurting in all directions, filling the air with a crimson mist. Such was the intensity of the fight, the ground rapidly turned to scarlet as it pooled on the ground.

The warriors on the chariots jumped from their vehicles as the skilful horsemen pulled their charges around sharply, causing the wheeled machines to almost spin on their axles and face the opposite direction, before being urged to gallop away from the battling forces. As they headed out of the battle, a warring Celt jumped on board and was whisked out of the foray to rest. He alighted as the chariot was turned once more, replaced by a fresh sword-bearing fighter, and transported back into the very heart of the struggle. All the chariots were being used as transport, supplying fresh troops to the battle as it raged.

Cerialis with a few of his mounted officers and about two hundred cavalry soldiers, were behind the front ranks of the Legion. The cavalry came up to surround Cerialis and protect him but were overwhelmed by the hordes of Celts who vastly outnumbered them. When Cerialis saw they were being defeated he ordered a retreat, and he along with a few of his officers and about half of the cavalry raced up the slope on their fast horses and escaped the carnage. In the heat of the battle they slipped away easily. They rode until they were safely inside the walls of a Roman camp and were the only Romans to survive the attack.

The aquilifers in the rear few ranks realised the fight was futile and screamed at their soldiers to retreat, only to be rushed from behind by the last of the war chariots. The timing of the attack to the rear was carried out with such precision that any choreographer would have been in complete awe at the sight. The two-ponied chariots charged into the rear of the column at full gallop and smashed into the cohorts with such force that the last three ranks were killed outright before they could react. The mounted warriors followed the chariots, slashing swords, and battle axes indiscriminately into any flesh around them. The height advantage the charioteers had standing on the floor of the vehicle, or the horsemen had from the saddle gave them a better reach than their opponents as they struck out at the Romans ahead of them. The chariots slowed, the tightly packed legions ahead of them brought the vehicles to a near stop so the charioteers turned their ponies around to take them out of the fight. The warriors jumped off and, as the war machine retreated, a wounded fighter hopped on to be taken to safety. The action of the skilful Celtic charioteers ensured the men in the fight were fresher than the exhausted enemy.

The ambush was over almost as quickly as it began. The number advantage that Boudicca had, coupled with the warrior's bloodlust, meant the attack was swift and fierce. The writhing mass left by the initial attack as the Celts withdrew, was soon motionless as the attackers systematically moved through the Romans. Every one of the invaders was slain where he fell. The Celts showed no regard for the dead Romans, in fact they had complete contempt for the infantry they had destroyed. Orders had been given that there were to be no witnesses. When Boudicca was satisfied all were dead, she ordered the men to search the bodies and take anything of value. Every weapon was gathered and placed on carts and chariots, along with every helmet. The prizes from the ambush would be evenly shared between the Kings and Boudicca later that evening. The armour would be melted down and remade into their own weapons. The shields, which were mainly of wood, would be burned on a victory pyre, honouring the Celts who had died in the battle. The war chariots were laden with the fourteen dead warriors killed in the raid, and they slowly made their way back to the camp so they could be prepared for their final journey.

It was to be a full traditional funeral, presided over by the Druid priests, to honour and respect the fallen as they started their journey to the land of the ancestors.

Oliver noticed just how quiet everything seemed as he perched on a log, not even the birds seemed to be singing. He was certain he could hear the noise of battle in the far distance, but he could not be sure. Was it the screams of the battle that he knew was going on or was it the memories of the horrific sight and sounds that he had witnessed first-hand in Colchester echoing in his mind? He could not be definite. Did he really bear witness to the butchery at Colchester, or was he dreaming? He must have been dreaming… There was no way that anybody could wage such savagery. Only in dreams, films, and games.

Oliver suddenly jumped up with a start, 'That is it,' he thought, 'that MUST be it, I must be dreaming.' He pinched himself in the hope of waking. 'Or maybe I am caught in a game, that is why Boudicca seems so cold hearted and murderous.' The thoughts just kept tumbling over in his brain as he desperately tried to make sense of the situation that he had found himself in. 'I must be dreaming or trapped in the imagination of a flashy game developer, after all Boudicca is a mother, and NO mother could be like this.' His thoughts continued on this strange tangent, 'well apart from Graham Finch's Mum!' Oliver had never met her, but Simon Crampton had been for a sleep over once and said she was so scary, she made a werewolf seem like a friendly family pet! "If this is a game, it is bloody fantastic," Oliver mumbled to himself, "bloody being the operative word!" He chuckled to himself.

"Why are you grinning like an idiot?" enquired Aiden. "Have you gone strange in the head?"

"Nooo," smiled Oliver.

Aiden examined the features of his pal. "Good!" he exclaimed. "We had an uncle who suddenly started smiling and talking to himself, it did him no favours you know!"

Oliver was perplexed by the statement. "Why?" he eventually queried.

Aiden picked up a stick and had started to whittle it idly. "Well…" he began slowly. "The Druid priests claimed he was special you see," he paused as he threw the cut stick to one side and examined his sgian. "They took him under their control and led him away," he paused again as he looked around for another stick. "They treated him like a King, feeding him, giving him medicine and clothed him in rich clothes."

"Well, that does not seem so bad!" Oliver interjected.

"It was for him in the end!" Aiden exclaimed with a heavy sigh.

Oliver glanced at his friend with a puzzled expression.

Aiden picked up another stick and started to whittle again. "He was sacrificed to the god of the harvest!"

"OH...HAHA..." Oliver sarcastically grimaced. "Anyhow, I am not bothered." Oliver huffed, "Because I know this is a game and you," Oliver declared as he raised his arm and waved it from side to side, "and all this is not real!"

Aiden punched Oliver with all his might in just the right place to deliver a 'dead arm'

"Ouch…" Oliver cried out, "What the...?"

"You felt that didn't you?" Aiden laughed as he jumped up and started to run off.

"I'll get you!" screamed Oliver as he gave chase, his arm flapping around uncontrollably as he did so.

Aiden stopped dead in his tracks, Oliver nearly ran into the back of him, as the cavalcade broke the tree line. The blood-soaked warriors slowly and wearily approached the encampment, as the previous rush of adrenaline had drained their energy. Shouts rang out at the sight of their return; the whole place fell silent as all stopped their activities and conversations and ran over to greet the returning men. As the horde got closer, they stopped on either side of the column and bowed their heads in respect, as the fourteen bodies headed the procession. The chariots were greeted by the priests, who took hold of the ponies' bridles in silence, and slowly guided them towards one tent. Several of the men who knew the dead searched out the dead men's families.

Oliver had a sudden rush of sadness overcome him at the sight, his hand reached up involuntarily, and rested on Aiden's shoulder as Boudicca approached the spot where the two friends stood. She pulled sharply on the reins, making the two ponies stop immediately in front of them. Oliver was surprised by the number of wrinkles on her face, framed by swathes of neatly plaited red hair. Each one tied off with a different cloth, carrying the colours of the four tribes that were now standing alongside her in her fight. Oliver carefully studied her features, committing them to memory. As he looked at her vivid blue eyes, he realised that she was staring directly at him. He was transfixed, he tried to submissively look away, but he could not, he was entranced. Her face was sad, her eyes were dead; they had no expression at all.

Oliver snapped out of his trance as the Queen smiled briefly before she looked away, arched her back, pulled herself up to her full height and filled her lungs.

"MY WARRIORS..." she screamed, "MY PEOPLE..." Boudicca theatrically threw her arms open. "MY FRIENDS..." she shouted as she looked around at the faces surrounding her, making sure she had everybody's attention.

"WE HAVE HAD A GRRREAT TRIUMPH!" She drew a huge breath and paused dramatically, "WE HAVE DESTROYED A ROMAN FORCE!" Boudicca paused again as she acknowledged the cheers at the news. "A FORCE THAT WAS SENT WITH A PURPOSE." She dropped her hand and grasped the side of the chariot as one of the ponies shifted its footing, causing the chariot to jolt suddenly, before she continued, "THAT PURPOSE WAS TO DESTROY US." The gathered crowd all started to boo at the revelation as Boudicca bent down and retrieved an item from the chariot floor, "BUT TODAY I HAVE GIVEN YOU..." she cried out as she lifted a single Roman helmet clasped in her right hand. The helmet of Cerialis, the Roman officer in charge of the decimated force. "VICTORY!" she screamed as she punched the helmet into the air. Boudicca looked around her and she cried out again, "VICTORY!" as she punched the helmet in the air. "VICTORY!" This time she punched the helmet in the air and held it aloft for all to see, soaking up the crowds' cheers.

Every man, woman and child cheered. A frenzy of elation broke out amongst the crowd. Oliver felt all the hairs stand-up on the back of his neck and goose pimples raced all over his body as became swept up in the moment, "YEESSSSSSSSS!" he screamed. "Hurrah!" he bellowed as his hands punched the air above his head, and he started running and dancing on the spot.

Chapter Fourteen

Laenus drew a deep breath, "I am so bored of this game, I can't remember the last time I was warm!" he mumbled as he thrust his hands towards the fire. "I have forgotten what the sun feels like."

Festus looked over and scowled, "It could be worse. Think of Cato, at least you did not have all those stitches in your thigh!"

"Anybody know how he is?" asked Decimus.

Marcus glanced over in Decimus's direction, "Doing better than us!' he chuckled. "I saw him earlier when I went for my ablutions." He grinned, "He was lying back, relaxing on a cart back there." Marcus stated as he threw his head back in the direction of the carts bringing up the rear. "When I saw him, I have never seen him smile so broadly and he gave me a nod!" The Roman revealed, "He was being tended to alright! Fed by one of those female slaves, very pretty she was too."

Festus grimaced as they all huddled around their small fire, "Ablutions? Ablutions? Why are you using words like ablutions?" He grumbled, "Why can't you be like the rest of us and go for shave and a shit?"

"No wonder the malingerer was smiling," Decimus interjected. "I would be thanking *all* the gods if I was in his shoes."

"Yeah! I would be milking it all I could if that was me," Aelianus added. "I have seen the slave that is looking after him" He pursed his lips and wolf-whistled, "And Wow, she is a real looker!" he smirked.

Decimus tutted loudly, "We know you would be in no rush to get back on duty!" He quipped lightly, "I have seen your wife and she makes Medusa look like a decent catch!"

Marcus appeared with some food he had 'found' and passed it over to Lucanus, who was cooking, "I thought Aelianus's wife had been chasing stationary carts!"

The banter flowed as Festus piped up, "Well, what would you expect?" he guffawed. "A fine handsome specimen like my dear friend Aelianus here, is obviously a dream catch!" he mocked as he placed his arm around Aelianus's shoulder.

Aelianus genteelly lifted his hand to his mouth and coughed lightly. "My dear Festus, I do believe you are envious of my rugged good looks," he announced in his poshest voice. "After all, compared to me, you look like you fell out of the ugly tree!" He smirked, "and obviously smacked your face on every branch and bough all the way down!" Aelianus waited for the smirks and titters to quieten before delivering the punch line, "And it was obviously a very, very long fall!"

The group fell about laughing at the banter, but the friends all secretly wished Cato was back with them. Not only was he the glue that bonded them all, his smile and humour was something they all appreciated in their own way.

Cato was the youngest of the group and had a deep respect for every one of the men. He openly admitted that he had been too young to join up and had lied about his age to get into the army. He never really talked about his background to anyone, despite numerous attempts from the group to make him divulge his past.

Festus looked puzzled. "Where did you say Cato was from?" he queried.

The group looked at each other, all shrugging shoulders and shaking their heads as they searched for the answer in their heads, nobody was entirely sure what the answer could be.

A voice in the crowed ventured, "I always thought he was an orphan."

Decimus shook his head. "No. His father is a respected leader in Egypt!" he revealed, "I am sure that is what he said." He paused, "Or perhaps I am making it up!"

A gruff voice to the side of the group pitched in, "I thought he was the son of a whore, who was the daughter of a whore," snarled Albus.

Maxetius growled, "I would have nobody else looking out for my back in this world or the next," as the others moved quickly to restrain him from punching Albus. The men scrabbled to hold on to him. "Aye!" they all agreed as they held him back.

Albus revelled in rousing anger in others, "Oh... Have I touched a nerve?" The boss asked with a sly smile stretching over his face.

The group released their grasp on their friend. "Be very careful," warned Decimus under his breath. "If I get chance, I will slit your..."

It was a thought they all shared as they tried to stop Albus from saying any more.

He turned slowly and walked away nonchalantly, tapping a wooden handled whip against his armoured shoulder protection as he wandered off.

Aelianus hated to see his friends look so dejected. "Look on the bright side boys," he piped up, chirpily in the hope that it would lift the mood a little. "With Cato incapacitated there is more food for the rest of us!" And if anything lifted the mood it was food!

The faces of the group brightened as Aelianus continued, "And there is a bit more space in the tent!"

"ALRIGHT!" shouted Marcus. "You have made your point, let's finish off this lovely breakfast that Lucanus has very kindly made," he blurted out as he shovelled another spoonful into his face. "We will show him our appreciation by washing up all the pots," he muttered through his mouthful of oats, "He very kindly *baked* the oats in," covering his colleagues with a mix of spit and half masticated porridge. "Won't you Laenus?" Marcus smirked as he finally swallowed the remnants left in his mouth.

"Agreed!" declared the rest, as they too lapped up the last of the breakfast.

"Good, it will keep Laenus's tortured mind occupied; and hopefully stop him from moaning!" Marcus gargled as he took a large mouthful of water in an attempt to wash his breakfast down. "As for the rest of us, let's get this tent down, put the fire out and prepare to move out." He continued like a clairvoyant sage, "The order will be given at any moment, just you wait."

Lucanus glanced up, "Oh... He's good," he jested, "He's very good!" He leered, "I have known my friend, Marcus, for many years now and every time he makes this prediction, we end up doing as he has foretold!" Lucanus quipped, "Is he truly a sage? Or is it because we break camp EVERY BLASTED MORNING?!" he joked.

The early morning mirth and banter was definitely the best way to start yet another hard day.

Marcus and the band of soldiers were not wrong, the cohort from the Ninth were the first to be marched out of the camp at double pace. Before long they had caught up with Gaius Suetonius Paulinus, his entourage and the two legions under his command, Suetonius was determined to carry out the Emperor's wishes to the letter. Making himself incredibly wealthy in the meantime, and where there was wealth there was power.

The man had no patience, and his reputation for being a cold-blooded killer preceded him. All the officers had heard rumours that the 'slightly unbalanced' Emperor-appointed Governor of Britannia was coming to oversee the defence of Londinium and take command, but none of them had expected to see him quite so soon, or for him to arrive with such urgency. Nor had any of them expected to see so many carts and people traveling with the man, his entourage was simply staggering.

Suetonius always ensured his favourite slave travelled with him. In order to keep up with his mounted master the slave was almost jogging. Suetonius leaned towards him. "This is going to be a case of 'Smash and Grab'. The sooner we crush this scum, the sooner we will be back enjoying the sunshine at home, hey Corinulus." The slave could see the greed in his master's eyes, as the Governor rode alongside his horse-drawn armoured carriage as it buffeted along the barely made-up road. He looked at his master's face but was careful not to look directly into his eyes. He had seen many who had made the mistake of glancing too long into his eyes. He had scrubbed so much blood off the marble floors, mosaics, and soft silk furnishings to know that you *never* looked at the master directly. Even when he talked to you like you were a human.

"Yes Master!" he replied as he bowed his head.

Suetonius righted himself and took a few moments to enjoy the gentle roll of Apollo's gait as the horse marched purposefully along the half-made-up road. "*So, tell me, how much further do we have to travel*?" Suetonius screamed at the officer to his left. The man considered the question carefully before replying to his psychotic chief. He was also very careful not to draw attention to himself and anger the man who had the power of life and death over him.

The gang started to join the column, "Looks like we finally have met up with our Lord Governor and Emperor's mouthpiece!" grumbled Decimus as he nodded towards a brightly decorated wagon.

Laenus spoke in a very hushed tone, "Is that the Psycho Suetonius riding beside that ghastly coloured box?" he asked cautiously.

Marcus nodded, "Psycho? You got that right. He does not know when to stop." He looked furtively to his left then right. "Apparently, he murdered the toddler son of one of his slaves because he kept coughing. Suetonius claimed it kept him awake," he mumbled in an informed manner.

"Yes," Decimus added, "I heard he summoned the woman along with the child to his private garden. All his slaves from the household were ordered to gather. He marched out of his apartment, gladius in hand, and with one blow, cut the child's head off in front of them all. As he turned away, he said just one word. 'Peace!'"

"I heard that story as well. Apparently, the reason this tale is even more horrific is that it was believed that the boy was his own son!" volunteered Lucanus.

"What a bloody scandal!" Festus interjected.

Maxetius glanced over to his mate, "What? The fact that he was a cold-blooded murderer, or the fact that the child was his son?"

"Both," Aelianus, Lucanus and Maxetius all remarked in unison.

"What a charming man! We'd better make sure we stay well out of his way, eh boys?" declared Maxetius.

The gang had not noticed the approaching figure, "We will be just fine. After all, we have been in worse company, I am sure!" Albus mumbled to the group, as he joined them and marched with them towards the area identified for the next new camp.

"Right, you lot put your shovels down. It is the time of day that you all love so much. Fall in with full uniform. It is… fight time!" barked Albus. "Collect practice shields and gladii from the supply master."

Maxetius forced the tip of his spade into the ground and leant on the handle, "Those blasted things are so heavy. Why can't we use our regular kit?" he queried.

"You know full well why," Festus replied.

Lucanus clambered out of the freshly dug ditch. "They are weighted with lead because it increases their weight," he interrupted, before expounding, "When you increase the weight, it makes you work harder. When you work your muscles harder, they get bigger and faster!"

"And when you are the fastest, you will survive!" boomed a familiar voice from behind them.

The group spun around to see the broad smile on the face they all knew so well. "Cato!" they cried in unison before approaching the fellow, patting him on the back and shoulders. "It's great to see you. Welcome back. How are you? How's the wound? Are you staying with us? Are you marked fully fit?" The group surrounded the tall black figure and bombarded him with heaps of questions, as each of them greeted him in turn.

Cato had to literally fight them off as he tried to answer the barrage, "Hey. One at a time! Yes, thank you. Better. Yes, I am." nodding at each as he continued, "Yes I am, and before you ask Festus. No, you can't! I think that's all the questions answered!" Cato said with a huge grin, showing off his large front teeth. "I've had enough of being on my back. I need to move and work my body, otherwise you bunch of reprobates will be taking advantage of me before I know it!" The giant bowed in reverence at the gathered crowd, "Praying to the gods is just not enough to make sure I stay alive!"

The group cheered at his revelations, all unaware of the approaching decanus.

"Ah... Cato... I guess the gods were not ready for you, so that means you are still *mine!"* the man snarled sarcastically. "Believe me... You will wish you were dead!" Albus then turned his attention to the rest of the group, "All of you grab your full kit, and move to the training ring." The boss growled, "Cato, you are first up to fight and your opponent?" Albus glared, "Is... *me!*"

The pair armed themselves with the practice weapons that every soldier knew so well. They strapped a weighted shield to their left arms and held a wooden gladius that was weighted with lead, and about double the weight of the swords used in battle, in their right hands. Albus moved in quickly without warning and threw all his weight into the first strike of the lead-weighted wooden gladius on the right side of Cato's torso. The move almost caught Cato off guard. The tall soldier managed to block the blow, but the force drove him backwards and off balance. Albus moved his weight forward and forced the shield into Cato's exposed chest. The force of the impact expelled all the air from Cato's lungs, making a loud 'urghhh' as the gasses pushed up through his voice box.

Cato spun his tall body a full 360 degrees with the agility of a ballet dancer and smashed his sword at the shield of his opponent. The combination of the blow and the noise of the strike grabbed the attention of people who were wandering nearby. Albus tried to counter, but his sword arm was blocked by Cato's shield. He tried to push Cato to the side, but the black figure would not be caught again. Instinctively Albus stepped back, and Cato knew he had his foe. All he had to do was execute the killer blow. He moved forward, thrust his blade between the two shields, and found its intended target… Albus' rib cage. The impact winded his opponent, forcing Albus to yield. The pair stood facing each other, staring intently into each other's eyes for what seemed like ages. A round of applause from the friends snapped the pair out of the face-off that was going on.

The rest of the soldiers in the group numbered off and paired up with the other cohorts. It was not good practice to fight the same opponents over and over, so the legions always fought different pairs at every session. The fighting was not always one on one either. To mix things up from time to time you could find yourself with two opponents, or you might be told to fight with no shield, or even just a shield and no gladius. The more practice you had, the better and sharper your skills would become and in Britain you had no real idea who your enemy was, or how they would attack you.

"Arggh!" groaned Decimus as he took the full force of a strike to the ribs, "I wish I had not eaten so much of that blasted breakfast this morning!"

His opponent momentarily revelled in his victory, "You are trying to say that you are this slow because of your breakfast?" he sneered, "You are wrong, fat old man!" Decimus responded by catching his shield under his opponent's chin and forcing his head back. "Would you like to repeat that? he asked.

Chapter Fifteen

Oliver and Aiden spent increasing amounts of time with Boudicca's house-guards, the pair had practically been adopted by the trained fighters. The boys had really stood out because of their willingness to learn how to move, advance, retreat, attack, defend as a group, and, coupled with the speed they learned rudimentary sword skills, they had made remarkable progress. All of the training had occurred in close proximity to the Iceni Queen.

Oliver glanced over to his right as they were going through some blocking moves when he witnessed a half-naked Boudicca emerge from her tent. The bright red scars on her back were clearly visible as she moved into a patch of light. The celebrated Queen opened her hands, outstretched her arms, and lifted them towards the skies, throwing her head back as she did so, allowing the bright sunlight to bathe her pale skin and the suns' rays to penetrate her long, flowing auburn hair as she revelled in the momentary peace. She closed her eyes tightly, took a deep breath and exhaled slowly as she gently moved and pulled her body into various shapes and positions, unabashed by her form as she did so. She always exercised within sight of her guards.

As she moved, the Queen reflected on recent events. She knew her task was only half finished, but the objectives so far had been achieved with great success. She knew that the Emperor Nero had sent one of the most feared and dangerous of all his Senator Generals, Gaius Suetonius Paulinus to be the Governor of Britannia. He had shown himself to be a capable and ruthless General and had tamed the Druids in the north-west. The reputation that superseded him would have shocked just about anybody else, but if Boudicca was worried at all she did not show it. Her spies had informed her that this man had been dispatched to kill her, and all those that were deemed to create 'problems' for Rome, but this did not faze her at all. On the contrary, the sense of danger excited her, and the thought of mortal combat made her skin erupt in goose bumps as she visualised a fantasy fight in her mind.

The admiration and support of ever more numerous tribes, with their armies swelling the troops behind her, only added to the addictive thrill of danger and heightened her euphoria. The more victories she gave the tribes, the more her reputation grew. The more her reputation grew the greater the army she commanded increased. The bigger the army, the more power she wielded. The energy and growth were self-perpetuating and no Roman, whoever he or she might be, was ever going to throw her, or her people, off their lands. The very lands that they and their forefathers had nurtured, raised crops and cattle on, had toiled and sweated over, sacrificed to the gods for, fought and died for. These treasured lands were not going to be stolen from them! *No Roman* was *ever* going to claim them or take them as prizes.

Boudicca was not alone, her actions were witnessed by a small crowd, along with the Chief Druid and several assisting priests, as she let the bright sun gently warm her skin. Later the same crowd would watch the priests sacrificing a goat and dedicating its life to the gods.

The beast was first ceremoniously paraded through the camp. As it reached a makeshift altar, it was lifted by its hind legs. As it hung head down, the Chief Druid recited ancient rhymes as he stabbed a sharp, narrow blade into its throat. The blood surged from the puncture wound and was captured in a shallow bowl by one of his minions. A secret concoction of herbs was added and mixed before the fluid was slurped by the Chief Druid who then passed it to the other priests. Each drank a mouthful of the mixture from the bowl and passed it on. Finally, the bowl was passed to Boudicca who drank and dutifully passed it to the chiefs from the other tribes. They all took large mouthfuls of the liquid while it was still warm and had not yet begun to congeal.

As this macabre scene was going on, more bunches of herbs

were placed on the fire in front of them. The acrid pungent smoke swirled in the air. The smoke filled their nostrils and made their eyes sting. Heads started to spin as the mixture was inhaled deeply and filled their lungs. The Druid took a curved-bladed knife in his hand, and he mumbled prayers to the gods as he reached up, violently stabbed the razor-sharp blade into the beast's lower stomach and dragged it sharply down towards the goat's throat. As the wound opened, the intestines fell to floor. The Druids keenly examined the mass of the intestines as it uncurled before it landed on the ground. The Chief Druid scrutinised the mess that lay at his feet before he threw his hands to the skies, his head theatrically thrown back as he did so.

These were holy men, men who conversed with the gods, and the gods spoke and channelled their demands through them.

"You will be victorious... The gods decree it!" the Druid wailed, with huge, exaggerated gestures, throwing his hands in the air as he did so and starting to dance around the stinking pile of blood and guts on the floor like a man possessed.

The flock of people surrounding the spectacle cheered and broke into a spontaneous round of dancing and saluting at the news. All had heard exactly what they needed to hear from their spiritual leader. The druid priests had confirmed that their gods were with them!

Boudicca gathered the tribal Kings and house-guard captains together to discuss the next move to be rid of the Romans for good. Once the company quietened down, she cleared her throat and slowly began to speak as she studied each face in turn. "Gentlemen, we have them on the run. We have made our voices heard. Their gods have deserted them, and the time of leeching the wealth of our people is over. We have them on the back foot, we are on a roll. We will not stop until they have departed from our lands and our dead have been vanquished. With every passing hour we grow stronger, while they grow weaker!" Boudicca declared with an imposing power in her voice.

The brief silence was broken. "We need to be wary," Brawley interjected. "If we think the Romans are on the back foot, do you not think they know that too?"

"This is true," Donnchad added. "The Trinovantes have pledged to follow you till our last breath, and we will. But I must ensure that all our warriors don't end up dead warriors, and that, ultimately, the Romans do not triumph and unleash their unbridled revenge."

Volisios looked at the pair and raised his hands. "Brawley, Donnchad I think we need to listen carefully to Boudicca," he commented calmly. "The Priests have confirmed that the gods are pleased with Boudicca, and that they are with her," he confirmed as he slowly raised his hands. "I know Boudicca is dedicated to seeing the invaders run off our land, and like you, I too want to make sure we all see the Romans gone from our shores." The King paused as he judged the looks on the faces of his fellow Kings and warriors. "I am also positive that Boudicca does not want to see her people destroyed, but to see her warriors live full, long and prosperous lives," he added as he politely bowed his head towards the other men in deference to them.

"Indeed!" agreed Boudicca. "We have wiped out the families of the best part of two legions and a garrison while they slept." Her voice dropped as she continued. "We have made whole cohorts just simply disappear, as if by magic. We have ensured that nobody survived, nobody escaped to raise the alarm." She rose from her seat. "There is nobody to report on what we have done, what we are doing, or what we might be planning!" She spoke gently as she moved around the room, pacing the floor with purpose, her hands clasped firmly behind her back.

"I have had news," Boudicca declared as she halted and turned abruptly towards the huddled gathering. "Our numbers grow every day and I have had word that our numbers are going to be swelled again. The house-guards and warriors from the Regnenses, Cantiaci and Belgae tribes from the south and east are joining our fight."

Voices murmured within the group as they nodded at the good news.

Volisios's voice was clearly heard over the mumbling. "I have heard that we have been joined by men from the Dumnonii Tribe from the far southwest coast," he declared.

Boudicca's face brightened and a large grin caused the corner of her lips to turn upwards at the revelation. "That is why we are on the move south, and on to our next target." She paused for dramatic effect as the gathering hung on her every word. She led them over to her campaign table and unravelled a piece of velum that had a drawing etched on it as she proudly announced, "Londinium, the Roman trading post is going to be sacked, and razed to the ground!"

Her announcement caused an audible gasp from the warriors before whispers and mumbling started up once again from the band of men, only to be broken by the booming voice belonging to Brawley. "Londinium?" he queried, "Do you not think that the Romans know how important it is to them as a port and trading post. We all know it contains great wealth and riches, and as such, do you not think it will be heavily guarded and defended by Roman legions?" he continued as the others nodded, many looked quite concerned at the prospect of attacking such an important stronghold.

The Queen nodded sagely. "I know you all have concerns and I understand," assured Boudicca. "But I will remind you that we have several advantages in our favour." Her words caught the attention of the room causing each man to fall silent as Boudicca continued. "We have the experience of taking a town; Londinium is smaller than Camulodunum and our force has grown exponentially." The Warrior Queen knew she had captured the imagination of her fellow collaborators. "We will keep it simple, use a similar tactic and attack at night. In five days time we will have a full moon, so that is when we will begin the offensive." Boudicca used her favourite tactic of nodding as she spoke, and as she looked at the leaders in the room each subconsciously started nodding in agreement. Their action proving that they had all bought into the idea without really being aware of the trick.

All apart from one. "I hope you appreciate this may not be quite as simple this time," interrupted Donnchad. "Londinium is protected by the mighty Thames on one side, so to attack from all fronts at once will be impossible. Also, don't forget that the approach from the North is treacherous and difficult to navigate because of the bogs, as well as the deep ditches that have been dug to try and drain them." He informed the crowd with certainty, "It would be perilous and foolhardy to attempt to navigate them in the dark, even in a full moon period."

Boudicca heard the King's words and quickly reworked her first plan in her head. "That is why we are not approaching it in darkness!" Boudicca informed them with an air of self-assured confidence. "We will make our way towards Londinium in full view of the garrison, and more importantly, in full view of the people within the city walls." The revelation stunned the audience into silence as she continued, "Every man woman and child will make as much noise as possible. The noise will make us appear an even larger threat than we are already and put the fear of their gods in them." She grinned and nodded at the men as the vision flashed across her mind. "We will stop just out of range of their war machines and be very, very visible, I want the horsemen from all the tribes to work together, charging the gates and retreating before the enemy can fire upon us." Boudicca's voice grew louder with every word, "They will hear us. They will see us." Her voice reached a raging crescendo, *"They will fear us!"* she cried out, her words met with a rousing cheer from the captivated audience.

Their response spurred her on. "They will hear our cries and they will hear our pipes. We will make the ground tremble with our thunder!" She was on a roll. "They will be unable to control their bowels as fear grips them. Men will be shaking women will be crying and children screaming with fright!" Boudicca continued as a look of menace flashed across her facial features. "As the sun sets, they will see our fires and will be distracted as our fine warriors slip into the darkness and approach the walls." Her adrenaline started to rush as she constructed the battle in her mind. "A handful of men will remain around the fires and continue the illusion of the camp numbers remaining the same with the women folk, banging drums, wailing, screaming, and playing the pipes, making it seem like we are all still around the fireside. But we won't be!" The subterfuge intrigued the group as Boudicca continued, "The bulk of our force will be on the move towards their walls."

The Queen looked over to the Catuvellauni King, "Brawley, I want you to take your forces to the south and begin the attack. I have made provision with the King of the Atrebates, who control the lands that the Thames runs through to the southwest. He will provide boats and men to take you downstream. He will also send warriors to assist you in the attack." She watched Brawley think though her details for moment as she pointed to the map and paused, "You are to start the attack on the south bank of the Thames. It is imperative you take Southwark and destroy it before you assemble your men at the great bridge on the south bank." She looked up at all assembled, and asked, "What is the best way to take a bridge?"

The assembled leaders looked blankly at each other, all trying not to catch Boudicca's gaze as they pondered the question.

"Both ends at once!" she answered with an air of disappointment as she searched the features of the glazed-looking faces around her. "Brawley, that is why you will have a separate small force join the skilled boatmen of the Atrebates. They are to remain hidden until you have razed Southwark to the ground and are ready to storm the bridge."

"A flotilla of boats will bring your main force downstream at the setting of the sun and they will land the bulk of your forces on the south bank." Boudicca pointed her index finger at Brawley before pointing it at the map and using it to indicate the point of the drop on the map as she continued with the plan. "As the moon begins to rise a small force will be landed on the north bank, which is the soft underbelly of this rich cow. They are to remain hidden until you start your attack on the south side of the bridge." Boudicca had to be clear on the timings to ensure the success of the start of the offensive. "When you start your assault, your men on the less protected north side are to commence their attack and overrun the small force that guards the bridge. Your forces are to take the bridge, and once taken you are to take the gates as we did in Camulodunum." She paused again as she gauged the faces around her. "The bridge is important as it will allow us an escape route if we need it, and more importantly, prevent any of the enemy from escaping. Any questions so far?"

"No," Brawley replied and smiled as he shook his head. "This is second nature to my men. They are used to boarding and launching themselves off boats. They can do it before they can walk!" His land was made up of a lot of marshland and waterways, and to get anywhere you needed great boating skills. The mark of a man was to be able to build his own craft. The chosen craft was coracle-like. It was a small half-sphere shape; the frame was made of hazel sticks that were bent into shape and woven in and out of each other to create a frame. This was then covered with the hide of a cow, sheep, goat, or deer, which was stretched over the frame and covered in pitch to make it watertight. A plank was fitted across the middle as a seat, and a simple oar was carved from a single plank and was used to both guide the boat and power it by paddling the water in front of the craft.

Volisios, you will have your Corieltauvi numbers swollen by the Regnenses, and some from the Durotriges tribes. You will attack the gates and walls to the east. Taran of the Regnenses will lead you through the land north of the town, past the Roman burial grounds until you reach the main gate on the east wall. You will need to be in place by the time the sun sinks. The warriors of the Regnenses and Durotriges will join you at the gate.

Boudicca drew the attention of the group to a map laid out on the table in front of them. "As the sun sinks and before the moon climbs the night sky we will edge towards the walls and prepare to scale them. We need to get men over the walls to secure the gates from the inside as your main forces wait to charge them from the outside and enter the town. Donnchad, you will take your men of the Trinovantes, whose ranks will be swollen by the Dobunni and Cantiaci tribes and move to the south-west side and attack the gate there. Do you have any questions?" she asked her closest and most loyal friend.

"No." A sudden puzzled look furrowed his brow, "Apart from just one." Donnchad could see a problem but paused as his mind searched for a solution. "It is not a question so much as a suggestion." He smiled as his contribution seemed so obvious, "When we are all prepared to move, can we have a visible signal in order to orchestrate our movement and ensure we all attack at once; similar to the previous attack?"

"Of course!' Boudicca replied as she slightly bowed her head in acceptance of the comment. "We will be moving into our starting positions while Brawley takes Southwark. Once the bridge is secured, Brawley is to shoot a single lit arrow into the sky. This flare will be the signal to begin the assault on the main centre. You will brief your men who will be scaling the walls that when they see the flare, they are to rise up and charge the wall with their ladders, while your remaining forces fire arrows over their heads to give them protection," Boudicca exclaimed as she busily moved her hand over the drawing, picking out the various points as she spoke.

"When you, Volisios, and you Donnchad, see your men safely over the walls you begin your attack by firing flaming arrows over the walls and into the city itself before you make your charge towards the gates." Boudicca needed to explain the details in such a way that all were completely sure of their positions and orders, so she paused once again. "I will lead my main force of the Iceni, the Dumnonii and the Belgae in through the west gate. Once inside, we will attack towards the north, and charge at the main gates of the garrison. Their numbers have been greatly depleted recently as troops were sent from here to Mona," she revealed, "so they should be swiftly overcome. The forces from the river will be making inroads by this point, that the other gates will be less well defended as the Romans will be rushing to the south to defend the weakest point that is under attack. This will give *us* the element of surprise. We will be attacking when their attention is being diverted and the main force is being pinned down, or should I say, 'Entertained'!"

The gathering all broke into light laughter as the plan became clearer, the mood lightened at the realisation that the bulk of the planning had been carefully worked out; conveyed clearly and precisely; the reconnaissance had been properly carried out and the prospect of failure was not an option and had not even crossed anybody's mind. Victory was to be theirs!

Boudicca was visibly lifted by the reaction in the room. "The other point is," Boudicca continued, "I have my spies, they have reported the walls are much lower and far less defended than we would expected them to be. They are more a statement to the 'Glory of Rome', a decoration if you like." She beamed, "They are not a practical defence for the city beyond. They are poorly defended and the gaps between the viewing points are much longer than in Camulodunum. The number of soldiers guarding at these points are drastically reduced compared to Camulodunum." Boudicca drew attention once again to the sketch, "The reason for this is because the Romans are acting as 'Guardians', policing the area if you like. Londinium is an area made up of an eclectic mix of peoples, traders, classes, wealth."

The Queen looked up once more at the faces around her as she explained her reasoning. "Camulodunum was different, it was Roman, an outpost of *Rome* itself that was in *our* land.' She could feel her anger start to boil at her own words, "The moment you entered the gates you were immediately in Rome, its laws, its life, its language, its people, all contained inside the walls." She drew breath and closed her eyes as she fought to keep her temper. "The families of the soldiers attacking us, taking our lands were based in Camulodunum. It was *their city.* That was the reason we had to attack there first. The choice was simple... Kill and exterminate the blood line of all who threaten us."

Boudicca paused, her eyes closed, as she had a flashback of her two daughters being hurt. "Strike pain and fear into the very men who have attacked us, killed our people, made our kin slaves." Boudicca's voice raised in both pitch and volume as the anger flushed and contorted her features, giving her the appearance of an ugly gargoyle. "We will continue to exact our revenge on their women and children. We will inflict pain and suffering on them all. We will send their loved ones to *hell*." She paused as she took a huge, exaggerated breath. "Each and every one of them will know the fate of their loved ones before we send them on the same journey." Her fists punched the table in rage. "They will experience the heartache and all-engulfing pain as we have - the physical pain of our blades." Boudicca gasped before her face turned crimson as she screamed, "The Romans in their ignorance, have vastly underestimated our strength, our numbers and our ability." Boudica's body was shaking uncontrollably. "KILL THEM ALL!" she screeched.

Chapter Sixteen

London was buzzing with the news of the sacking of Colchester. Wild rumours flooded the temples, the markets, and the public baths. With each telling the stories became more exaggerated and more lurid. Like any bad news, the word travelled swiftly through the town; speculation quickly followed which, in turn increased a growing sense of unease amongst the population. The Roman town of Londinium had been deliberately built on the River Thames. It was in a place that was easily accessible from land and sea via the great river. It was a designated trading post as opposed to a garrison town and had become a hub for the exchange and purchase of goods from all over the known world. The town itself was renowned as a trading and meeting place, not just of people, but of cultures, creeds, and religions. The place had, by and large, become one of harmony and did not require a heavy military presence.

Boudicca and her followers had very different ideas. Her allies, the women, children, supporters, and warriors, had massed together and were impatient for action. Oliver and Aiden stayed close to Jannon as they all started the journey towards the town, united by one objective, to sack the place and strike more fear into the hated invaders. The fact that harmony existed within the walls did not matter. In fact, in Boudicca's eyes, cavorting with these unwanted invaders was a more heinous crime than being a Roman. The more she could put to the sword and rid them from her land, the happier she became. But Boudicca had given her word and she stood by what she had said. She gave the order to halt the force at a respectable distance from the town. Near enough to be very visible to the town's folk, the mere sight was enough to strike fear into the population as panic started to spread. The people of Londinium started to pack belongings and fought to get on to the boats moored on the Thames. Items they could not carry, or did not want to lose, were buried or hidden in safe places, the owners ever hopeful that they would be spared and able to retrieve them once the dreadful savages had retreated.

The Roman Procurator, Catus Decianus had heard of the dreadful slaughter and the destruction of Camulodunum, and he knew the Celts were taking revenge for his actions against Boudicca. He feared for his own life so, taking the treasures he had amassed for himself, he fled Londinium and crossed over to Gaul. An Acting Governor, Felix Dominius Gillis, replaced him temporarily until the new Governor arrived. Gillis watched the horizon to the north with dismay as it filled from east to west with the hostile tribes. Boudicca moved her tribes towards the outskirts of the town walls and created the panic she desired.

He gave commands for the gates to be barricaded and issued directives for every single man under his command to report for immediate deployment, and for veterans to make themselves known. He was acutely aware of the danger that lay ahead and that he needed every Roman soldier to be on full alert on the walls or in cohorts ready for attack. He issued commands to the groups of veteran soldiers and sent them into the streets to keep law and order. He required the public to be reassured and that the army was in control, that the residents needs were being catered for and that they were safe. The Governor was more than aware that he needed to confront the hordes that had gathered on the outskirts, to establish the reason for the sudden attention that Londinium had attracted. He ordered his horse and a small escort to accompany him as he prepared to venture out, beyond the protection of the towns' walls. As he mounted his horse the Governor looked towards the Commander of the Roman forces in the town, "If these scum move to kill me, you are to unleash hell and cut them all down, is that understood?"

The Commander did not utter a single word. Instead, he pulled himself smartly to his full height and saluted the Governor in acknowledgment of the order.

"Good!" the Governor mumbled as he pulled his horse around and headed in the direction of the North Gate. Six of his personal bodyguards mounted their steeds and a cohort of foot soldiers massed at the front gates in full armour and carrying lances. The order was given to open the gates as they approached. As they passed through the wooden frame the Governor kicked his horse forward, closely flanked by his mounted guards and doggedly followed by the foot soldiers who broke into a near sprint to keep up. As he neared the edges of the encampment, he slowed his beast and cautiously continued forward as he searched out his adversary. All of Boudicca's men gathered ahead of him slowly stood up, weapons clasped tightly in their hands, silence falling over them as they faced the approaching men with a growing sense of unease at the perceived danger.

The boys had travelled with Boudicca's house-guards and helped set up the camp, got a small fire lit and were relaxing around it as they waited for their dinner. Aiden stood up and tapped Oliver on the shoulder as he was crouching close to the fire. He got Oliver's attention alright. "Bloody hell!" he exclaimed as he saw Romans close up, in daylight, for the very first time. He could not believe his eyes or ears.

The elegantly dressed man on the leading horse halted and as he did so Oliver heard a heavy Sicilian Italian accent boom out. "My name is Felix Dominius Gillis, Acting Governor of the town of Londinium. I demand that you make it clear who you are, and I demand that you make your intentions known!" the Governor yelled as he kicked his horse forward once more and made his approach towards the gathered tribes, while signalling to his men to remain where they had stopped.

Boudicca's men all stood firm. Nobody moved or spoke as the Governor slowly drew nearer until a voice eventually rang out, "That is close enough!"

The shocked Governor stopped dead in his tracks. It was not so much the words, but the fact that it was the voice of a *woman* that surprised him. Boudicca rode forward on her chariot and the lines of warriors parted as they stood to one side to reveal Boudicca in her full battle regalia. Her two war ponies walked forward obediently, pulling her chariot, as she made her way towards the Roman. As she reached the front of the line she pulled the two war ponies to a halt, almost knocking Oliver over. Oliver followed Aiden's lead, as he instinctively grabbed hold of the ponies' bridles and stroked the animals' noses to steady them. He could not believe he was actually holding Boudicca's pony and was about to witness the great Queen converse with a Roman.

Boudicca looked the Governor up and down from her chariot platform for what seemed an age before she broke the uneasy silence, "*Your name is of no importance to me!*" Her voice echoed around the marshy plain. "For you will all be dead soon enough. But know this," a look of disgust flashed over her face, "Your life will be taken by me, and it will not be a quick death!" Boudicca declared loudly as she threw her head back, causing the locks of her hair to fly back and expose her features for the Roman to see clearly for the first time. "Know this Roman, history is written by the victors." Boudicca looked down her nose at the man mounted before her, "*Your name* will not be remembered." She growled with contempt, "Your blood and the blood of your spawn will flood your homes and flood the streets of Londinium!" The anger boiled in her blood as she bellowed, "Hear my name and fear me!" She paused melodramatically before continuing, "For I am Boudicca, Queen of the Iceni and this is my army." As she paused, the Governor could see her chest move in and out heavily as she fought to keep control of her rage. Then she continued, "Remember my face, for it will be to me that you will be begging for death!" she screamed.

The Governor, along with just about everybody else in Londinium and beyond, had heard of the legendary savagery this beast of a woman and her tribe had inflicted. As the words rang out, he signalled to his men to remain calm, knowing that a wrong move at this critical moment would mean certain death for him, his men and the town would be destroyed without further warning.

The Governor considered his words very carefully and he cleared his throat before replying, "We are a peaceful trading town, not a garrison. We have many different people, women, and children. The population is made up of many different races, many different people like yourselves, some of whom may well be your brothers and sisters. I do not know why we have attracted your attention," the mounted Roman proclaimed, "We have nothing that would benefit you. If it is riches or food you desire, make your demand and we will give you all you require and see you on your way." He watched Boudicca closely, hoping to see any small sign that she might capitulate on her threat, "but I beg you to leave the town and her people untouched!" he concluded.

Boudicca listened to the request, but she was not for changing her mind, in fact the Governor's pleading only deepened her resolve. She arched her back and threw her head back as she pulled herself up to her full height, drew a breath and asserted her position. "We are the Iceni, the Catuvellauni, the Trinovantes, the Corieltauvi and we are joined by a host of others. We stand united." She raised her left arm horizontally and swept it round theatrically, pointing out the horde of men around her. "We have one goal, and one goal only." Her eyes narrowed as she growled, "To rid our lands of you and your kin." She hesitated briefly to allow her words to reach all in earshot before roaring, "Hear our battle-cry!" The words quickly followed by whoops and cheers, a bawl of concurrence from her troops as she screamed, "And shudder in fear!"

As the noise rang out, Donnchad moved close to the Queens' chariot, leaned in towards her, "Boudicca, don't forget our agreement about the children," he ventured quietly.

Boudicca slowly turned her head and looked her friend square in the face, her eyes cold and emotionless as the staunch warrior stared unflinchingly ahead. He was not sure if his words had penetrated her mind. Boudicca froze for a moment before she looked slowly at her confidant. The hard look subsided and the warmth that he knew so well momentarily returned to her features as she looked into his eyes. She gave a regal nod before looking back towards the Governor.

"I am Queen Boudicca." She announced fearlessly, "I am benevolent. I *will* allow women and children of our tribes to pass through our lines." She looked hard at the Roman as her eyes narrowed, "But *only* those from our tribes and *only* if they swear allegiance to me and our cause."

The revelation caused the gathered force to let out a huge cheer as Boudicca shook the reins in her hands. The boys released the ponies' bridles, and she pulled her chariot around, urging her ponies forward. The warriors moved to either side to let her pass, before moving back and closing the gap caused by her vehicle as she rode off into the distance.

The Governor was momentarily frozen to the spot. He could not believe what he had witnessed. This woman had dared make her wild demands, then had the audacity to turn her back on him and just disappear. The fact that someone turned their back on him was the height of insult as far as Romans were concerned, but to have a woman do it! The Governor's blood boiled. He pulled his mount around and kicked it forward towards his guard. "Get back to the gates!" he growled in anger. "This bloody woman thinks she can destroy me!" he bellowed, kicked his heels hard into the animal's girth and charged back to safety inside the walls.

The Governor slowed to a canter as he passed through the gates, his mounted protectors in close formation behind him. He drew up beside the Captain of the Guard at the small garrison fort. The officer saluted his superior and informed him, "Sir, I have heard that these savages show no remorse and have the blood of innocents and infants on their hands." The officer was not sure if he was speaking out of turn, but he was determined his voice needed to be heard, "They have slaughtered indiscriminately and must not be trusted," murmured the Captain of the Guard in a hushed tone, eager not to be overheard by his men.

The mounted Governor looked straight ahead as he listened before snapping, "I have heard the rumours, Captain... And that is just what they are – *RUMOURS!*" The ill-tempered Governor shouted in anger.

The Captain had expected this response but was not going to be dismissed so easily. "Sir, if we can get some of the women and children out, we may be able to get a message to Suetonius and his troops," pleaded the officer. "Perhaps we can hold the Celts back long enough for them to relieve us."

The Governor silently considered the request. As he did so his thoughts were abruptly interrupted by a messenger, who informed him that more savages and barbarians could be seen in every direction. The town was surrounded! The revelation helped him make up his mind. "Send for my daughter!" he ordered as he turned and headed towards his residence.

He reached the imposing villa and paced through the building, searching desperately for his wife as he did so. He eventually found her standing in the courtyard looking mournfully at the rose garden in the centre. "Minerva!" his voice snapped her thoughts back to reality as she handled one of the dead blooms.

"Oh darling, look at this poor thing, I just don't know how to keep them alive," she informed him in her usual soft tone. Her face filled with shock and horror as he snapped, "NOT NOW!"

He could see the tone and volume unsettled the delicate woman who was now physically shaking in front of him. The sight of the poor figure and the effect of his harsh words immediately filled him with remorse as he reached out and took her hands in his. "Minerva, I am sorry, but I have to tell you, you must leave this place while you have time." The Governor gulped and he looked lovingly into her eyes as he tried to explain the desperate situation as calmly as possible. "I believe that an attack on Londinium is imminent, and I think it is going to end badly."

His words caused his wife's eyes to fill with tears as she fought to remain upright and stop her knees from buckling from under her at the revelation. The Governor continued calmly, "You know you and our daughter are the most important and precious things in my life and my one purpose in this life is to keep the pair of you safe." He half whispered the words with a growing sense of regret and sadness in his voice.

His wife composed herself and slowly looked up into his eyes. "My husband, I took sacred vows to be by your side, and I will *never* break those words," Minerva replied with a tremble in her voice.

The Governor shook his head at his wife's insistence to remain, "As your Governor and as your husband, I demand that you leave. I have instructed your personal slaves to follow and look after you."

His words were met with a strength he had not witnessed in his wife for a very long time. Her eyes narrowed. "How dare you *demand*?" she snapped. "I am not a servant nor a slave. I am a free citizen. And as such I can make my own decisions." The anger welled up inside her, "I am *not* leaving you. Don't you ever tell me to do so again!"

The Governor dropped her hands. "You will die if you stay here!" he growled, "Do you not understand?"

"Then I will die by your side," she replied calmly. "Death has no fear for me, but life without you does."

The Governor looked deep into his wife's eyes. He could see that she was determined to stay, and realised it was futile trying to change her mind. He held out his hand once more towards her, she took it gently in hers and pulled it to her lips.

"I love you, my husband, I always have. I will spend eternity in your arms and by your side. If the gods demand we are to die together, then so be it," Minerva whispered.

The Governor tried to smile, but sadness was etched on his face. He let go of her hands and walked out of the courtyard and towards his study as he felt his heart break.

He sat alone and contemplated the very short time he had left, as he busied himself preparing for the inevitable. He completed papers freeing his slaves and read over his will before locking it away in a metal strong box. He was sure all his business was just about in order when his beloved daughter, Valentina, swept into his room and filled it with life and passion. It was her presence that he would miss the most. "You sent for me father?" her tone was light, almost as if she was about to burst into song.

The Governor watched his beautiful girl glide around the room. His heart felt as if it would burst with the love he felt for her, but his joy was heavily tinged with the prospect of never enjoying her company ever again. "Indeed I did, my dear, darling girl." His eyes watched her every move, studied her every detail and hung on her every word, desperate to commit them all to memory as he continued, "We have a situation that I don't think we can control. Outside the walls lies a danger, the likes of which I have never encountered before." He rose from his chair and slowly walked towards his beautiful girl and wrapped his arms around her. "Never forget, my child, I have loved you from the very first moment I held you in my arms," he paused as he thought back to that very moment, "and my love for you will never wane."

Valentina looked up at her father's face and hugged him back as he continued calmly. "The walls will not protect us and keep the hordes out for long. I fear for you and your mother. Your lives are in danger." He closed his eyes, pressed his face into his daughter's hair and breathed in her perfume, again committing his daughter's aroma to his deep memory. "I need you to break through the savages and find Governor General Gaius Suetonius Paulinus," he instructed softly. "He has gone to the northwest to fight the Druids." As he spoke the Governor lifted a parchment from his desk, "You will need to hide this about your body." The Governor pressed the sealed letter into his daughter's hand.

"You must give him this letter," he instructed with a sense of urgency. "It gives you my authority to explain that he needs to return urgently as we are under threat. You will need to cut your hair, my darling, and dress as a slave. You are to take

Herion and Felicia with you. They have known and loved you since you were born, and I know they will defend you till death."

He looked up and tried to hide the tears that were now running down his cheeks, "I will announce that all non-Roman women and children are to leave the city at once. I have been promised that they will be allowed to leave unhindered." He tried desperately to control his breathing and contain the cries of sadness that were desperate to escape. "This will give you a chance to pass through the lines. Once you are clear, you are to find, beg or steal a horse and ride as hard as you can to Suetonius. Every moment you waste, the nearer death comes to all of us." The Governor found it hard to hold back his tears, as he knew he may never see the face of his most precious child again. He released his grip and stood back to see her beautiful face one more time, as the girl started to sob at the news. "Do you understand?" he stuttered as his voice started to waver.

Valentina nodded solemnly as the Governor reached out hands and placed them gently on her cheeks. He pulled her towards him one last time and gently placed a kiss on her forehead. "Go! Kiss your mother goodbye and travel with the speed of Mercurius!" the Governor said as he turned away in order that she did not see his tears.

Outside the garrison the Governor's orders were given, the troops and administrators marched through the streets announcing the news that all Britannic women and children were to leave and to gather at the gates of the town. They would be allowed to travel unhindered through the marauding masses that were causing great unease with their menace. The announcements triggered a lot of very difficult discussions to take place behind closed doors.

Back at the rebel camp Oliver and Aiden looked at each other, "What do you think is going to happen?" Oliver asked.

Aiden shrugged his shoulders, "I don't know," Aiden mumbled as the pair turned and watched the preparations going on around them. "We had better stay near father though." Aiden suggested, "We don't want to get lost in the lanes of the town, especially with all those Romans running about." He thought for a moment, "They will be as angry as a swarm of bees when we go charging in… And I can't wait!"

A voice sternly rang out, "Oh yes you can!" Jannon replied sharply. He had approached the boys from behind and had heard every word they had said. "Your role is very important. You are to guard the women and children." Placing his hands on their shoulders he said, "We think the Romans might have a force heading back to Londinium. If they arrive and find your mother and the other women unguarded, they will kill them." He looked at the boys, "I need you to guard them for me. Is that clear?"

"Yess," the pair replied sulkily. Oliver looked at his feet as he scraped circles in the dirt. "S'pose so," mumbled Aiden.

Jannon knew that the chance of Romans suddenly arriving without warning was very slim, especially as he knew that many legions had been sent far and wide across the country. The real reason was that he knew the forthcoming battle was going to be very dangerous. Fighting in the streets at night would cause the whole place to be full of peril, particularly if it was a strange town to you. It would be easy for the enemy to appear from doorways and alleys behind you, almost as if by magic. It was definitely not a place for his young charges. No, they would be far better staying with the supporters. Jannon did not like to say no to the boys again. The disappointment in their faces had been hard enough to take the last time when the Trinovantes had been stood down. He reasoned that asking them to guard the wagons and pointing out that they would be responsible for other people, might make them feel valued, making them feel like men who had an important job to do while he was away fighting. He was right.

Chapter Seventeen

Valentina rode hard with her companions. She was riding for her life, the life of her family, the life of Londinium. The fact that she had got through the lines of the savage tribes was a miracle itself. She was absolutely convinced that every savage knew who she was; and she knew that they were all looking out for Romans trying to escape, making the chances of her making it out of the lines alive next to nil.

Make it she did though! Her support hung back as they all mingled with the crowd of evacuees fleeing Londinium. Each one had been briefed with the mission to get word to Suetonius with the utmost speed. They were warned of the danger if they were identified or captured, not only to themselves, but to the entire population of Londinium. The brief was to help and protect Valentina, but if she was identified, they were to break away and do their best to reach the force and get a Roman legion back to Londinium as quickly as possible.

Her father had given her coins to buy horses and food en-route, but as she mingled with the crowds, it dawned on her that the coins she possessed had the picture of Emperor Nero stamped into them. They were *Roman coins*. Coins of the very people the natives were revolting against. Valentina surmised the only option she had, once they slipped passed the Britons surrounding them, was to steal some horses. This sounds easy in principle, but if they were caught it would mean death for sure. Valentina jumped as a hand touched her shoulder, she froze and closed her eyes tightly as a rush of adrenalin surged through her body. She turned slowly and breathed a huge sigh of relief as she saw the familiar face of Felicia smiling back at her. Herion watched from a distance and shadowed the pair until it was safe to join them and so help her mistress to safety as the Governor had requested.

As the group approached a small settlement, they could see a paddock containing several horses that would fit the bill rather nicely. Valentina had found a great hiding place which gave a commanding view of the homestead and beckoned the two servants to join her. Felicia was first to kneel down beside her and, as she did so, Valentina whispered to explain the situation that they now found themselves in. "As you know, we must reach Governor General Suetonius with the greatest of speed, but we have a problem. My father has provided me with money to buy horses and supplies," she explained as she looked furtively around her. "The problem is they are Roman coins and there is a good chance that these people will be sympathetic to the uprising. We could be deemed to be the enemy, and our mission would fail before it really begins," she explained in a half whisper. "I think we have no option but to steal the animals and make good our escape."

"Mistress, look!" Felicia ventured as she pointed towards one of the roundhouses.

Herion had half heard Valentina's explanation and had taken it on herself to find a quick solution. The pair remained under cover and could only watch in horror as they witnessed their companion running towards the roundhouse door, as she did so she signaled back to the pair to move. "I think she is creating a diversion for us!" Felicia ventured.

The pair broke cover and grabbed the halters of the ponies that had gathered around a water trough, and led them quietly out of the paddock, into the nearby woods where they waited in silence. They did not have to wait long before Herion joined them holding a bag.

"What the hell were you doing?" hissed Valentina angrily.

"Mistress, you need horses and food. I went to the house and asked for food to sustain us as we were following the brave fighters. She naturally thought I was talking about Boudicca, and she gave me this bag of food and bread as well as pointing me in the direction of the savages. She also told me that her husband and her sons had joined the force one day's walk to the east of here, so I think we should all ride in the opposite direction to make sure we do not accidentally run into them," she explained as she pointed to the north-west. "Did I do wrong?"

Her mistress looked to the heavens and rolled her eyes, "No, you did a very brave and courageous thing." Her emotions were mixed as thoughts rolled around her head, "but a very stupid thing because you could have got us all caught." Valentina probed the slave out of curiosity, "How did you know they sympathized with the uprising?"

Herion puzzled for a moment as she considered her mistresses queries, "Oh, I did not!" she grinned, "I said I was in search of the brave fighters." The slave shrugged her shoulders, "and the lady started talking about the Romans being defeated by the brave men of Britannia, so I made out I was seeking Boudicca. If she had said she was worried about the poor people being attacked, I would have told her I was seeking to help the Romans," Herion panted. "Anyway, she gave us bread, cheese and meat to help us on our way, which was very kind, don't you think?"

"Only because she thought we were fighting the Romans!" countered Valentina. "Now get on the horses and let's get out of here. I trust you can both ride bareback?"

The girls nodded dutifully, even though they had never tried, and they mounted up and followed their mistress's lead.

The journey led them along narrow paths and lanes until they finally came across a Roman road. At last Valentina could relax a little, knowing that they would eventually come across a fort or town and be safe under the protection of Rome once more. Not letting her guard down, she kicked her horse on and ensured the pair sent to protect her remained close. Her instinct was correct, and as the sun was starting to set and disappear over the horizon, they came across a cohort camped for the night.

Valentina approached the gate, identified herself and passed the seal her father had given her a few days before, to the sentry. The group was ushered in, and the gates closed behind them, they were directed towards the Tribune's tent. They dismounted just before it and Felicia and Herion were taken to a tent to freshen up and wine and food was ordered for them. Valentina was asked to follow the centurion, who led her to the tent door and asked her to wait while he spoke to the Tribune.

As the door flap parted again, a voice called out from the dimly lit interior, "Come in girl! I understand you have come from Londinium, and you are trying to find Suetonius Paulinus," said the young Tribune. He inquired, "Can you tell me why?"

He listened intently as she explained the whole situation, along with the reason why as a Roman, she was dressed in the clothing of a tribal woman, and riding on a native pony rather than a Roman horse. She hurriedly showed him the sealed letter and even in the dim light the Tribune recognized the detail and shouted for his decurion.

"This is Lexinus, and he is a brave veteran of these lands. He is the decurion in charge of the cavalry unit here." The Tribune explained, "He will take your letter directly to Gaius Suetonius Paulinus with the speed of the gods, and make sure a legion is returned to Londinium to save your family and the city."

"No!' snapped the girl. "I can't do that!" she shouted, much to the dismay of the Roman officer. "I cannot allow this letter out of my sight until it is the hands of the Governor General himself." Her face took on a purpled hue and the veins in her neck stood out as a raging temper took hold, "My father was most insistent, and I gave my word."

"This is no task for a lady, I insist you leave this to the professionals," insisted the Tribune. "I urge you to remain under my protection and let us do our job."

Valentina was not one for taking orders, and, coupled with the fear of not seeing her beloved parents again and lack of sleep, her temper erupted. "The fate of Londinium is no place for women and children!" she yelled loudly in a very fierce voice. "If my father had a son, he would have sent him, and I am sure you would not patronize him in this manner," Valentina growled as she leaned her face towards the Tribune's, "but he does not, and *I* will not fail him or my people!"

The Tribune stared in disbelief for a moment. He was not used to Roman women speaking to him in that manner. He could see the determination on the girl's face and knew he was unlikely to win.

"Lexinus, get this girl a proper mount, then select your six best riders and make arrangements to leave at once. You are to take Valentina to the Governor General who, I believe, is to the west of here and moving south. I will send a force of two hundred immediately to sort this scum out, and that will be the end of it."

The decurion punched the clenched fist of his right hand on his chest, over his heart, and dropped his head smartly in salute before twisting around and marching out of the tent.

"Two hundred?" Valentina queried incredulously. "Two hundred?" she barked, "the Britons have a force of thousands, tens of thousands. They will be slaughtered along with the people in Londinium," Valentina declared as tears welled in her eyes in sheer frustration. "My people."

Her words fell on deaf ears, "Make sure you get something to eat before you leave," the Tribune instructed. "I will ensure that your travelling companions are fed and looked after in your absence. Now go and may Hermes bless you with speed," The Tribune concluded as he looked down at some papers on his desk and vaguely waved his hand in a gesture to dismiss Valentina.

Towards the end of several days of hard riding, the troop finally caught up with the Governor General. He stood in silence, not amused by being woken out of a deep sleep, as he was presented with the letter and read it slowly before turning his back on Valentina and Lexinus.

"How many are there?" he finally asked as he continued to read.

"There are many tribes that have joined Boudicca and the

Iceni. They have surrounded Londinium completely." Valentina closed her eyes as she mentally envisaged the sight she had left. "There are tens, if not hundreds of thousands of warriors and followers," Valentina said in a hushed, almost whispering voice.

Suetonius reread the letter as he absorbed the girl's information, "And what did the Tribune do when he heard the news?"

Valentina was unsure of the direction of the questioning. "He ensured that I had safe passage to find you and to give you the news direct," she replied.

Suetonius glanced up from the scroll with a look of irritation. "About Londinium?" he screamed. "What has he done about bloody Londinium?"

Valentina was taken aback by the Governor's reaction, "He ordered two hundred soldiers to leave for Londinium and intercept the troublemakers." She stammered.

The Governor General shook his in disbelief. "Two hundred?" the man mumbled as the rage made his blood boil. "Two hundred?" he shouted. "The man is a bigger fool than I thought!" The Governor's fingers curled into fists and scrunched the parchment he was still holding, "How in Mars's name does he think two hundred can overcome this swarm of bloodthirsty barbarians?" He raged, as he threw the letter to one side and violently kicked his campaign chair over. "I bet he has sent them and stayed at the camp himself in order to 'protect those under his command!'" The veins in Suetonius' neck became obvious and his complexion turned crimson as his hands started to shake in anger. "By all the gods I will make him pay for his stupidity!"

The Governor General was never in the best of moods. He was a very intelligent man, a man with very high standards, a man who believed he had never met a person that could equal him, and so far, he had not been proved wrong. He treated all those under him with complete contempt, and this situation enforced this belief. He started barking a string of orders at his orderlies, "Rouse all officers at once and prepare the camp to move!" He screamed.

Valentina had seen her father in a bad mood but had never witnessed anything like this.

Word got round to Albus that the camp was going to be on the move, and he took great delight in screaming at the sleeping crew. "Up! Up! Up! The gods may not want you today, but I do!" he shouted as he kicked the various cots around him, "We break camp in five minutes!"

The gang snapped out of their comfy dreamworlds, "Did you say something darling?" Lucanus asked as he stretched his body.

Another body twitched into life, "By all the gods! I have gone blind! I can hear the voice of devils but can't see anything. Where am I?" joked Aelianus as he lay on his back flailing his arms in the air.

"More like 'Who are you'?" tutted Cato. "Just think, I could be in my bed with hot and cold running slaves tending to my every need. But, Oh No!" he cried out, "I had to get back to join you lot of buffoons!"

The tent filled with the noise of men scrambling out of their beds and packing all their kit in an ordered manner. The army was always on the move so erecting and striking the camp was second nature. It was a well-rehearsed action, and all knew the routine, even in the dark.

Cato stood up and stretched his arms above his head, arching his back and cracking his knuckles as he did so. He took a deep breath, relaxed and bent forward. PHAAAARRRRRRP…

"Oh, you dirty son of erghhh… euh… eug…" spluttered Decimus. "That was right… Urrghhh… in my face."

The tall African grinned, "I said the food the slaves brought tasted good. I did not say it agreed with me," he exclaimed. "I feel so much better now!"

203

Maxetius retched as the gas reached him. "Man, it stinks like something has died up your backside," he gurgled. "Open the door flaps before we all get overcome by the stench, and by the sake of all the gods don't light a lamp or we will all be blown up!" he continued as he fanned his hand in front of his face in a futile attempt to waft the smell away from under his nose.

Festus sat bolt upright and unintentionally got a nostril full of fart as he took a deep breath. "Urgh… I think you are still very ill," he gasped as he started to gag, "You need help!".

The rest of the camp was also busy in what looked like organized chaos as tents were dismantled and loaded onto carts, along with nonessential equipment that was required to keep the army on the move. Pots were put over embers and water was quickly boiled up to be added to oats, making porridge for each tent.

Lucanus took his turn at overseeing the breakfast and filled the patera bowls of the other seven as the jovial banter began again.

"Hey Festus, are you wearing your subligaria? Or are you going to dress like the savage natives and wear nothing under your pteruges leather skirt?"

"Why? Have you pissed in yours Aelianus? After all, it would not be the first time!" Festus quipped.

"How would you know what savages do or don't wear, Aelianus?" enquired Decimus.

Festus leaned over to stir the oats. "Rumour has is that barbarians and savages 'let it all hang out'!" he said.

"It is true," Lucanus butted in, "Curiosity got the better of me, I had to check and see. I had a pugio stuck in one once and I had to struggle to get the bloodied dagger out, and so I sneaked a look!"

"And?" Decimus and Festus both asked simultaneously.

"I can confirm that it did not wear underwear, but I am still not sure if it was male or female!"

"Ha, ha, ha, ha! Are you sure you know the difference?" Cato laughed as his large frame appeared in the half-light.

Lucanus looked up from the embers, "Hope you feel better for that?" he idly enquired as he passed Cato his patera of porridge.

"I am pleased to announce, for all of those interested, that my bowel movements are normal," grinned Cato. "Well, for the time being anyway. But I am sure that this porridge will change that!"

"Why you cheeky...," Lucanus started as he raised the ladle above his head and was about to hit Cato with it. Marcus grabbed his hand. "Now, now children, play nicely!" he quipped, making the others laugh out loud.

They quickly cleared their equipment and loaded it on a wagon before they joined the rest of the legion in removing the sudes, or wooden stakes with a sharpened end, that were used to make a protective wall or fence around the camp. The latrines were filled in and fires extinguished as the whole area double-checked for equipment that might have been missed.

While all this organized mayhem was going on, the officers attended Suetonius in his tent in the centre of the compound. The General marched smartly into the tent where they had all been ordered to gather. "Gentlemen, I have received information that changes our whole expedition," he began without looking up from a scroll he was studying. "I can confirm that the rumours we have been hearing are indeed true. Camulodunum *has* been attacked. I do not have any accounts with regards to deaths or casualties, but I do know the garrison has been raised to the ground." Suetonius paused as the assembled group gasped aloud on hearing the information and started to mumble among themselves.

"Gentlemen, please…," Suetonius continued as he raised his hand to silence the group. "I have also been reliably informed that this is *not* the work of some raiding party, but the work of an organised and very motived militia consisting of various

Celtic tribes of warriors and primarily led by the Iceni tribe." Suetonius fought to keep his temper under control as the words tumbled out of his mouth. "Their numbers are unknown, but I have been told that they have moved to attack Londinium, where, it is reported, they are now completely surrounding the town."

The group started to mumble and looked at each other in amazement at the news of the audacity of the tribes. Once more Suetonius raised his hand for silence before beginning again. "I am sick of this scum. I will not have any more Roman blood spilled. We march back to Londinium, and we will wipe this scum from the face of the Earth." His blood pressure was rising alarmingly, "WE WILL ERASE THEM FROM HISTORY!"

The assembled crowd cheered before Suetonius dismissed them to their duties to complete the preparation to move out.

The legionaries completed the loading of the equipment. "Here we go again. I wonder where we are going today?" grinned Decimus. "I am sure it will be fun wherever it is!"

Maxetius glanced at his companion, "Decimus, why are you always so blasted positive?" he enquired.

"Well... I have porridge in my stomach, I have had a good sleep, I am surrounded by a bunch of reprobates that I consider my family and I had a good shit this morning. What's not to be happy about?" Decimus grinned as he shrugged his shoulders.

Lucanus looked up to the sky, "I wonder about you sometimes Decimus. I really do!" he joined in merrily.

"Why do you worry about me?" Decimus retorted, "There are so many other things you should be concerning yourself about." He smirked, "Like learning to cook the porridge better!"

"Ha, ha, ha, ha! That would be a good start," giggled Festus.

The tall African interrupted the joshing. "I have just heard we are being moved back to Londinium. Some rebel upstarts have angered the Emperor … Or something like that," chipped in

Cato.

"Hey Boss, do you know what is happening?" Decimus asked Albus as the man ran past the gang while they double checked their equipment.

"I will in a minute. We have all been summoned by our centurions Albus called out. "I will tell you what I find out. In the meantime, make sure you have everything packed away and are ready to move out!" he barked as he ran into the distance.

It was not long before Albus doubled back to his charges. He seemed very distracted, his shoulders drooped, and he had a blank look on his face. With furrowed brows, he slowly approached them. "Listen!" he snapped. "We... We..." He stopped and took a deep breath as he desperately struggled to compose himself. "Squad, Attention!" he snapped, bringing the group to full alert. He looked through the men as he spoke very slowly and purposefully, "I have news. A force of local barbarians in the east of this cesspit land have risen against the might of Rome." He paused as he drew a deep breath and rehearsed his next sentence in his mind. "We know the cowards attacked Camulodunum when it was unguarded," he swallowed hard. "And... And... Camulodunum has been burned to the ground."

The news stunned the friends as they all started to look at each other, desperately hoping for someone to break the silence. They all had family and, having been stationed there for a couple of years, had many friends in the town.

Albus could not look up from the ground as the unbelievably shocking news dawned on him. He too had family there. His voice started to tremble. "There are no survivors..." he blurted out before turning sharply and walking away from his charges.

Cato placed his hands on the shoulders of Maxetius and Aelianus who were standing on either side of him. They all bowed their heads, partly in shock and partly in silent prayer for the slain.

"Barbarian Celts!" Lucanus mumbled under his breath.

Albus stopped, pulled himself up to attention and composed himself before turning back to the group. "They are moving on Londinium, and we have orders to move south and wipe the scum from this earth." Albus drew himself to his full height. He drew his shoulders back, filled his lungs and lifted his chin. "Who are we?" he asked.

"The *Ninth*."

"Who *are we?*"

"The *Ninth!*"

"*Who aarrre we?*"

"*The Glorious Ninth!*" they all shouted in response.

"MOVE OUT!" Albus ordered.

The group all raised their right fists and punched their breast plates over their hearts before turning to the left and breaking to join the ranks.

Chapter Eighteen

As the light began to fade, Aiden and Oliver willingly took up their posts, as they had been shown, with a sense of pride. From their position they could make out the boats that contained Brawley's attacking force as they made their way downstream heading towards the south bank of the Thames. None of the men could be seen from the banks, as they were all hidden under blankets and waxed cloths so they could slip towards the town without giving advance warning of the impending attack. The view of the army preparing to battle stirred up a sense of excitement in the pair, they became quite animated and chatted incessantly to each other. The enthusiastic boys did not realise the time had passed as quickly until the conversation was interrupted by a familiar voice.

"Boys, your food is ready," called Mardina from the fire side.

Aiden tutted and let out a loud sigh, "Oh Mother! You know we can't leave our posts. Father told me that we were to guard you at all costs." Oliver nodded in agreement. "That is true, Jannon said he would be very cross if we failed to watch over you," he added, "and it does look like the battle is about to kick off any moment."

"Boys, I am sure that nothing is going to happen in the next ten minutes, and as my guards you can both stand down," Mardina ordered. "All will be fine."

"Awww… Mother…" pleaded Aiden, just as the delicious aroma of cooking bacon reached the boys nostrils.

"Awww nothing. The food is ready. I'm sure the two of you are starving. Besides you will need all the strength you have to protect me and the babies if the Romans come this way."

"When…" corrected Aiden.

His mother smiled and she gently nodded her head as she agreed with her young protector, "*When* the Romans come this way." Mardina looked back at the food, turning it and making sure it did not burn from the intense heat. "I know our guest is hungry too. I can hear the stirrings of hunger starting to rumble in your stomachs from here!"

"Well…" started Oliver as his stomach was so empty it was starting to make him feel faint. "I am not sure if we can take an order from the person we are protecting." He paused as he considered the situation, "I am sure that is not the right protocol!" As he spoke, he started to doubt his own words as they fell from his grinning lips.

Mardina continued watching her food cooking, staring intently at the pan and griddle as she remarked, "Can I just say, I have cooked some of the bacon. It would be a real shame to see it go to waste."

Before Mardina could finish her sentence, she was quickly joined on either side by two eager characters, their grimy faces beaming at her, noses raised as the pair sniffed the smoky air deeply, determined to absorb every bit of scent from the food that was being readied on the edge of the fire's embers. Mardina glanced to her left and then to her right and tutted at the visions, "And if you think, for one moment, you are eating my food with dirty, grimy hands and faces as grubby as this, you can think again. Go and wash."

The two boys' faces dropped as they glanced over to each other.

"But Mother, we are staaarrrving!" protested her young mud-splattered son, to no avail as his words of protest fell on deaf ears.

"And here…" Mardina called out as she grabbed a cloth and threw it at Aiden, "Use this cloth to dry yourselves." And she took no notice of the further protest.

The two friends looked at each other again as they realised that this was a battle they just could not win.

"My mother's cooking is like that too," Oliver shrugged as the pair turned to face the tree line and started to wander towards a fast-flowing brook.

"Yeah. Bet she's a better cook though!" Aiden giggled and smirked.

Oliver forgot himself for a moment and blurted out, "That may well be true, but then my mother does not cook on an open fire."

Aiden stopped dead in his tracks at Oliver's unexpected revelation. "Really? How does your mother cook?"

"Badly!" Oliver laughed as he thought about home. "In our house we have a fully fitted out kitchen and my mother is still appalling at just about everything she attempts to make!" Oliver began laughing as he continued, "I say most things, I am not exaggerating when I tell you that my mum can burn salad!" he gleefully exclaimed, imitating an old-time music hall comedian in full act, "but she is definitely a whizz when she rescues an ice cream tub from the deep freeze!"

Oliver closed his eyes as he searched his memory. "The way she grapples with the lid, growling as she tugs and pulls with all her might, culminating in a victorious 'yes', as the lid is forced open with a crack; a spoon is crashed into the frozen creamy mixture within, twisted and pushed until a large dollop is separated." He murmured dreamily, "She then slowly withdraws the large spoon, balancing the sweet mixture in the spoon's bowl. As it hits the warm atmosphere it develops a fine shiny liquid coating, and it is delicately splatted into the centre of the dessert bowl with all the finesse of a burly bricklayer slopping a trowel of mortar on to a row of bricks!"

He tutted and dramatically threw his head back before spinning on his heels and pretended to draw an imaginary pistol from an imaginary holster, pointing his empty gun hand at his friend, "And boom, a strawberry is unceremoniously rammed onto the top as a crowning glory, and a squirt of strawberry flavoured syrup smattered across it. Just as it is thrust into your hand and a metal spoon thrown into the mix, clanging as it crashes against the china bowl!

"What?" interrupted Aiden. "Why are you suddenly talking in

tongues? What is a kitchen? A freezer? Ice cream?" Oliver's confused companion loudly exclaimed. "What are you saying?"

Oliver froze in horror as he had unwittingly given himself away, "I, er, I mean, um…"

Aiden stared unbelievingly and in complete confusion and awe at his friend, "I am sorry," he gabbled, and he dropped onto his knees, fearing he had overstepped his position and offended his visitor and the other gods.

Oliver quickly gathered his thoughts and grabbed the young Aiden by the elbows and pulled him up to his feet before anybody could see, "A kitchen, the kitchen is a room that we do our cooking in."

Aiden's face crinkled as he mused over Oliver's words, "You cook in a different room?" Aiden was really confused now. He had usually lived in buildings consisting of one big room. Sometimes a woven blanket or skins were spread open and supported by a couple of poles if you needed sleep or rest, but never separate rooms. His curiosity got the better of him, "Why, why do you cook in a different room?"

Oliver shrugged his shoulders as he pondered the question. "Mum says that when my father cooks, the mess he makes is contained in one area, also it stops the smell of burning filling the whole house!" he smirked.

"Your father COOKS in the house?" Aiden was shocked at the revelation.

"Yes. He often cooks for us all at the weekend. But he is not as good a cook as my mother."

"My father is okay at cooking food when we go out on a hunt or journey, but never cooks at home."

"I know. I have tasted his food!" Oliver laughed as the pair headed towards the stream. "My father also cooks outside in the summer when we have a barbeque."

Aiden felt as if he was losing the plot, "There you go again, what is a barbeque?

Oliver glanced at his friend, "A barbeque is a sort of party that we have in the summer if the weather is nice. My mother makes some salads, and my father lights a fire, and cooks food such as chicken, sausages, or burgers. We don't need fires in the kitchen because he has a big old oil drum on legs, and he builds a fire using charcoal and cooks on that."

Aiden was shocked at this information. "You don't have a fire in your kitchen?" he quizzed, "So how do you cook in this room if you don't have fire?"

"Well…" Oliver thought very carefully, "How can I explain this?" he mused, "Every house has a big box that is used as an oven, which is heated by gas or electricity."

"By what?" Aiden abruptly interrupted. "What are you talking about?" he enquired. "You are talking in riddles again!" Aiden was puzzled.

"Gas is fire in a way. We either have big metal jars full of gas or it comes out of pipe, and we set it alight and cook with it." He looked about him for a cow pat, "Here let me show you. Have you got your striker with you?" Oliver asked as he picked up a dry pat.

Aiden burst into a fit of laughter, "No!" He exclaimed at the sight before him, "NO… Wait… You cook with cow shit?" Aiden guffawed.

"No, of course not!" Oliver retorted, "I want to show you the gas… That's all."

"We also use electricity. And before you ask, electricity is an invisible power that we have, which travels in wires. Do you know what a wire is?" asked Oliver as he put on a voice impersonating his schoolteacher as they wandered back to the wagon where Aiden's mother was cooking.

"Of course, I do,' Aiden countered. "I am not stupid you know!" he replied in a mocking voice.

"Well, this power moves along these wires. It can't be seen, can't be smelled, touched, or seen, is very dangerous, but gives us light, heat and allows us to cook."

"I am very confused! You can't see it. It does not smell, and you cannot feel it. It is very dangerous but gives you light and heat. You are lying. Nothing like this exists." Aiden looked very puzzled as he looked at the ground as they walked, aimlessly kicking loose stones as they wandered back. "Thunderstorms?" Oliver declared, "You know thunderstorms?"

Aiden tutted, "Of course, I do!" he moaned. "Mother does not like them, and says it is the gods fighting!"

"Well. You obviously have seen a flash of lightning?" Oliver explained as he observed Aiden nodding with a puzzled look. "Well, that is electricity!"

"You just said you can't see it, feel it or touch it. Now you say it is made up of lightning, and we can see that. Then you say you use lightning to cook and then you say you have light. I think the gods are keeping a lot of things from us!" Aiden sulkily looked down and watched his feet idly kick some dirt around as he contemplated Oliver's explanation. Oliver concluded that it was better to stay quiet at this point and not say anymore. His stomach was really making funny noises as the pair approached the wagon, both clean and eager to eat. The pile of food did not take long to disappear as the boys rammed the grub into their faces with no manners. Oliver was so hungry that his table manners were definitely not at the forefront of his mind!

The boys wiped the bacon grease from their lips with their sleeves as they both lay back on the ground, tummies swollen with the meal as Oliver started thinking about the gas. He hated being called a liar and would demonstrate he was right when it came to him. Oliver sat bolt upright and announced. "I can prove that I am right about the gas," he announced confidently. "Watch this!" And he jumped to his feet and gathered a small pile of dried cowpats. Oliver picked a lit stick from the fire and touched a cow pat. Immediately it emitted a blue flame in a flash.

"Wow!" gasped Aiden. "Does all cow shit burn like this?"

"Yep. We use a gas like this to cook on," Oliver said with a sense of pride.
"That is amazing!" Aiden sputtered incredulously. "Can I come with you and see it?"

"It is not that simple…" Oliver had a lump in his throat as he suddenly became very homesick as he thought of Grandad, his Mother and Father. He was even starting to miss Michael!

Mardina glanced at the two boys, who were deep in conversation, when she witnessed Oliver suddenly go quiet and look very sad. "Oliver, what's wrong?" she asked gently as she could see the tears welling up in Oliver's eyes.

Oliver was suddenly very embarrassed at the enquiry. "Nothing!" he snapped as he tried to pull himself together.

Mardina could not bear to see anybody upset. "Come here," she said softly as she beckoned him towards her. Oliver slowly walked towards her, and she wrapped her arms around him and pulled him close. She ran her fingers through his hair and pulled his head into her shoulder to comfort him as she searched for some comforting words. "Oliver, you have come into our lives, and I am pleased to have you with us," she assured him as she lightly stroked Oliver's hair. "I do not pretend to understand you, or where you come from," she murmured as she felt his body convulse as he fought to keep his tears back. She continued, "But what I do know is that even the bravest and strongest of men cry from time to time. It is nothing to be ashamed of." she whispered in his ear as the tears started to flow. He tried to stop himself, but could not, and he started to cry into her chest. "There," she comforted. "Don't you worry. It is all going to be fine," she whispered gently in his ear as she continued stroking his hair.

A single voice rang out, "OI!" it screeched.

Oliver suddenly was snapped out of his feeling of sorrow and self-pity and looked in the direction of the exclamation. His eyes were so teary the figure was just a blur.

The voice rang out, "What are you doing with my mother?" Aiden mocked, before he realised his friend was really crying.

Oliver tore himself from the warm embrace, "I... I... I will be all right," he stated bravely as he swallowed hard and wiped his cheeks with the bottom of his shirt. "I miss my home and my mother. I am scared I will never see her again." Oliver managed to explain through his light sobs, trying desperately hard not to start wailing again.

Aiden placed his arm around his friend's shoulders as he tried to reassure his pal, "My father has promised to return you once we have had victory over the Romans, and my father has never failed to keep a promise!" he announced proudly.

"I hope so," Oliver replied. "But I am not sure he can help me. I don't even know where home is anymore... Or how to get there."

"Here you are boys. Drink your drinks, it will soon be getting dark," Mardina said with a smile as she passed two cups to them.

The two lads were just starting to settle down for the evening when one of Donnchad's guards came running over to them. "There you are!" he panted. "We have been looking all over for you two. King Donnchad is insisting you join him. After all he would not want to go into the fray without the talisman sent by the gods!"

The two could hardly contain their excitement as the warrior explained to Mardina that the lads would be safe under his watchful eye and the guards would be forming a ring around the King with Oliver and Aiden in the centre.

The boys abandoned their cups as they sprung up and hurriedly said goodbye to Mardina as they headed off with the House Guard back to Donnchad's encampment. As they approached, the guards surrounding their King gladly waved them past. No sooner had they arrived than the pair were ushered through and finally found themselves face to face with the King himself.

The King glanced up and smiled broadly at the two grinning faces, "Ah boys, glad you made the party!" Donnchad raised his right hand and made a signal to one of the supporting warriors. "Of course, it is going to be an adventure, for sure, but I expect my lucky talisman to be close."

As he spoke the boys could hear some clattering getting louder. Oliver spun around to see a house guard laden with shields, armour, and helmets, and as he did so he elbowed Aiden and whispered, "Look!" as he nodded in the direction of the guard.

Aiden obligingly spun his head around and his audible gasp was so loud it made all the men in the room smile and laugh at the boys.

Oliver and Aiden quickly had armour plates secured around them and helmets of various sizes plonked on their heads in a desperate effort to find a good fit for them.

The boys were the centre of attention for a few minutes while the room filled with the senior house guards and officers, all of whom had been summoned to hear the final plans for the attack. Donnchad went through the proposals in the finest of details and timings with the men as Oliver and Aiden listened intently. The pair looked at each other, their mouths dropped, their eyes widened as the King revealed that he would be heading the attack, on his war chariot, flanked by his senior house guards his horsemen and… the two boys!

Aiden and Oliver could barely contain their excitement, not only were they dressed in full armour for the first time, in the presence of the King, but they would be rushed to the front… on a war chariot, with charging ponies! The pair were in complete awe as they observed the speed and efficiency of the tribal army's preparation; the professionalism of the force as they took up their positions ready for the assault. They all seemed to know where they should be and what they were doing with the minimum of orders needing to be issued.

The boats that had lain in wait on the south bank of the Thames had the blankets and waxed cloths thrown back and the warriors underneath jumped to the shore and charged forward. At the same moment a couple of brigades, war chariots and horsemen charged from the south, slashing, and striking down anybody that stood in their way. The Roman guards on the north bank hurriedly ran towards the city defences, shouted for the gates to be closed and sealed as they scrambled a small force together in an effort to try and hold the bridge connecting the two banks.

Southwark was left to its fate as the sheer number of attackers soon overcame the defenders and razed the buildings to the ground before heading to the only connecting bridge that spanned the great river. The signal was given, the Britons leapt out from their hiding places on the north side of the river, charged up the banks and up on to the bridge, cutting the Roman defenders off from the safety of Londinium's walls. The Romans came face to face with the barbaric militia rushing at them from the front and their rear. Panic overtook the inexperienced defenders as they tried in vain to use their shields to create the famed 'Tortoise' defensive square, but the size of the attacking force and the momentary hesitation from their officer led to them being quickly overcome and each brutally put to death in full view of their comrades who watched helplessly from Londinium's defences.

As Brawley's men stormed forward a single flaming arrow streaked into the darkening skies, quickly followed by wave after wave of lit arrows being sent up over the walled defences and striking the gates and the buildings inside. A single shout was heard in the distance and was quickly followed by the roar from thousands of men and women as they jumped up from the ground and charged at the burning gates. The force suddenly split into numerous groups, diverting from the gates and heading along the walls on either side. Men with ladders had been sent under the cover of darkness and waited, hidden in the scrub and undergrowth near the Roman walls. Jannon glanced up from his position to see his King, Donnchad, standing proudly on his war chariot as he took the lead and headed up his force charging to attack the south-west gate.

The sense of pride quickly turned to panic when he recognised the two armoured boys hanging on to the hooped side of one of the chariots behind. Aiden and Oliver were whooping and cheering with blue woad patterns painted on their faces. Before Jannon could jump up and try to stop them the attack was sounded, the fight was on, all the warriors suddenly sprang from the vegetation and started charging towards the walls.

Jannon scrambled to his feet, his back to the wall and forced one end of the ladder into the ground, grasped the side rails (he did not want his fingers stamped on) and leaned back along with the other ladder bearers. The attacking force climbed up at lightning speed, jumping over the balustrades, weapons at the ready, they made quick progress along the defences, easily overcoming the woefully unprepared defenders. Outnumbered, their forces had been further depleted by men being sent to the burning gates, as it was believed that was where the main attack would be happening. Defiantly the Romans continued in vain to hold back the ever-increasing number of attackers. Each soldier and veteran determined to defend to the last, to deny Boudicca of victory and kill as many of her army as possible before he, himself, would be slain.

Boudicca had once again timed the attack to perfection, all her forces expertly coordinated the push forward at the opportune moment. This coupled with an element of surprise panicked the whole town inside the walls as it came under the savage attack. The Roman defenders had been wrong-footed and quickly realised that they were now trying to fight battles on fronts they had not expected. The defenders' main concentration had been placed at the various gates around the perimeter, as they wrongly believed the Celts would try to storm those to gain entry as the main front of the initial attack.

The Celts sent flaming arrows indiscriminately over the walls, some hitting civilians and soldiers alike as they scrambled for safety. Gravity eventually overcame the traveling projectiles' initial trajectory and pulled them back to earth, landing with audible thuds and thwacks as they hit. Some of the incendiary arrows struck wooden buildings and caused them to ignite. The resulting yellow and orange flames soon started licking upwards and lit the darkened night sky. The first wave of Celts ascended the walls, and they drew their preferred weapons as they scrambled over the top and conquered the parapets. Some wielded swords, others brandished battle axes as they participated in the close hand-to-hand fighting. The Romans caught on the walls were a highly trained and disciplined force but were lightly armoured and were relatively easy to overcome by the vast numbers that just seemed to keep coming at them. Officers and senior soldiers barked orders at the men under their command and the legionaries desperately tried to regroup and start a counterattack, but to no avail as the copious blades of the Celts slashed and stabbed at them viciously.

The dense air started to become heavy with the stench of burning as the fires started to rage out of control. Fire storms were created in some of the streets as the heat whipped up winds, causing a deafening whoosh as they funnelled through the grid pattern streets. Civilian men, women and children had become trapped within the burning shells of the buildings as roofs started to collapse, sending showers of embers high into the skies. Others found themselves caught up in the fighting and were slain where they stood by the crazed invaders, struck down without mercy. Some witnessed the sight and retreated behind the closed doors of their burning houses, hoping that the thick toxic fumes would extinguish their senses before the wild flames disintegrated their bodies into unrecognisable piles of ash rather than being hacked to death.

The Celts amassed in their tribes, followed the orders given to them and finally turned on the gates. The attack had gone to plan so far. The loss of their own men was comparatively light compared to the numbers of Roman and civilian bodies strewn around the streets. The fire-damaged gates were finally opened from within, allowing the rest of the waiting hordes to flood in.

Donnchad and the boys tore through the gates, along with numerous other chariots and mounted warriors, the King's chariot slowed as he rendezvoused with his men who had scaled the walls. He jumped off and raised his sword to the heavens and bellowed a huge war cry. Oliver and Aiden followed suit and were quickly surrounded by guards as the King made his way through the streets, heading in the direction of Boudicca's Iceni.

The vast numbers systematically ransacked the remaining buildings one by one, striking down anyone alive, stealing anything of value and setting the houses alight as they went. Orders from Boudicca were simple, Londinium was to be destroyed and all life extinguished. Carts were loaded with treasures, medicines, and food, and taken to the various camps outside the walls. There they were unloaded and then returned for more as the militia army methodically pushed forward from street to street.

Brawley and his men had busied themselves pillaging Southwark before setting it alight as they waited impatiently for the south gate to finally be captured and opened. The gallant Roman defenders inside continued their gigantean effort to repel the overwhelming indigenous forces, but their valiant defence started to falter and fall as persistent attacking came from all directions.

The situation seemed impossible as it appeared they were trapped with no chance of escape when the *Primus Pilus* or commanding centurion, realised they were close to the south gate. He rallied the troops and ordered them to keep falling back and guided them to the closed and barred gate. It was the only chance for them, perhaps if they could get out, they might have a chance to raise the alarm or perhaps meet up with other cohorts, regroup and start a counter offensive.

They courageously tried to hold back the attacking native forces as they manoeuvred their escape. Many had only their gladius to protect themselves as they battled, but they were a professional army, trained every day in hand-to-hand combat. This training, combined with a deep belief in themselves, their comrades, their legion, and the Empire, meant these dedicated men were a formidable force to be contended with. But the sheer numbers against them meant that they would soon stop being united and it would descend to being a clear case of each man for himself if the primus pilus allowed the discipline to break down. They had reached the south gate. The plan was to try and sneak out and raise the alarm, hopefully to be in time to save what little was left of the walled city.

Brawley was on the bridge with his men when a cheer went up as the gates started to creak and complain as they were being strained open. The battle raged as the gates started to move slowly as they were opened from inside.

Brawley, keen not to let the people opening the gates know of their presence, quickly silenced his men as they waited, eager with anticipation at finally being able to gain access to Londinium, joining the other tribes in liberating the rich bounty inside the walls.

He was not sure who was more surprised as he viewed a gang of Roman soldiers slowly emerging from the opening gates. The Roman commanding the legionaries peered through the smoky mist. The shocking sight of a marauding army, painted in blue symbols, paused like statues, ready for the battle ahead, caused him to stop and lower his sword, partly in shock, as he realised the fight was futile. His action was quickly repeated by the rest of his men as they realised death was fast approaching and impossible to avoid.

Brawley could not help himself gloat as he shouted, "Thank you, centurion for opening the gates." He looked around at his entourage. "It is very kind of you to allow us entry, but why did it take you so long?" he queried sarcastically.

His words were not acknowledged, the primus pilus briefly looked to the skies and gave a short, silent prayer to the gods before ordering his men into a battle formation. The battle was savage but short-lived. The aggressors were not in the position, or frame of mind, to be taking prisoners and both sides were fully aware of this. Every man knew the fight was to the death, and the Thames waters were soon tainted with the blood and bodies of the Roman soldiers.

Boudicca was determined she was not going to miss this fight and had led her group of Iceni house-guards through the streets from the north-west gate. The garrison had been easily overcome as every Roman soldier had been ordered to defend the town. She now had only one goal on her mind, the capture, torture, and ultimate death of the Governor of Londinium.

The Governor's Palace was normally heavily guarded, but it was not long before she was at the gates with the main force of her house-guards. The fighting had been intense, with pockets of resistance offered up by the few crack troops stationed in Londinium, but ultimately it was the sheer numbers and raw aggression that gave the assailants the final advantage.

"I want the Governor *alive*!" she screamed as the last palace guard fell, leaving nothing between her and the palace doors. "Nobody else, just the Governor!"

The horde charged the front doors with a large lump of timber, finally bursting through on the third attempt. The double doors had been barricaded with a heavy metal bar that was hinged on one side and had a retainer on the other. It had been lowered into place behind the doors and locked, but it offered no real security. The mortar it was mounted into crumbled and gave way. The door hinges that had been screwed into the brickwork were simply ripped out. The avenging mass stormed into the building. Slaves could be heard screaming as they ran in all directions, trying to get away and hide from the invaders, but nobody was safe. Axes were thrown into the backs of many, the thud and crack of shattering spines and ribs filled the air along with a fine mist of blood. The screams stopped, as those who were hit dropped to the floor in pools of blood. The invaders surged after them, retrieving the battle weapons by pulling the bloodied blades out of writhing bodies with a single action, as they strode by.

The Governor and his wife looked at each other in silence as they heard the commotion caused by the savage horde as they broke through the front doors. They could hear the screams fall silent as panic raged through the palace, and the sudden death of many innocents. Minerva was shocked at the violence she was hearing but was relieved her darling, precious daughter would not suffer the absolute brutality going on around them and prayed to the gods to keep her safe. Minerva and her husband had made hasty provisions for their departure from this life by ordering the Governor's most trusted servant and slave to attend them. The Governor had instructed the pair that he, and his wife, were going to take poison and that they were not to be taken alive. He had appreciated their dedication, and as a reward for their service, arrangements had been made and papers prepared for their release from bondage. They were to be free citizens of Rome.

The two released servants remained. They knew the gesture was well meant but it would make no difference to their life span. They knew they would be dead at the hands of Boudicca, but obediently attended their former master's bedroom to the rear of the palace. They observed the couple embrace and look deep into each other's eyes. Minerva and her husband grasped a goblet each from the dressing table, each laced with a deadly poison that had been prepared for them. Minerva mouthed, "I love you!" as she offered her goblet to the Governor's lips. He whispered, "Forgive me," as he raised his goblet to her lips. The pair drank the liquid and climbed onto the bed, holding each other tightly as the deadly potion did its work.

Boudicca crossed the threshold of the palace and was immediately outraged, disgusted with the wealth and opulence that was displayed in front her. In her eyes this was stolen, not only from her but all the native people of her land. The more she saw the more enraged she became. As she strode through the palace, she could hear the sound of her own voice echoing in the corridors as she screamed in utter rage, "*Bring me the monster who thinks he owns us!"*

The house-guards ahead of her burst into the inner sanctum of the Governor's bedchamber to be greeted by the sight of the two servants and the dead bodies of the Governor and his wife. Shouting that they had found him. Boudicca broke into a sprint towards the doors and came to a sliding halt as she witnessed the sight.

"No… No… No. No. Nooooo! Seize those two!" she screamed to her house-guards, pointing to the servants. *"Who are they?"* She yelled into the face of one servant.

"My Master and Mistress," the girl sobbed.

"They have children?" Boudicca screamed at the girl. Her rage spilled from her with such force that her spittle splattered the servant's face. The girl shook with fear, which took her voice, all she could do was shake her head.

The second slave blurted out, "They have a daughter."

"Where is she now?" Boudicca bellowed.

The slave shook her head. "I don't know!" she cried. "She is not here. I think she left along with the women and children."

"Women and children? WOMEN AND CHILDREN?" Boudicca was incandescent with rage. *"Our women and children?"* Boudicca was exasperated. *"Get me the kings… NOW!"*

Boudicca breathed heavily as she fought to control her wrath. She raised her hand and pointed to the two servants. "These two… KILL THEM!" she demanded as she looked down upon the scared and trembling pair as they cowered in front of her.

Boudicca steamed out of the palace in a complete rage. How dare she be robbed of her sadistic pleasure of seeing the face of Rome meet his death at her hands. Screaming for retribution, and for her Council, she could not think clearly as she stomped through the corridors and back into the street. The blood lust had overtaken her completely. The job was not done until Londinium was erased both physically and mentally from the population. The order was given, torches passed around as the orders to set the whole establishment alight were carried out. The only people to walk out of the gates were the warriors who had put every living person to the blade.

Chapter Nineteen

The gang of friends trooped south in the footsteps of their comrades. The occasional shout of, "Sinister, Dexter, Sinister, Dexter" from the senior centurions kept the men in time as the miles passed. A loud clunk echoed as every metal-studded leather-booted step touched the Roman road surface in unison with thousands of others. Each stride was the same length as the men's in front, to the side and following behind. Leg muscles were marched and marched for miles every day and were used to the effort, the length and speed of the stride was pure muscle memory.

"I prefer marching with a purpose, it's much better than the everyday training march!" grinned Lucanus.

Marcus glanced to his left and caught the smile on his friend's face as he tutted, "I know why!"

Maxetius could almost hear Lucanus's smirk, "Could it be because you are lazy, and we are marching with a lighter load?!" he quipped.

"I know!" Cato exclaimed. "It is because with every step you are getting closer to death!" he snapped, causing a hushed pause as his words hit a chord with everyone around him. "Good, perhaps now we can get some peace from your irritating comments!" the African growled through gritted teeth.

A sarcastic voice called out, "Aw, don't be like that, I know you love me really!" "The way you tower over me in battle, your scutum held so perfectly over my head, offering some wonderful protection, and keeping those awful missiles away from my precious head," Lucanus parried.

"Well... Until the stupid fool goes and gets stabbed!" Decimus cheerfully pointed out.

"Yes!" Festus turned with a puzzled look, "what exactly did

happen Cato?"

Cato was incensed at the hint of accusation. "Some stupid legionaries in front of me, let the arm of a dirty Celt past their shield!" he snapped, "*They* side-stepped it, neatly avoiding the arm and the bloody blade attached to it, as it thrust forward into me." Cato imagined punching the man responsible in revenge. "Unfortunately, he did not warn the poor guy behind him, *ME!* that a blade was coming in at speed." He paused as he stared into the back of the culprit's head. "Did you Aelianus?!" he growled as he pushed Aelianus's shoulder as they marched in formation.

Aelianus turned his head to look over his left shoulder. "Now, now darling," he tutted. "I did say I was sorry and after all, it was only a flesh wound!"

Cato's face scrunched up as he snarled, "Flesh wound?" He was almost beside himself with anger. "As if your apology makes it any better!" He almost began to hyperventilate with rage as he gasped, "It still stings when I bathe."

"Bathe?" Marcus butted in, "I did not realise you bathed Cato!" he mentioned casually.

"I don't!" snapped the tall soldier. "Not now; thanks to that bloody idiot and this bloody wound!"

"I did not think you bathed much before that!" smirked Decimus.

Cato knew he was not going to win as he reasoned, "You only *think* because you don't know!" His temper was subsiding. "The reason is that I refuse to spend any more of my time with you than I need to!" huffed the African. "Ahh. Is that because you have something to be embarrassed about?" teased Laenus.

The African glanced a puzzled look at him, "What?" Cato was suddenly confused and overwhelmed by the comments flying around. "No... I would not want to show you all up!" he countered as he stared straight ahead.

"Aww. Do you fink you haf sumfink dat would make us

blush?" Festus mocked.

"Well, it did make your mother blush!" Cato retorted in a flash.

A squeaky noise rang out, "Ooooh…" Festus taunted. "Get you Mr. Smart-gob!" He could not stop grinning at Cato's poor retort, "Shame your mother only had a fleeting experience with your father, and she did not catch his name!"

Marcus guffawed, "Well, she was very busy that night!"

Cato flexed his fingers, stretching them out and pulling them into tight fists, "I have something that will make you all bleed profusely if you don't shut up," he growled.

The group smirked and chortled as the tall black soldier started to pout. If Cato wanted to deflect attention, he was going about it the wrong way. The joshing was only going to continue getting worse. The group loved to beaver away if they found a chink in someone's armour; and they had certainly found it with Cato.

Decimus waved his hand in front of his face, pretending to shoo a bug away. "It would be nice to march and not be followed by a swarm of flies from time to time!"

Lucanus reached up and grabbed Decimus's oscillating digits, "Leave them alone. Those flies are Cato's fan club!"

Cato could not take any more, "Right that's it!" he declared as he started to go into full melt down. "One more jibe, go on!" he sneered. "Just one more, and I will not be held responsible," Cato snarled.

Marcus reached out and firmly grasped Cato's shoulder from behind. "Calm down Cato," he soothed. "They were only trying to take all our minds off the news about Camulodunum." As he continued to squeeze Cato's shoulder.

Lucanus realised he had overstepped the mark. "We did not mean any harm by it."

Cato gruffly snorted, "Get off!" as he jerked his body away from Marcus's hand. The message was clear; he did not want any contact. His mind was on his wife and child who had been living in the town when it had been sacked. Marcus let his companion battle with his thoughts and let his hand drop down by his side as he struggled with his own feelings. The silence seemed to last for hours as the march continued. It was eventually broken by the sage voice and words of wisdom that Lucanus always seemed to orate. "I am positive all our families are safe. The gods have protected them, I am positive that I can still feel their souls in my heart."

Cato glanced at his compatriot and observed the sincerity in his eyes. The look reassured him, and he started to calm down. He took a few deep breaths as they maintained eye contact before he nodded his head in agreement as the words swam around in his mind. His bad temper ebbed away and was replaced with his usual cheery persona.

The friends all shared Cato's concerns. Every one of them, apart from Marcus, had wives and small children living in Camulodunum. Every one of them thought of their loved ones. All felt the same way as they each prayed silently and yearned to hear the voices of their loved ones once more.

The hush was broken by a single voice, a voice that was gentle and measured, "Lucanus is right," Festus murmured. "I know my Cecilia and the girls are alive, and I know in my heart they are safe."

Cato was silent as he searched his heart and prayed hard, desperate for some confirmation, some feeling. He slowly came to a grim conclusion "I am not so sure," he gulped. "I cannot feel them. I have prayed to the gods, and I don't think they have heard my prayers or are even listening," Cato declared with a heavy heart as he looked down at his feet while they continued their march.

The legionaries rendezvoused with men from other legions as they continued the march south. All came under the direct command of Suetonius, who only had one thing on his mind - to take on the rebels and destroy them once and for all.

As the legions met, Cato double glanced at some of the

strangers. "I recognise some of those guys!" he said as he nodded his head in the direction of some of the legionaries marching towards them. "They are from the Fourteenth. Keep your eyes on your valuables."

"As if you have never 'lightened somebody's wage pouch' before!" smirked Festus.

Cato's face started to beam as a smile turned the corners of his lips up, "Ahh! all was done fairly," he said as he lifted his finger, making a point, "If you can't follow a ball under a cup, that is hardly my fault, is it?"

Festus grinned and patted him on the shoulder. "You did 'relieve' Albus of three month's wages!" "Luck!" Cato exclaimed as he winked craftily.

Maxetius tutted and rolled his eyes at the memory of the occasion being recounted. "Lucky for you!" he loudly exclaimed, "You nearly got us all on company punishment!"

Cato pondered, "Ahhh, yes!" He put his hand on his chin and looked up at the sky deep in thought. "He never paid up!" he suddenly declared as his face started to light up.

Marcus leaned towards his friend, "Nice to see you smile again." He half whispered in Cato's ear, "It has been a while."

A figure busily marched past. "Hey Albus! What is happening?" Decimus called after the man. "What's the news?"

The figure completely ignored the question as Decimus jumped up, caught up with Albus and started marching alongside him. "Come on Albus, spill the beans!" he pleaded, "I need to know."

The decanus glanced over at his charge, "Are you on a 'Need to Know' list?" Albus probed as he turned his head and looked to the front as he continued to walk. "Oh come on," Decimus begged. "I'll bet you know more than you are letting on," he insisted.

Albus tutted as he glanced at his unwanted companion. "Bet?"

he asserted. "Have you been taking lessons from that bloody Cato?"

Decimus was thrown for a moment. "No!" he blurted, "I mean you... I mean..." He completely lost his train of thought.

"Confused?" Albus announced with a wry smile, "That is why I am YOUR Decanus!" he smirked. "And that is why you do as I say and NOT the other way around!" Albus remarked as he continued on his way. He took a couple of steps, stopped, and spun back around to face the soldier.

"We are heading towards Verulamium," he announced with certainty. "We have it on good authority that this where the Barbarians who have been sacking our towns and slaughtering our people, are heading."

On hearing the news, the remaining seven all looked at each other and one by one their eyes widened, and broad grins broke out over their faces. "Yeeeeeesss!" they cried in unison as they all punched the sky. Albus heard the roar and smiled to himself as he made his way forward. A short time later the order came to set up camp for the night.

The hares that Aelianus had snared earlier, tasted really sweet that night, as the crew sat around their fire. Cato had liberated some wine from the General's supply, which complemented the fresh meat. They polished off the meal with such gusto, no conversations took place as they gulped and rammed the morsels home, sucking the bones clean before throwing them on the fire. Lucanus placed his bowl on the ground, pulled his stomach in and arched his back. As he relaxed, he let out a huge belch. It was so loud numerous bodies from the other fires spun around to identify the noise and the culprit. One by one the gang followed suit as the rubbed and patted their nicely full tummies and belched in various volumes, keys and tempos, much to their own amusement!

Decimus stared into the embers, "I cannot wait to get this over and done with," he stated. "I want to watch the agony on their faces as I twist my blade in their bellies, and watch the life leave them as I pull my gladius from their guts."

His companions watched the dancing flames and one by one they nodded in agreement.

Maxetius picked a twig out of the fire, the tip had just caught alight as he pulled it from the flames and tapped it impatiently the ground. "I can't wait to put them to my sword," he snarled.

"Show them the mercy they have shown to our families!" agreed an aggrieved Cato.

The men all turned in, but little sleep was had. The excitement of the forthcoming battle and taking revenge for the Roman dead on these tribes, especially on their female leader, occupied their minds.

Chapter Twenty

Boudicca's temper consumed her whole being, she was incandescent with rage that just would not subside. She was furious that the Governor of Londinium had taken his own life. The man had denied her the pleasure of seeing him beg for mercy for his wife's life. She had planned to make him watch her cruelly tear his wife's guts out in front of him. She had wanted to witness the man's mental anguish and pain before inflicting physical pain upon him, hearing him beg, plead, and scream as she killed him slowly.

The house-guards followed her dutifully as she turned her back on the bodies and crashed out of the chamber. She screamed, slashed at the walls with her sword, kicked furniture and destroyed objects in her way as she finally stumbled out of the palace. As soon as she hit the fresh air her whole demeanour changed immediately as she viewed the devastation around her. Boudicca paused, drew a deep breath and looked to the heavens as her house-guards caught up with her. The group made their way towards the gates of the city, carefully picking their way through the burning buildings. They were joined by some of the raiders and hailed by others, who continued executing their orders as the great Queen passed by. All her entourage were very aware of her orders, and they stabbed and slashed at lifeless bodies as they passed, just to double check that they were dead.

War chariots were unceremoniously piled up with bounty. Carts and wagons, that once belonged to the now dead people of Londinium, were loaded with provisions and treasures from the mass of destroyed properties. Boudicca wanted to make sure that all her men and accompanying families had plenty to eat and drink. She knew that they were better fighters and happier men with full stomachs and full goblets! The wine and mead ran freely that evening as the camps celebrated the victory and commemorated the fallen.

Boudicca was still seething with rage, it boiled inside her as the Druid priests performed the rites for the dead and lit the pyres for the deceased. Families of those who had lost their lives in the sacking of Londinium gathered as they said their last farewells to fathers, husbands and sons as the souls journeyed to join their forefathers. The pyres burned long into the night as the tribes continued to revel in the glory of the past days, eventually greeted by the rising sun as dawn arrived.

Boudicca had taken her leave and rested for a few hours before she emerged and ordered her house-guards to summon the Kings for a meeting over the first meal of the day. Some of the gathered group of chieftains were indifferent to hearing the plan of what was coming next. Several had privately thought and even mooted the idea of leaving the uprising. The thought of ridding the lands of the invading force was the reason they were there, the bounties were obviously a bonus, but the fact that they were executing women and children was difficult to take. Each was a warrior king, and as such, was starting to look ahead to a time when the Romans had gone. It was obvious to all that a power vacuum would be created, but should Boudicca and the Iceni fill the void and continue to control all the (for now) united tribes?

Each tribe had a different answer! The fact Boudicca was a woman only added to their frustration, plus a certain amount of distrust was starting to show as each King believed he was not being favoured in the same way the others seemed to be. Jealousy is a powerful emotion, and each King had his own personal reasons why he should take over the role of 'Overall Commander' of the combined forces instead of the Iceni and their Queen. One by one they started asking themselves what her ultimate goals were, and more importantly, who exactly would benefit from them?

For now, all acknowledged they had taken an oath, and appreciated that the only way to rid the land of the Roman invaders for good was collusion and cooperation with the other tribes.

The chiefs were talking to each other in a tight group, Boudicca was very astute and could sense the tension as she breezed into the room for the gathering. "Thank you all for coming this morning," she began a with a disarming smile. "I know it is early, and I know we are all tiring from the recent trials and onslaughts." She continued as she wandered around the group. Boudicca would touch, smile, or wink at each as she passed. Boudicca was a battle-hardened fighting general, she could outthink, outmanoeuvre, and outfight many a man, but she also was also very aware of the effect her womanly charm had on each of them. When she turned on her charisma, they became putty in her hands. Just a kind word and flirtatious smile and these men were all enchanted and were under her spell, under her command. Her will would be done. She knew when a kind word or a coy smile was more powerful than a sword, and she knew exactly how to push the buttons on these mere, weak men. A woman's ability to convey an aura of helplessness, of weakness, a need to be protected, had worked for time immemorial, and the tactic would continue to be worked as an advantage for all eternity.

"These vile invaders are easier targets that I ever imagined they would be," Boudicca sighed, almost as if she bored by the lack of resistance. "We are sacking their towns, spilling their blood." She read the expressions and body language of the group as she spoke with an air of authority. "Blood lines have been stopped with the spilling of their blood and the blood of their loved ones," raising her voice with the rhetoric. "They are powerless to stop us!" She slammed her palm on the centre table as she turned theatrically to face the chiefs. "WE ARE VICTORIOUS!"

Brawley could not contain himself, his temper snapped as he retorted, "Do you really think the total force of the Roman Empire was in these sacked towns?" He could feel himself start to tremble with anger as he made his opinion clear. "They have crack troops here in this country, but they are all in the north of our lands." Brawley was not normally a passionate orator, but his anger and frustration exploded as he kicked the table and growled. "These are hollow victories, victories against second rate troops and innocents. Victories that have happened because we greatly outnumbered the, the... *PREY*!" He stared directly at Boudicca as he bellowed, "We are stirring up a wasps' nest."

Boudicca spun on her heels. "Crack troops?" she retorted with disgust, incredulous at the claim. "Such as the much revered Ninth Legion?" she interjected sarcastically as she shrugged her shoulders. "The so called 'Legio IX Hispana'?" she hissed. "The infamous Spanish legion that carried the coveted Eagle standard of the Emperor?" She snarled, "Soon to be known as 'THE DEFEATED LEGION'?" Boudicca paused as she closely examined each man's face before turning back to Brawley, "You know, the 'crack legion' that we destroyed... Brawley?" Boudicca growled sarcastically into his face.

She rocked back, took a very deep breath, and looked away as she gathered her senses before she aggressively spun round to face the gathering and addressed one person in particular. "My dear Brawley," she bellowed as she looked him directly in the eye, "Are you saying you no longer have the fight in your belly?"

Brawley took offence at the accusation and looked coldly at the Queen. "I have never walked away from a fight, as you well know." He steadied his temper before continuing, "But my fight is with the Roman invaders, not with the innocents, killing women and children is *not* what I, or my nation, signed up to."

Boudicca tutted as she threw her head back, her auburn hair whipped round and slapped her back. "Innocents?" she exclaimed, "Innocents?" Her voice was rising in pitch and volume. "My daughters were innocent!" she howled. "Were they shown any compassion when they were being raped and then beaten by these degenerates in full view of my people?"

The room fell silent as the words caused every man present to hang his head. Some of those gathered shook their heads slowly at the revelation as she continued, "Have our people been shown any benevolence as they were being murdered?" Tears welled up in Boudicca's eyes and started to roll down her cheeks, "What benevolence was I shown by these 'men' when they did this?" Boudicca's voice trembled as her fists reached up towards her neck. Her hands grasped the top of her shirt and ripped it apart as she turned her back on the Kings, only to reveal the terrible red scars all over her back. The room gasped in unison at the horrific sight before them.

Boudicca covered her body as she marched over to Brawley. Their noses nearly touched as she barked in his face, "This is not over Brawley, believe me." Her breathing was very erratic as the anger raged inside her. "Do you wish to make an enemy of me?" she hissed as she stared, unblinkingly, into the man's eyes.

A sheepish Brawley looked away and bowed his head. "No," he whispered like a child who had been scolded. "I gave my word that my people will follow you and rid our lands of this invader." He slowly looked up at the Queen, looking for her approval as he continued, "I stand by my word, my support remains."

Boudicca added a proviso, "At any cost Brawley, the only way to end the Roman occupation must be at any cost." Brawley thought for a second before he nodded and repeated, "At any cost."

Boudicca nodded her approval at Brawley's confirmation of the continued support from his tribe. "Gentlemen, this is not over. We are not finished," her voice calmed as a smile turned the corner of her thin red lips upwards.

Volisios rose to his feet and spoke out, "We are going to be facing the full force of the Roman Empire soon. I fear we will never be at peace."

Boudicca looked hard into her allies' eyes, "Dear, dear Volisios, I hear your words, but ask yourself this, have we ever been truly at peace?" Her piercing blue eyes drilled through to his very soul. "Will the lives of your people be harmonious after you are dead?"

The man thought hard as Boudicca continued, filling the silence, "The answer is NO!" She enforced her observation with a shake of her head as she spoke gently, "Your lands will be taken, your children will be abandoned and your people will be turned off their land, is that what you want?" Volisios shook his head along with Boudicca as he unconsciously participated in a masterful lesson in mind control. The Queen continued her oratorial performance. "Of course, it is not my friend, we will remove Rome from our lands, from our lives and the lives of our future generations." Boudicca paused dramatically and she listened to the silence in the room before she continued, "Our children and their children, who will be free to find peace without interference." She released her grip as she stepped back and looked around the room. Her eyes fell upon the one ally among the group who had remained silent. "How about you Donnchad?" she asked as she walked towards the man who was leaning against a post, concealed in the darkness among the shadows. "You were childhood friends with my dear husband. Do you feel reluctant to continue?" Boudicca asked her closest supporter.

Donnchad stood up straight, unfurled his arms, and paced the tent in silence, deep in thought for what seemed like ages. "Boudicca," he said as he turned to her and bowed his head. "We are all friends and allies here. We have all been behind you and supported you," he began sagely. "We have all shared in the victories and the glories of the battles. Our peoples have fought hard and have benefited from the spoils." The tall man raised his eyes to the heavens, closed his eyes and drew a deep breath as he reflected on the last few months. He continued, "We have profited from the attacks you have planned and executed against the Romans. We all want to see them evicted our land." He strode about with his hands clasped firmly behind his back; a look of contemplation etched across his face. "Our friends fear that retribution will destroy us all; that our peoples will either be slaughtered or made slaves in retribution by the might of Rome."

Boudicca seized on the words and knew how to spin their fears and keep the men on her side. "That is exactly why we must make sure that we continue this campaign and see them off our shores!" she countered cleverly. "There will be NO FAILURE!"

Volisios jumped up, "We are talking about the Roman Empire. *They* will not simply give up," he screamed. "Even if we destroy the legions and their families on our lands, the Romans…" He was desperate to make his views heard, "They will simply keep coming back and back, this will *never* end!"

"Volisios!" barked Boudicca. Her voice immediately stopped him in his tracks and silenced him. The man, quite sensibly, could tell from her body language that the leader in chief was not in a mood for polite discussion, as she continued through gritted teeth, "The fate of the Corieltauvi was put into doubt the moment you signed the treaty with Rome." Her words growled in an almost unhuman tone. "Now *you* have underlined your fate the moment you encouraged your men to raise your swords." Boudicca paused briefly as she threw an accusing look at every chieftain before focusing on Volisios. "What has been done cannot be undone!"

The Queen pulled herself to her full height and drew a breath that filled her lungs to bursting, then she continued, "We have all assigned the fate of our people, our kin, our kingdoms to this fight. The moment we began our righteous uprising against the tyranny of Rome, we all knew what we were getting into." Boudicca was on a roll, "But it is better to die a free people rather than suffer under the tyranny of this evil Empire." She worked the room expertly and drew from the collective energy as she recognised the positive reception from even the most hardened of doubters. "Now let's finish this, once and for all. We move to the north and attack Verulamium."

One individual was dismayed at the revelation. "But Verulamium is a peaceful Celtic trading town," Brawley pointed out.

"It is a ROMAN town!" Boudicca bellowed as she corrected the chieftain. Her fists violently thumped on the table around which many of the Kings were sitting. "With Romans in it..." she stated as she looked into the eyes of each man in turn. "It has enormous wealth." She paused to let the news sink in, "And my spies tell me that the armouries in the town have been making and stockpiling all the weapons to supply the Ninth, the Fourteenth and the Seventh Legions, all of which are based on our lands." She leaned in towards the seated men. "If *we* have their weapons..." she ventured, "What are they going to use to fight us?" Boudicca purposefully started to walk around the men again, "Just think on this." She paused and smiled, "How sweet will it be to see them die at the hand of their own javelins, their swords, their crossbows?" A look of sadistic pleasure creased her face as the vision of the slaughter and ultimate victory crossed her mind. "As we attack them with *their* shields and weapons?"

The room was silent for what seemed an eternity before Volisios rose to his feet and spoke. "I am Volisios, King of the Corieltauvi. My father was King and his father before him. My son will be King of the Corieltauvi, and he will die, like me, King of my people." The man stood tall as he exclaimed, "Not as a puppet of Rome!" Volisios slowly and meaningfully strode over to Boudicca. In a powerful, visual statement he held out his hand as he looked into her piercing blue eyes. "I offer my hand in eternal friendship and I pledge my house-guards and warriors to be at your command."

Boudicca grasped his hand and placed her other hand on top as their eyes watched intently for any wavering, as deep down neither entirely trusted the other. Each believed they were better than the other but realised they depended on each other as they battled the common enemy to achieve a common goal. Smiles broke out across the surrounding leaders as their hands locked, the remaining Kings rose to their feet and moved around the table behind Volisios, queueing to do the same, keen to reaffirm the pledges they had made to the Iceni Queen.

Donnchad was the last in line and observed the unplanned

ritual as it played out before him. He slowly viewed all the other faces around him before he loudly declared, "I also reconfirm my allegiance to you, Queen Boudicca, until we finally have peace among us."

Boudicca reached out her hands and clasped Donnchad's right fist in her fingers, "Thank you my dear friend." She smiled as she shook his hand, "That means a lot to me and to our peoples."

On Boudicca's orders, food and drink was brought into the room as they all retook their seats. The discussions continued for hours as they talked through the plans to move the army and its supporters north to take the next Roman target.

Jannon, still very traumatised by some of the sights he had witnessed, made his way wearily towards Mardina and the wagon she had successfully made into a quite comfortable home. His clothes were damp and stained with sweat, spattered with a mixture of blood and grime and he reeked of burning. Jannon had scaled the walls with the second wave, rather than being just a ladder bearer this time and he had followed the assault through Londinium. His sword, which his late father had presented to him, had seen action in this raid and needed a bit of attention. It had collected several nicks in the blade, battle souvenirs caused by crashing and smashing into other iron blades during the violent and furious hand-to-hand fighting.

He had acquired a couple of Roman gladius swords and had carried them back with him as souvenirs. He was going to let the two boys have them, but he was a bit perplexed after seeing the pair charging after Donnchad. The fighting had been a hard strenuous onslaught. The Britons had battled relentlessly as they forced the defending guards back and into total annihilation. The combat is always harder and more perilous than the reports reveal afterwards. His whole body ached, and the smell of death and the fires that had been lit as Londinium fell, filled his nostrils.

Jannon could feel his energy leave him as the adrenalin, that had given him almost superhuman power, was replaced with lactic acid. His whole body was hurting and cramping. He could barely lift each foot as he slowly approached the two boys, who had seen him coming and had run forward to greet him.

"Father!" Aiden loudly exclaimed as he threw his arms around the man, and pulled him into a tight hug, making the man groan in agony.

"Hi boys!" he grimaced, "how was your battle!?"

Jannon could have screamed as pains shot around his body with every slight touch but hid it as best as he could. "You obviously had an adventure, judging by your smiles!" he exclaimed as he rubbed Aiden's hair and smiled at Olive. "And you obviously brought our King some luck!" Jannon casually announced.

"Yes Jannon," Oliver announced eagerly. "We witnessed some of the battle first hand, but the house guards stayed so close we could barely see a thing, but the noise was deafening!" Oliver continued, eager for Jannon to say some more, hoping he would reveal gory tales of danger while recounting stories of heroics.

Mardina could see the pain in in Jannon's eyes. He was desperate not to reveal his agony, but Mardina knew why he looked so pained. "Now boys, leave Father alone," She requested as she smiled kindly, while she too made her way towards her husband. The look on her face was one of sheer joy and relief, as she had believed she would never lay her eyes on his smiling face or feel the warmth of his gentle touch ever again. She felt as if a part of her died when she watched him walk into the distance and finally disappear with the other men that made up the militia. Later she had had to deal with the boys being hijacked by the King. The pair wrapped their arms around each other and pulled each other close, their lips touching gently.

"Aww… Father... Mother!" exclaimed Aiden in disgust as both

boys looked away in embarrassment.

Jannon jolted himself awake; his subconsciousness remained on high alert as he slumbered on the makeshift bed that Mardina had made in the back of the cart. It was just as well he slept so lightly as the house-guards strode through the camp, rousing all the men and calling them to arms as they did so.
Boudicca's reputation and rumours of the success of the resistance to the Roman occupation had spread far and wide and were rising. Warriors, men, women, whole families abandoned villages and homesteads to join the rebellion. A force numbering hundreds of thousands was on the move. All heading with a sinister purpose. All heading towards the next objective, to annihilate… Verulamium.

The main thing the whole camp was getting better at with every move, was breaking camp and being ready to move at a moment's notice. Oliver and Aiden helped Mardina pack everything onto the wagon and prepared to move on, while Jannon attended the meeting that had been called by his chief.

Oliver aimlessly looked up to the skies as he helped loading the wagon. "I am glad these long days of summer are dry," he remarked out of the blue. "Just imagine how much fun this would be in the wet!"

Aiden shuddered at the thought. "Brrr, all that cold air, freezing water and mud everywhere," he shivered, "It does not bear thinking about. I hate it when you get really soaked. The wet chills you to the core and you just cannot warm up."

Oliver nodded sombrely. "We learned about a war that happened. It dragged on and on." He paused as the horrific images he had seen on fading sepia photographs and black and white flickering film of the fallen and dead from the First World War, the 'Great War'. The photos portrayed a real, living hell on earth. A hellish realm that men, millions of men, were caught up in, witnessing and unable to avoid the horror. Oliver tried to choose his words carefully, "These two gigantic armies faced each other and battled for months. The two sides were quite evenly matched, and it eventually became a stalemate." Oliver could see that Aiden was transfixed by the story as he continued, "Both sides 'dug in', opposing each other and created massive defensive trenches that spread out over hundreds of miles. Winter came and all the land quickly turned to thick cold mud. The trenches filled with water, so the men could never get properly dried or clean."

Aiden was mesmerised and listened intently but did not really understand what Oliver was trying to tell him. "Why did they not wait for the rain to stop?" Aiden wondered. He found the whole idea preposterous.

Oliver pondered the point for a moment, "I really don't know." He was not sure if Aiden was joking or not, "Well, because if one side got up and left, the war would have been lost I suppose!"

Aiden scratched his head, turned away and carried on pottering about, but his mind kept returning to Oliver's last statement. "How long did this war go on for?" he asked casually as he went about his duties. "Four years."

Aiden stopped dead in his tracks. "Four years!" he loudly exclaimed. "No fighting season lasts for four whole years. You are wrong, even I know the war season ends in the last quarter!" he laughed, "Four *years*!"

"It is true." Oliver exclaimed, "We don't have 'fighting seasons'," he countered. "We have big wars that last until one side or the other wins. We don't stop for tea you know!"

Aiden shrugged and tutted, "You gods are definitely a funny lot!"

Oliver decided to leave the conversation at that. He had forgotten that Aiden and the rest of the tribe thought he was sent from the gods.

Jannon trudged wearily back to the family from the group meeting. He had bumped into one of their neighbours from home and shared a flagon of mead with him before he finally found his way back to the wagon. He patted the boys' heads as he wandered past and crept up behind Mardina, threw his arms around her waist and planted a wet, smacking kiss on her cheek as she tried to turn around to face him. "The rumours are true," Jannon mumbled. "We are moving on to Verulamium..." He let go of his wife and she finally spun to face him. Her eyes were smiling at the thought of his words. A smile broke across Mardina's face she wrapped her arms around his neck and kissed him. "And then we will be going home?" she asked hopefully.

Jannon paused, "Yes, well we are close to wiping the Romans out." He smiled, with a hint of relief in his voice. "We are moving to take and the destroy the town," he shrugged his shoulders. "We are going take the treasure from the tax collectors based there, and more importantly, take the weapons the Romans have stored in the armoury." A grin appeared on his face. "If *we* have their weapons, they will not be able to keep us under their rule!" Jannon looked towards the heavens, "Then Donnchad said we will be near to our homesteads so it looks as if the wars may be over." He smiled as his eyes caught Mardina's.

The boys overheard the conversation. "Not four years then?!" Aiden smiled as he nudged Oliver in the ribs with his elbow.

"Four years? What are you talking about?" enquired Jannon.

Aiden tutted, "Oliver said armies fought for four years where he came from."

Jannon took a double look at his son, "Wow. I am glad I am not a god. I am tired out after a couple of months!"

The warrior Queen was surprised to hear the news from her scouts. They had been sent forward to Verulamium to report on the number and positions of the guards protecting the town. She could not believe her ears at the news that came back. "Are you sure?" she quizzed.

The house-guard kept his head bowed, "Yes, my lady. The town is almost empty. The news of the attack on Londinium has reached Verulamium and many have left. There is a small guard made up of old service men on the gates to the town, but much of it is empty. The people seem to have simply disappeared."

A second scout continued with the report. "We believe they have left for other towns further away from Londinium. Others, we believe, have simply dispersed, and vanished into the countryside."

Boudicca contemplated the news as she paced around her tent, "Are you sure this is not a trick?" she demanded.

The pair shook their heads. "NO! It is most definitely almost deserted!" they insisted.

Boudicca strode around her maps and tables, so deep in her thoughts that she did not hear Donnchad enter the tent and catch the news. He cleared his throat, the sound broke Boudicca's train of thought. She looked over to her old friend, "I suppose you heard the report?

Donnchad nodded as she spoke. "Yes," he replied. 'I am not sure, though," he paused, "This, this could be a trap." He asked, "How do we know if the information is correct?" Boudicca froze as if she was in a trance as she considered the King's reply. He studied her pose and jumped as she suddenly took a deep breath and raised her hands up and clasped them behind her head. Her eyes were firmly closed as the numerous possibilities tumbled around her brain and she became motionless once more. Boudicca suddenly dropped her hands by her side and took a deep breath. "Right then, we know what to do!" she suddenly blurted out as she clapped her hands together and rubbed them hard. "We rush the town by force and confiscate the toys in the armoury before the place is eradicated!" She smirked as she ordered her house-guards, 'Spread the word and gather the Kings." She turned towards her friend, "This will be the easiest victory to date, I can feel it!"

Her guards carried out her request to gather the commanders and the Kings while she and Donnchad shared a meal as they reminisced and talked fondly of her late husband. The exchange moved her at times, but the warmth of Donnchad's words brought her comfort and provided a pleasant distraction from the fighting and war.

The dialogue was disrupted with the arrival of the Kings and numerous house guards. They had received her request, and all attended the Queen at her invitation. Among the group were some new faces. Word of Boudicca and her successful uprising against the now detested Romans had spread far and wide. The account of the Queen's punishment and the violence her daughters had endured at the hands of the Romans was fast becoming legendary. Many knew a similar fate awaited their own tribes if they did not act. With many other tribes rising and revolting, now was the time. The tribes were all united by a single cause. Driving the Romans out gave them all a sense of solidarity.

The gathered force listened intently to the plan for the attack. Most of the details imitated the previous attacks. Boudicca went through the details in great depth, not just for the sake of the new members but to also ensure everyone was in the picture and so ensure that the assault was to be faultless. Objectives had been explained, and targets identified. The strike was designed to create as much destruction and damage with the minimum loss to the raiding force. The massed army was to move out at the closure of the meeting and head north.

Once again, the army was to camp in plain sight of the town, make lots of noise, burn fires and move about to ensure the inhabitants would be riled and a sense of panic would prevail. The timing was the key again as there were to be attacks on all sides at once. It was tried and tested and had proved to be extremely efficient for the rebel militia.

Distribution of the bounties and provisions had been agreed and the captured equipment was to be shared equally with the eventual victors. The question was raised about the welfare of the women and children that were bound to be present.

Boudicca's reply was brash and direct. Her retort shocked

some of the new faces as she justified and reinforced her words by explaining that only hard-core Romans remained in the town. Her spies had confirmed that those who did not oppose their struggles had escaped the tyranny of the Roman Empire by leaving the town.

The rebel army moved at a swift pace and set the camps around the perimeter of Verulamium, once again just out of reach of the Roman artillery and set about taunting the souls inside the boundary walls. Walls that should have given protection for those contained within but would soon be overrun by the sheer numbers at Boudicca's command. As night fell the Iceni Queen gathered the Kings and commanders prior to the final assault and ran through operation ahead, updating all of them with minute details before dismissing them and allowing them to organise their own men.

Finally, the moment approached, Boudicca ordered her gathered men forward. "The Kings all know the plan," she declared at the top of her voice. "Give the word and let's get this over and done with!" she shouted as she mounted her war chariot. She gathered the reins in her hands, grabbed a spear and raised it above her head and screamed out, "By the grace of the gods, Verulamium will not be left standing!" The words were met with a huge cheer from the two hundred thousand Britons as the assault began.

Boudicca was correct. The town was soon ransacked, relieved of all its provisions, its population slaughtered, and the buildings razed to the ground. The buildings were left ablaze as the great army turned its back and left it far behind. The rebels were like a plague of locusts, leaving nothing behind but devastation and dust.

Chapter Twenty-One

The sun shone brightly and glinted off the highly polished imperial helmets and the shoulder protection. The metallic points of the pila and javelins reflected the sun's full rays, creating beams that fired into the darkness of the woods surrounding the Roman road.

Festus held his hand up in front of his face, "What's that bright disc up there in the sky?" he questioned as he protected his eyes from the sun's bright light.

"Ohhhh, hold on Festus..." Decimus replied eagerly, "I recognise it, I think it's called, err..." he pondered, "No, don't tell me...!" He paused for a moment, "It's on the tip of my tongue."

Marcus had also raised his hand to shield the bright light from his eyes, "Ahh yes, I am not sure, but I think it could be the ... sun!"

"You know, I think you could be right!" Laenus agreed with a big grin.

Lucanus threw his head back to allow the rays to warm his face, "Nice to see a bit of sun. I was beginning to think the gods had abandoned us," he stated as a smile brightened his face. "Oh, Apollo! Oh, how I love you!"

Cato could feel his mood lift with every step in the glorious sunlight. "I am glad we have our focalia around our necks. I don't know about you guys, but it stops the sweat running down my back," he sighed. "At least it stops the armour chafing my neck. I will never get used to that."

The gang were all secretly relieved to hear Cato's words, not only because he was right and it was nice to have the sun's golden rays beat down on their faces, but because the friend they all admired and held in high esteem, was back with them in body and soul and was obviously feeling better.

Lucanus looked over to the gang on his right. "Thank the

gods!" he grinned.

"Sorry?" Cato asked, "Did you say something?"

Lucanus glanced back and pointed to his chest, "Who, me?"

"If it was not you, it must have been a ghost that has your voice!" Cato quipped.

Lucanus looked up to the skies again as he retraced his thoughts, "Oh yeah, I was just thinking how nice it is to have my brother back." He nodded. "Rather than the miserable big fellow that we have had invading your space in our tent," he grinned, much to the amusement of the others.

Cato looked around and burst into laughter, his rich, deep, booming voice travelled up and down the columns as they marched.

The stomp of every man's foot as it hit the ground, the rattle of every man's protective mail and the clunking of the body armour was amplified thousands of times and reverberated around the trees. The sight of thousands of highly trained, and heavily armed troops marching along the road known as Watling Street was something to behold and was guaranteed to strike fear into any enemy.

Suetonius had just received the news of Londinium and the recent sacking of Verulamium. He was aware that the rebels had stolen all the weapons they could carry. His spies had also informed him that the rabble was heading right towards them and were itching for a final conflict.

The main question that occupied Suetonius was not how he was going to destroy them, but where. He needed to find somewhere that gave him the advantage and had sent out teams on horseback to survey the land in order to identify the perfect place to launch an attack. He needed a place that gave him the high ground. It was easier to fight going down a hill than it was fighting uphill. Being on the high ground would also give arrows and javelins a longer reach than those being fired upwards! He also wanted an area that narrowed into a valley, so Boudicca's men would be funnelled towards him. This meant the numbers would be even to begin with so he could kill as many as they could without risking his troops. The valley needed to widen out behind so that he could push the rebels back to allow his cavalry to come into play. He would be able to widen his lines and then outflank these upstarts and wipe them out for good. The enemy would be forced back into the open, allowing his men to draw them in. Even a natural barrier like a lake or a cliff would be useful. Suetonius knew a natural barrier could double the strength on the outer flanks. He did not mind whether it was a lake, or cliff, river, or marsh, as long as wherever it was, he could create an advantage.

He commanded the Fourteenth and Twentieth legions as well as a cohort from the Ninth. Together with his cavalry his army numbered about ten thousand. His spies had told him that Boudicca commanded one hundred thousand souls and might be nearing two hundred thousand. They may be considered 'just simple farmers' as well as women and children, but Suetonius knew his enemy. He knew they had chariots, cavalry, and well-trained soldiers. They may have lacked the finesse of the Roman guard, but they were determined, well-armed and highly motivated, a combination that made them very dangerous.

The General was clad in his gold decorated armour. He rode his stallion with his two high-ranking Legatus Legionis alongside him. As they rode, they discussed the finer points of the land before them and the forthcoming battle, which was becoming ever more inevitable. One of his scouting parties galloped towards them, pulled up and excitedly described an area they had identified that lay about fourteen miles ahead. The cavalry rider manoeuvred his horse around, kicked his mount forward and the Commanders followed suit.

To the surprise of Suetonius, they were right. The area ahead of the force was perfect. As he surveyed the open space, he described what he had in mind to his officers. The force was to continue forward and when it was at the point where the road opened out, the first five cohorts, and only the first five cohorts, were to stand with one in the centre and two on either side. They were to halt and hold their positions while the remaining cohorts and cavalry were to remain hidden. When the rebels showed themselves, the order would be given for four further cohorts to move forward and reveal themselves. This would give the illusion of him having a larger force than he really had.

On the cornua and tuba calls, the centre cohort was to move forward and create an equilateral triangle, its centre point facing the enemy. The next call would be the signal for the rear cohorts to move forward at a steady pace and fan out. When they drew parallel to the blocks of cohorts on either side, all were to move forward in unison. The triangle would split the enemy into two separate armies as they charged. At this point the flanking sides were to move in and surround the divided mass and compact them into a tight area, creating two killing zones. All this would be happening while the mighty Roman Emperor's standards flew above them so the dying would have no doubt who the victors were as they were being slain.

Oliver found himself moving forward with the tribes. Suetonius was not the only leader who had spies. Boudicca had learned of the large Roman force moving south and she knew that this was going to the final showdown. Boudicca was to face the Governor General of Britannia, the Emperor's champion, the foe the Druid priests had foretold would come. This would be her chance to get rid of him and the Romans forever. She had her huge army, far outnumbering that of the Roman General, and she was making plans to finally destroy the invaders once and for all. The tribes were all swept up in the moment, excited and desperate to witness the Romans being defeated on a perfect late summer's day, with warmth in the ground, glorious sunshine, and bright blue skies.

Oliver silently observed the hordes, listening to the light-hearted banter of the spectators and the trained armed men as they casually mingled together. Oliver jumped up on to a cart and threw his arms out as he balanced himself precariously and stood up. He looked forward and all he could see was a line of people, carts and mounted men stretching to and disappearing over the horizon. Oliver turned around slowly, there were at least six or eight columns of people on either side of him. He could feel goosepimples as he continued turning and could see the column stretching into the distance behind them. He had never witnessed so many people gathered in one place before. He had completely forgotten that he had learnt the result of the battle in history lessons at school.

The Roman front ranks filed into the opening and took up their positions. The eight friends stood firmly in the very centre of the first cohort. The mighty Ninth was still the pride of Rome, despite a large number of their colleagues disappearing from the face of the earth, and the eagle standard with them. The friends were proud of the uniform they wore, and all felt honoured to be serving their Emperor. They were standing shoulder to shoulder with their close comrades as the adrenalin started to flow through their veins. They were to have the privilege of leading the fight.

Decimus tilted his head back and exaggeratedly sniffed the air, "They're getting near, I can definitely smell the stink of their filthy bodies."

Albus noticed the front and second rows tilting their heads back and drawing in the air through their nostrils. "Hey, hey, hey. What on earth are you all playing at?" Marcus could not help himself. "Seeing if we can smell the scum as Decimus can."

Albus tutted at the comedic routine playing out in front of him, "Never mind all that, put your hands in your money pouches. Come on. Hand over all your monies, you know the custom."

The group all dug deep and every single one grumbled as they fished their coins out and tossed them into Albus' pot.

They did not have to wait long. No sooner had Albus taken the cash to the legion's actuaries, the administrator of wages and pensions, than the first of Boudicca's force started to make themselves visible, taking up their positions, jeering as they prepared for the forthcoming conflict.

The tens and tens of thousands of house-guards, warriors and volunteers moved forward in front of the spectators - the women, the children, the old and frail, sending them to the rear to find the best vantage points so they could see the action clearly. After all, when the Romans were finally slaughtered, they wanted to see every detail.

Oliver and Aiden were excited beyond words. They stood with Jannon towards the centre of Donnchad's army. The King once again had insisted the boys be near him for the final combat. The Iceni, Trinovantes, Catuvellauni and the Corieltauvi charioteers and horsemen all stood shoulder to shoulder in a slight curve with the Iceni in the centre front and the numerous newer additions to the force were out on the peripheries.

General Gaius Suetonius Paulinus rode slowly and purposefully up and down the ranks of the Roman Legionaries, with his back arched and his head held high. He looked like a god in his gold body armour and golden plumed helmet. Every man felt as if the General was staring directly at him personally and as he spoke pride swelled in their chests. He was eager to remind them who they were, their job as defenders of Rome and doing the Emperor's bidding.

"There!" he gestured towards Boudicca's force, "Finally… You see before you the mob who MURDERED YOUR FRIENDS, YOUR WOMEN, YOUR CHILDREN." He paused as he felt the rage and anger growing in his men. He needed them to have a blood lust, a red rage, and be so riled up that they would release such a vicious first strike on the mob facing them that it would decimate the opposition and make them run for the hills. Suetonius knew the numbers were not in his favour. His men were outnumbered by more than ten to one! Although he considered the rebels as an untrained, poorly armed rabble, they had a huge numeric advantage which he had to overcome.

Suetonius gestured at the tribes as loudly declared, "These are ANIMALS!" His words were having the desired effect as he watched the hate grow on the faces of his men. "They will suffer under our might, our courage and will be vanquished!" he hollered. "The gods are with us. The enemy will crumble under our power." Suetonius took a deep breath, gripped Apollo with his knees and shortened the reins on his horse's bridle to keep him under control, as he bellowed, "THE POWER OF ROME!" The shout caused the fine beast to rear up. Apollo's front hooves then thumped heavily back down on the ground,

Suetonius's rousing cry to battle was almost lost in the huge roar that materialised from the soldiers in front of him as they punched the air over their heads, their fists wrapped around swords or pila and javelins. Some banged the hand guards of their swords against the chest plates of their armour. Ten thousand men made a noise that would terrify the gods.

Boudicca stood on the footwell of her chariot, impassive for a moment, taking in the sight that was unravelling before her and watching the antics of the mounted figure. She started to laugh at the sight of a figure dressed as peacock as he fought to even keep the beast below him still. 'The arrogance of Rome will be their downfall,' she thought to herself. After all she had the huge number advantage and her force had grown exponentially with every victory. Boudicca took a deep breath and urged her ponies forward with a flick of the reins. The pair moved obediently at her command. As they did so they were pulled round and she trotted the pair parallel to the rows of gathered tribes. As the chariot moved, she looked at her men, nodding her approval as she did so. When she reached the end, she turned and rode back to the centre and stopped. With her back to the Romans, she threw her head back, filled her lungs and screamed at the top of her voice.

"See this 'Glory of Rome'?" she began. "Is this all they can muster?" She paused to take another deep breath, "These are the thieves who have robbed our lands and murdered our loved ones." Boudicca looked at the men and started to drive the chariot along the line again. She wanted all to hear her words. "Put these usurpers to the blade," she yelled, "KILL… KILL… KILL…!" Her rhythmic chant was soon echoed by her armies and the spectators, filling the whole area with their voices.

Boudicca's provoking and emotive speech raised the blood and determination of her troops to new levels and the horde screamed their approval. They raised spears, drew swords from their scabbards and stamped their feet on the ground. Nearly two hundred thousand feet stomping on the ground made a such a cacophony of noise it would throw the fear of the gods into any man, but would it have that reaction on a drastically outnumbered Roman army?

Suetonius addressed his officers, "Gentlemen, let us get this day done and erase this irritant once and for all!" He sank his heels into Apollo's sides and urged his mount forward.

The officer in charge of the Ninth cohort, Septimus, came riding over, "Ninth Cohort - *Wedge*!" The order was repeated and echoed through the legions via the Senior Centurions as the Legatus sharply pulled his feisty charge around and charged back up to be at Suetonius side to observe the battle.

The eight moved seamlessly, along with about four hundred and fifty other men to create a triangle pointing at the rabble at the base of the hill. The exposed rows moved their shields to create a solid wall all around the three sides. The men behind raised their shields above their heads, and all bunched in closer together so that the shields created a roof and covered the men in front of them.

"Cato, I know it is you behind me," said Festus.

"Is that because his shadow has blocked out the light?" grinned Maxctius.

"No, I can feel his breath on my neck!" Festus shuddered.

Decimus smirked as curiosity got the better of him, "How do you know it's Cato?"

"Easy," Festus uneasily revealed, "because I can smell what he had for breakfast"

"And what delights has our tall black friend been munching on?" inquired Laenus. Festus tightly closed his eyes as he searched for a description, "Dog poo!"

Cato wished he was not holding a covering shield and could use his fist to blacken Festus's eye. "I will remember what you have just said," he growled. "I just hope it is not the last thing I ever hear from you."

"So, you will make sure I survive this battle?" Festus smiled. "You can be my lucky guardian."

"Yes! It will be a pleasure to save you again," Cato snarled, "Just so I can kill you myself after the battle with my own bare hands!"

The group all laughed as they looked at one other, each secretly hoping it would not be for the last time.

Septimus gave the order for them to prepare to move forward, bringing silence and an air of deadly serious anticipation across the whole legion.

"With honour!" Marcus said out loud as he looked to the men on his left and then to his right.

"With honour!" The men around him all replied in unison.

The Senior Centurion looked and watched both the enemy and the officers for their signals. "UNUS!" he cried out as he saw Suetonius' second in command give the order to start the offensive. On hearing the order, every man took one step forward, leading with his left foot, then stopped and crouched down behind their shield wall.

The Senior Centurion bellowed again, "UNUS!"

Every move was well choreographed and had been rehearsed over and over as each man stood up, took one step forward and crouched down again.

"UNUS!" the Senior Centurion ordered once more.

Every man, in step, moved one pace nearer to the horde. The

thud of hundreds of shields hitting the ground in unison made the ground shake.

Boudicca turned her chariot to face the triangular formation. Loosening the reins, she directed the ponies forward at a walk. Her army followed in pursuit, trying to keep in line. Each man was staring ahead, eyes firmly fixed on the neat Roman triangular wedge of shields and the numerous rectangles behind. Mesmerised by the sight of so many obvious objects, seemingly solid but moving in time with each other not one of the tribesmen noticed the Roman Cavalry riding around them in the tree lines to the left and right of them.

From his elevated position at the rear of his troops, Suetonius had a clear view of the battlefield and with his senior officers and various runners on hand he could orchestrate and direct the battle efficiently. The position gave him a little more advantage.

He grinned to himself as the rabble began to gather pace towards his heavily armed and well-trained army. He gave the order and two blocks of men moved from the rear, positioned themselves over to the far left and far right and turned to face Boudicca as she led her men forward. The tribes picked up the pace and started to run at the wedge. Suetonius gave a signal, a wild flurry of heavy javelins and missiles were launched in waves into the air from a line of catapults and giant crossbows, over the heads of his own men and falling into Boudicca's first wave, shattering bodies as they hit.

The tribes rushed closer to the Roman wedge and their flanking support. The attackers quickly came into the range of the lighter spears and pila the infantry carried. Each Roman soldier carried two pila. The order was given, and another shower of deadly missiles rained down on the lightly armed Britons.

Most of the tribesmen carried small, lightweight shields, but once they had a weighty projectile stuck in it, the shield became unwieldly and useless and so were discarded leaving the Celtic warriors unprotected as they pushed forward with nothing more than a sword, battle axe or a dagger.

The metal-spiked hardware raining down on them had tips designed to twist or break on impact. Designed this way so they could not be picked up and thrown back at the Romans. What Suetonius failed to remember was that Boudicca had stolen a lot of the very same weapons and was quick to return the javelins back to the original owners. She gave the order and waves were sent into the Roman 'Tortoise' shield formations. Unfortunately for Boudicca, most of the projectiles bounced off the Roman scuta, and inflicted very little damage at all.

The tribes had tried to use the Roman shields that they had taken as victory prizes but try as they might to match the tactics of the foreign invaders, they found the scuta were heavy and cumbersome. The Britons traditionally preferred to travel and fight lightly armed, making their soldiers nimble. The advantage of speed and agility over the heavily armed and slow-moving opponents, coupled with the huge numbers that swelled their ranks, should make the final and decisive destruction of the Romans a forgone conclusion.

Oliver found himself moving forward with the tribes, swept up with the excitement and desperate to witness the Romans being defeated on a perfect late summer's day, with glorious sunshine and bright blue skies. Aiden and Jannon were on either side of him as the rows of men started to walk quicker and quicker before breaking into a run, so he did the same. He was not afraid at all; in fact, he was really excited and felt immortal as the adrenalin started to surge through him. In the distance he saw some spears flying aloft but did not see the devastation they caused as the men leading the assault literally ran into the deadly missiles. They continued to run towards the red wall of shields. Jannon, Oliver and his friend were dressed in light armour, and they followed the King, brandishing the Roman stabbing swords Jannon had presented them with days earlier, then suddenly became aware of the sheer numbers of men in front of them.

"This way!" shouted Jannon as he charged to the left of the

wedge shape. "Stay close to me." Jannon ordered as he could see the catapults and realised it was safer to get closer to the Roman shields. 'Not even the Romans would throw spears at their own men,' he thought to himself as he desperately tried to protect his two charges.

Suetonius subconsciously rubbed his hands together and a big broad grin spread across the psychopath's face as he viewed the enemy starting to fall. Their attack was beginning to fail under his carefully formulated strategy. He was prepared and ready for the second move. As he issued the next set of orders the archers ceased, the final trap continued to be set. Boudicca, on the other hand, was suffering huge losses as large numbers of her men had already fallen in the first rush, dead or badly injured.

The Senior Centurions could see the signalling from the collection of officers on the ridge and instinctively interpreted the order. "UNUS!" could be heard from numerous men up and down the Roman lines. The wedge again moved one pace forward, and then again with the flanking cohorts moving in unison around them. The cohorts flanking the wedge moved inwards, and the cohorts on the edges moved around, towards the triangle to squeeze the tribes tightly together.

The cavalry came out from the tree lines behind the hordes, taking Boudicca's forces by complete surprise. They trapped the divided forces against the heavily armed cohorts. Suetonius could see from his position that the tens of thousands of rebel supporters and onlookers had stopped at the entrance to the open lands. Quite unintentionally, they had blocked the only escape route open to the tribes. As he viewed the continuous and unrelenting moves from the Roman cohorts, he could see his plan playing out in front of him. It was working as he knew it would! His military tactics had created a perfect killing field, the bravado of the tribes suddenly turned into real fear as they were being cut down, the screams of the fallen filling the air.

The eight friends had launched their javelins, and now had their gladii drawn. First blood had been spilled as the first of the warriors had reached them and the short stabbing swords had found intended targets, sinking into the flesh of the tribesmen. The poorly armoured militia could not break free. Their sheer numbers pushed the front rows into the wall of shields. The men could not avoid the gladii as they were thrust out between the shields. The Romans kept pushing forward and as they passed over the top of the fallen injured, swords were plunged into the bodies that laid underfoot to dispatch the wounded and then trampled them underfoot. The Roman friends had been parrying blades and plunging swords in very hard fight. Thirst was kicking in and each movement was becoming more and more painful as blood sugars dropped and fatigue was starting to set in. Despite their near legendary fitness, all the legionaries were starting to feel fatigued as they continued to push the shrinking number of Celts back towards their own supporters.

Numerous members of the legions claimed to have seen a fearsome auburn-haired woman on a chariot leave the field, as they continued to move forward, pushing the warriors back against their own wagons and carts. Women, the elderly, and the children were being slain at the hands of the Romans. Revenge was sweet as far as the imperial cohorts were concerned as they refused to view the deaths of the innocents as murder. There were no innocents in their minds. They regarded it as vengeance for the deaths of their own families and loved ones.

Suetonius could see the end coming and the tribal forces were unravelling. It was time to finish the annihilation once and for all. He issued the order to break formation and finish the enemy. The Roman cohorts knew this was the moment the battle was won, and the final cleansing act was to be concluded.

Suetonius nodded sadistically as he screamed out, "OMNES INTERFICERE! OMNES INTERFICERE!"

This was the order, the eight friends looked at each other, not sure of what they had heard. Albus was just as surprised but urged his men to finish the job, "You heard. Kill them all!"

Oliver was not sure if it was luck, judgement, or both, but he, Jannon and Aiden were still unscathed after witnessing the horde of warriors being cut down by the Romans. He had seen women and children cut down as they tried to run away, but felt removed from the horrific scene, as if he were back in a computer game. From what he could see, the Romans did not seem to have any casualties or dead at all. Oliver became all too aware of what was going to happen to them all, as he could see the wedge suddenly open. For the first time he could clearly see the faces of the soldiers in the Roman triangle as the shields were lowered. He watched in horror as the red, armour-clad legionaries indiscriminately plunged swords into the bodies of the men he had heard laughing and joking only a few hours before. Fear took Oliver's voice as he stared in disbelief. He mouthed and mouthed and finally the words tumbled out as he witnessed Donnchad fall. "Jannon, Aiden, RUN!" he screamed as he grabbed wildly at his companions and desperately tried to drag them away towards safety.

Jannon turned and glanced at the young boy. "I can't abandon my people…" he yelled. Oliver scrambled over to the man and grabbed his shirt and pulled as hard as he could, "Your people are dead... Find Mardina!"

But Jannon reached down and yanked the material from Oliver's hand. "Aiden," Oliver shouted, "Stop your father!"

Aiden jumped deftly over a headless corpse and joined Oliver. The pair jumped on Jannon and screamed at him to stop and listen. The rage Jannon felt made him blind to everything going on around him. He just wanted to kill Romans, and nothing was going to stop him. Oliver had seen people being hysterical in films and being slapped to bring them back to normal, so he curled his hand into a fist, pulled his hand back and punched Jannon with all his strength. The resulting crack did the trick as Jannon stopped dead in his tracks. He looked directly at Oliver and heavily blinked a few times as he stared at the two boys.

Oliver grabbed the man by the elbow and tried to drag him away. "Jannon, IT'S OVER!" he pleaded. "Jannon, find

Marina and go!" as he pulled on his arm. Jannon turned and started to move back towards the wooded edge of the field. Oliver swung around to see his young friend frozen to the spot in fear. He looked up to see some of the armour-clad Romans breaking into a run towards them. His small friend stood still and silent in shock.

"Aiden, move!" Oliver screamed as he ran over to him, grabbed Aiden's shoulders, turned him away from the cohort and pushed him towards safety. His friend snapped out of his hypnotised state and broke into a sprint behind his father as Oliver reached for his sheathed sgian and followed suit. Jannon started to comprehend the loss of the battle and realised his days of being a warrior were over as he left the field and desperately searched for his wife. It was better for Mardina if he stayed alive. He glanced around quickly and stopped to wait for his two charges to catch him up. As they did so he tried to shield them as they all dashed for the woods.

Cato looked up to see Jannon and the two boys turn and start to run. "No, you don't!" he growled, and he caught the attention of Festus and Decimus and pointed to the three figures. "They're getting away!" he yelled. The three gave chase and as they neared Jannon, Cato reached for his pugio dagger. In one smooth action he tossed it up, grabbed the blade, pulled it back behind his head and threw it at the running figures. The heavy-handled dagger tumbled through the air and struck one of the escapees.

Oliver felt the thump on the back of his head and the force made his head jolt forward. His body started to turn as his legs could no longer keep up with his body's velocity. Everything went into slow motion as his body started to fall. He looked up to see the tall black Roman bearing down on him, the man's face distorted as he let out a blood curdling war cry. Oliver felt his knees buckle from under him as he fell. Everything slowed further still as his feet left the ground. He closed his eyes tightly as he waited for the earth to rush up and greet him with the inevitable, agonizing thud.

Chapter Twenty-Two

Lights flashed in front of Oliver's tightly closed eyes as his head smacked onto the ground, and a shooting pain ran from the back of his head to the front and behind his eyes. "NOOOO!" he screamed as the panic and fear made him thrash around as he tried to evade the inevitable, DEATH. He felt a heavy object land on his chest, winding him in the process. To his amazement, he was still breathing but could not move his arms. Oliver plucked up the courage to open his eyes, fully expecting to see a huge, powerful Roman legionary bearing down on him, only to be greeted with Michael's writhing body pinning him to the ground as he flailed his arms and legs wildly. He had landed squarely on Oliver's chest, winding him, and trapping him against the floor. As he did so the object Oliver held tightly in his hand was released from his grasp and shot under his bed.

Michael loosened his grip as his attention was temporarily distracted. "What was that?" he demanded as the object vanished out of sight.

Before Oliver could come to his senses and grab at Michael, he had jumped off Oliver and dived after it. Michael frantically finger-tipped searched in the darkness under the bed until his hand happened to come across the item. He grabbed it and pulled it into the daylight. The sight made him gasp audibly. He gazed at Oliver's sgian, "Ohhh! That's peachy!" Michael declared as he pulled the blade from its sheath and stared at the sharp, polished six-inch blade. "Wait till Mum finds out you have a knife!" Michael snarled. Oliver, extremely disorientated, struggled to come to his senses and make sense of anything that was happening.

Michael pushed the blade back into its leather case, jumped to his feet and ran out of Oliver's bedroom. "Mum!" he shouted as he brandished the sheathed blade in the air. "Mum!" he continued shouting as he ran downstairs, through the living room and into the kitchen.

Oliver desperately scrambled after his brother. "Stop! Michael!" he begged. "Please don't... Please!" Oliver shouted after his brother, but his pleading fell on deaf ears. Oliver, in a blind panic, shot out of his room, navigated his way over the dog, jumped down the stairs and out of the front door. He was in real trouble as he knew his Mum's opinion on weapons of any kind, particularly knives. His Mum would never believe the truth about how he managed to have it or where it had come from. The only person that could help him now was Grandad, who lived in a cottage on the other side of the village. He knew his Grandad would be at home. His white-haired hero would either be pottering in his garden or drinking tea in the kitchen. He was the only one who could stop his Mum from venting her full rage at him.

Oliver grabbed his bike from where it lay abandoned on the lawn. Without looking back, he jumped on it and pedalled for all he was worth. He rode for all he was worth, taking the shortcut down a pathway and nearly knocked Mrs Grayson over. "SORRY!" he yelled over his shoulder as he shot off into the distance. Oliver steamed along the side roads, up and down pavements and turned swiftly into the road that contained his Grandad's house. Oliver shot into the old man's drive and onto the gravel path. As he did so he wrenched on the back brake. It locked the wheel as he leaned to his left, causing the bike to slide around to a halt. He jumped off into the cloud of dust his manoeuvre had thrown up and slammed it to the ground.

Without losing a step he ran as fast as could. "Grandad, Grandad!" he shouted as he steamed around the side of the cottage and into the back garden. "Grandad!" he shouted again, only to be greeted by an earie silence. He opened the back door and called out again, but there was still no reply. The old man was not at home. Oliver paused for moment, took some deep breaths as he tried to control his panic. In his confused state it slowly dawned on him that the house was empty. There was only one other place the old man could be.

Oliver ran back towards the front gate, grabbed his bike, and started to run with it. He a threw his leg over the seat and sat in the saddle as his feet searched out the pedals. He pushed his toes hard down on the pedals with all his might as he sped towards the recreation ground. He could not get there quickly enough.

Oliver tore through the gates, through the carpark and dashed down the tarmac path which eventually led to the bowling green. A large wooden building loomed up quickly, the hut served as a tearoom and changing rooms for the keen bowlers and various visiting teams on summer afternoons. As he hastily zipped past the building, he could see a second little wooden shed in the distance and headed towards it as fast as he could, his heart beating so hard he thought it was going to stop.

As he got nearer, Oliver was sure he spied a clean-shaven, tall, familiar figure standing on the immaculately manicured grass of the bowling green. The figure was dressed in a white jacket, flannel trousers, with a straw Panama hat perched at a jaunty angle on waves of thick white hair that was slicked back and held in place with lots of hair oil. Sure enough, Oliver immediately recognised the man. It was his beloved grandfather. He felt a huge sense of relief as he dropped his bike and sprinted up to his hero. "Grandad… Grandad!" he shouted as he got closer.

Grandad was in full motion as he sent a bowl up the green towards the small white jack, "Hello boy-boy!" the portly chap chortled, as he glanced over and recognised the source of the yelling. The sight of Oliver always lifted his spirit but seeing Oliver sliding his bike to the ground and sprinting towards him was different, he instinctively knew something was obviously wrong. Breathless, Oliver ran up to the old man, threw his arms around him, hugged him tightly and revelled for a moment in the familiar, comforting smell of cigar smoke and his Grandad's favourite after shave.

Grandad was a bit taken aback with the greeting. "Hey! What's up? What's the panic for?" he grinned as he returned the hug.

Oliver gasped for air as his brain whirled in overdrive and he tried to get the sequence right in his mind. "I don't know where to start!" he blurted out. "I had a fight with Michael… and… and… a sgian fell from my hand… and…"

"Whoah! Hold up," Grandad said as he stepped back and waved his hand up and down at Oliver, indicating for him to slow down. "A sgian?" he asked. "A what?"

"I don't know where it came from!" Oliver blurted and stopped abruptly as he looked at his Grandad's enquiring face and noticed his hero indicating for him to quieten.

His Grandad was really puzzled. "A sgian?" he muttered. "What on earth are you talking about? What sgian?" he enquired as he continued with his efforts to calm his boy, who was obviously in some distress.

Oliver shrugged at the questioning; he was battling to find the right words as he struggled with his recent experiences. "Well, I am not sure, I think I do, but I am not sure!" he blurted. He was not sure if the adventure was real or not. He so wanted to tell, but the whole thing just seemed so far-fetched, he was sure nobody would believe him. He could barely believe it himself! But if he could tell anybody, Oliver knew his favourite Grandad would at least listen and not judge him.

Grandad gently reached up and put his index finger on his lips as the boy chattered, not making any sense. "Shhhh!" His action quietened the jabbering lad. Oliver stopped and looked into his Grandads' eyes; the action calmed him almost immediately. "Before you begin, a sgian-dubh is a knife, isn't it?"

Oliver nodded, "Well, you might not believe this… but …" Oliver swallowed hard as he looked his Grandad in the eye, "I had a fight with Michael, well he jumped me." He started the whole tale from the beginning while his Grandad nodded wisely as he listened intently to the whole story. He was intrigued to find out how these ramblings had anything to do with Oliver having a knife in his possession. The pair ambled over to the bench at the side of the bowling green and sat down as Oliver disclosed all the details. The seat was positioned under a mature cedar tree, its shade was a relief from the burning summer sunshine as Oliver recounted the entire adventure.

Grandad was a keen amateur historian; it had been a passion of his since he was a small boy. He nodded from time to time as the details tied up with his own knowledge of that period. Grandad had so many questions but dared not stop Boy while he was in full flow. Oliver's best friend patiently listened to the whole adventure as Oliver barely stopped to draw breath. He explained that he suddenly was under attack from a Roman one moment and the next he opened his eyes to see Michael's face and knew he must have brought the knife back with him.

"Now you see!" Oliver exclaimed. "That's why I had to find you. I can't go home. Mum is going to kill me!" he blurted as his eyes started to well up. "Please can you help me Grandad? I honestly don't know what to do. I don't think anybody will believe me, but it is the truth, I think I must be mad!"

Oliver closely watched his Grandad's face for clues as the old man drew in a deep breath and mulled over what had been said. Oliver hoped the old man believed him. He had never lied to him before and there was obviously no reason to start now, but even as Oliver imparted his experiences, he could hardly believe it himself! He hoped that fact that he had always been truthful with his Grandad would be taken into consideration as the details buzzed around his head and he hoped he would be given the benefit of doubt.

Grandad smiled and nodded sagely as he put his hand gently on Oliver's shoulder. The boy felt a real sense of relief as Grandad leaned towards him, put his arm around Oliver's shoulder and pulled him close. The old man stared into the distance for what seemed ages before he turned his head and whispered into Oliver's ear, "So, you did a little bit of accidental time travel then?" The man paused before he stood up, Oliver followed his lead, rose off the seat, and looked up at the tall, gentle man by his side. The old chap wandered back into the sunshine, his arm still wrapped over Oliver's shoulder, as his grandson walked in step with him. They had only taken a few strides when his Grandad cleared his throat, leaned towards Oliver "Boy... I thought I was the only one!" he gently disclosed. Oliver's jaw dropped as he stopped dead in his tracks, turned and stared hard at his hero. His eyes widened as the words slowly penetrated the fog of panic in his head.

Grandad appreciated that the revelation would be a shock to Oliver and paused for a few moments before breaking the silence. "This knife thing, it was a present from me, was it not?" the old man nodded sagely as he spoke.

Oliver mirrored the man's action as he agreed.

"Now," Grandad continued as the pair wandered over to Oliver's bike, "I want you to stop worrying."

Oliver bent down and retrieved it from the ground without breaking his stride, as they strode towards the immaculate flat grassed bowling green. Oliver halted near the gate and watched Grandad stride on, step over the border ditch and onto the green. The old man retrieved his bowls and bid a cheery goodbye to his practice companion as he loaded the four bowls unceremoniously into their carrying case and headed towards his waiting grandson. The two figures slowly strode through the park and finally along the footpath towards Oliver's home. Grandad looked at Oliver and smiled as they rounded the corner of Oliver's street, "You just you leave your Mum to me boy!..."

Glossary

Balteus – Military Belt

Balista – Large powerful catapult

Braccae – Woollen trousers

Caligae - Military Boots with metal studs on the bottom

Dexter - Right

Focale – Woollen scarf

Gladius - stabbing Sword 18-24 inches in length

Hasta - Throwing Spear 2.5- 3.5m in length

Gallic Helmet - Metal helmet with neck protection and side flaps to protect the cheek and jaw

Lorica hamata- Chain Mail

Lorica plumata -Chain Mail with feather plates

Lorica segmentata- Segment Armour made with large horizontal plates

Lorica squamata – Segment Armour made with scales of plates that overlap

Manica – Flexible arm guard, made up of interlocking metal plates

Pilum – Military javelin with a tip designed to bend on contact

Pilum muralis – Sharpened wooden poles designed for temporary defence

Pugio – Dagger

Tribulus – Triangular lump of metal designed to have a hooked barb facing up no matter how it landed

Scutum – Large rectangular military shield

Sinister - Left

Tunic – Made of wool and usually died red

Celtic Tribes in Roman Britain circa AD61

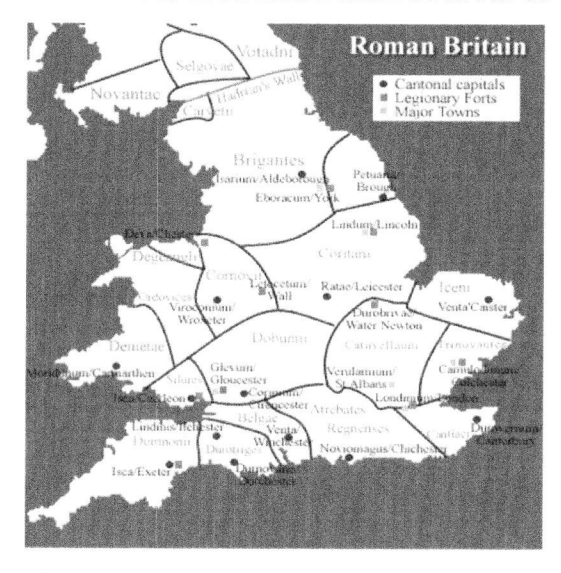

Keep up to date with Oliver's adventures at www.oliverboymason.com

The Oliver 'Boy' Mason Adventures series so far:

START – prequel to the series.

REVOLT

VICTORY (available soon on Amazon)

BATTLE (available soon on Amazon)

Printed in Great Britain
by Amazon